Iste Pauper Clamavit
Saint Bonaventure's Mendicant Theology of Prayer

European University Studies
Europäische Hochschulschriften
Publications Universitaires Européennes

Series XXIII
Theology

Reihe XXIII   Série XXIII
Theologie
Théologie

Vol./Bd. 390

PETER LANG
Frankfurt am Main · Bern · New York · Paris

Timothy Johnson

Iste Pauper Clamavit

Saint Bonaventure's
Mendicant Theology of Prayer

PETER LANG
Frankfurt am Main · Bern · New York · Paris

CIP-Titelaufnahme der Deutschen Bibliothek

Johnson, Timothy:

Iste pauper clamavit : Saint Bonaventure's mendicant theology
of prayer / Timothy Johnson. - Frankfurt am Main ; Bern ; New
York ; Paris : Lang, 1990
    (European university studies : Ser. 23, Theology ; Vol. 390)
    Zugl.: Rom, Univ. Gregoriana, Diss., 1989
    ISBN 3-631-42755-7

NE: Europäische Hochschulschriften / 23

BV
207
.J64
1990

ISSN 0721-3409
ISBN 3-631-42755-7

© Verlag Peter Lang GmbH, Frankfurt am Main 1990
All rights reserved.

Printed in Germany 1   3 4 5 6 7

This work is dedicated with love to my parents,
Burt and Mickey Johnson,
in whose home I first learned to pray.

Acknowledgments

The presentation of this dissertation brings to conclusion several years of research and writing. As I look back over the past years, I am once again conscious of the many individuals who contributed, in one way or another, to the success of my work. I owe all of them a debt of thanks.

Fr. Zoltan Alszeghy, S.J., guided my work from conception to completion. His insight and patience, themselves, no doubt, the fruit of his own theological research and many years of experience with doctoral students, were a continual source of encouragement to me. I thank him for his guidance, and the Institute of Spirituality as well, which allowed him to be my director.

Several confreres have assisted me in the preparation of the present text. The first friar who comes to mind is Fr. Oktavian Schmucki, O.F.M. Cap.. It was Fr. Schmucki who originally suggested that I investigate Saint Bonaventure's teaching on prayer. I am grateful for his advice and for the support he has given me over the past years. Three other confreres, Fr. Michael Blastic, O.F.M. Conv., Fr. Wayne Hellmann, O.F.M. Conv., and Friar Steven McMichael, O.F.M. Conv., read sections of my thesis at different points in time. Their reflections on the text, along with their suggestions as to its improvement, were of great assistance to me.

Just as several individual confreres played an important role in the successful completion of this dissertation, several communities of friars made a contribution to that end. In particular, I would like to mention the community of the *Seraphicum* in Rome and the community of *Sankt Anna* in Munich. While I was in Rome, the friars of the *Seraphicum* assisted me in numerous ways. The friars of *Sankt Anna* friary, for their part, generously offered me the space and time necessary for doctoral work. I owe special thanks to the librarian of *Sankt Anna*, Friar Bernardin Höhn, O.F.M..

Three people who made a notable contribution to the present dissertation are Fr. Reginald Foster, O.C.D., Ms. Marilyn Finnerty, and Ms. Diane Clough. I am grateful to them for the time and effort they dedicated to my thesis. Fr. Foster graciously accepted my request and reviewed the many translations that I made from the *Opera Omnia* of Bonaventure. Ms. Finnerty, who kindly proofread my work, made a number of suggestions which have been incorporated into this dissertation. Ms. Clough was most helpful in preparing the final text of my thesis for publication.

In conclusion, I would like to thank all the friars, friends, and family, who have assisted me during this period of study. I am grateful to my Province, *Our Lady of Consolation*, which has given me the resources needed to do research in our Franciscan tradition. I am thankful for the friends on both sides of the Atlantic who opened their hearts and homes to me when I was far from home. Finally, I want to express my deepest appreciation to my parents, Burt and Mickey, and to my sisters, Kimberly, Katherine, Kelly and Kara, who have been a constant source of support for me. In countless ways, they encouraged and enabled their son and brother to bring to completion his long years of study.

Table of Contents

9

Abbreviations

For periodicals, dictionaries and collections:

AFH	*Archivum Franciscanum Historicum,* Quaracchi, 1908-
Ant	*Antonianum,* Roma, 1926-
Aug	*Augustinianum,* Roma, 1961-
CChr	*Corpus Christianorum,* Turnholt, 1953-
CF	*Collectanea Franciscana,* Roma, 1931-
DF	*Dizionario Francescano,* Padova, 1983.
DS	*Dictionnaire de spiritualité,* Paris, 1937-
DtS	*Doctor Seraphicus,* Bagnoregio, 1954-
DThC	*Dictionnaire de théologie catholique,* Paris, 1903-
EF	*Etudes franciscaines,* Paris, 1899-
EJ	*Eranos Jahrbuch,* Zürich, 1933-
EsF	*Estudios franciscanos,* Barcelona, 1907-
ETL	*Ephemerides theologicae Lovanienses,* Louvain, 1924-
EWS	*World Spirituality,* New York, 1988-
FF	*La France franciscaine,* Paris, 1912-
FS	*Franziskanische Studien,* Münster-Werl, 1914-
FSt	*Franciscan Studies,* New York, 1940-

GL	*Geist und Leben. Zeitschrift für Aszese und Mystik,* Würzburg, 1926-
GR	*Gregorianum,* Roma, 1920-
HDG	*Handbuch der Dogmengeschichte,* Freiburg, Br., 1956-
IKZ	*Internationale Katholische Zeitschrift "Communio,"* Köln, 1972-
KD	*Kerygma und Dogma,* Göttingen, 1955-
LitJ	*Liturgisches Jahrbuch,* Münster, 1950-
LM	*Lexikon des Mittelalters,* München, 1977-
LR	*Laurentianum,* Roma, 1960-
LSB	*Lexique Saint Bonaventure,* Paris, 1969.
MF	*Miscellanea francescana,* Foligno-Roma, 1886-
MD	*La Maison-Dieu. Revue de pastorale liturgique,* Paris, 1945-
RTL	*Revue théologique de Louvain,* Louvain, 1970-
PG	*Patrologie grecque,* Migne, Paris, 1857-1866.
PL	*Patrologie latine,* Migne, Paris, 1878-1890.
RAC	*Reallexikon für Antike und Christentum,* Stuttgart, 1950-
SB	*S. Bonaventura 1274-1974,* 5 Volumes, Grottaferrata, 1972-74.
SBM	*San Bonaventura Maestro di Vita Francescana e di Sapienza Cristiana,* 3 Volumes published as Volume 75 (1975) of *MF* with Supplements I and II of the same year.
SFr	*Studi Francescani,* Firenze, 1914-

TD	*Theology Digest,* St. Mary, Kansas, 1953-
ThQ	*Theologische Quartalschrift,* Tübingen, 1818-
TRE	*Theologische Realenzyklopädie,* Berlin, 1976-
V V	*Verdad y Vida,* Madrid, 1943-
WissWb	*Wissenschaft und Weltbild,* Wien, 1948-
W W	*Wissenschaft und Weisheit,* Mönchengladbach, 1938-
ZKT	*Zeitschrift für Katholische Theologie,* Wien, 1876-

For Bonaventure's works

Apol paup	*Apologia pauperum*
Brev	*Breviloquium*
Christus mag	*Christus unus omnium magister*
Coll Jn	*Collationes in Evangelium Ioannis*
Comm Ec	*Commentarius in librum Ecclesiastae*
Comm Jn	*Commentarius in Evangelium Ioannis*
Comm Lc	*Commentarius in Evangelium S. Lucae*
Const Narb	*Constitutiones Generales Narbonenses*
De donis	*Collationes de septem donis Spiritus sancti*
De quin fest	*De quinque festivitatibus pueri Jesu*
De test Trin	*De triplici testimonio sanctissimae Trinitatis*
Ep off	*Epistolae officiales*
Hex	*Collationes in Hexaëmeron*
Itin	*Itinerarium mentis in Deum*
Leg maj	*Legenda major sancti Francisci*

15

Leg min	*Legenda minor sancti Francisci*
Lig vit	*Lignum vitae*
Myst Trin	*Quaestiones disputatae de mysterio Trinitatis*
Perf ev	*Quaestiones disputatae de perfectione evangelica*
Perf vitae	*De perfectione vitae ad sorores*
Plant par	*Tractatus de plantatione paradisi*
Red art	*De reductione artium ad theologiam*
Reg nov	*Regula novitiorum*
Regn Dei	*Dei regno Dei descripto in parabolis evangelicis*
Scien Chr	*Quaestiones disputatae de scientia Christi*
I, II, III, IV, Sent	*Commentarius in I, II, III, IV, librum Sententiarum*
Solil	*Soliloquium de quatuor mentalibus exercitiis*
Trip via	*De triplici via*

For distinctions in individual texts:

a.	articulus
an.	annotatio
au.	articulus unicus
c.	capitulum
coll.	collatio
con.	contra
concl.	conclusio
d.	distinctio
dub.	dubium
fr.	fructus
fund.	fundamentum
n.	numerus
opp.	oppositum
p.	pars
praenot.	praenotata
prol.	prologus
prooem.	prooemium
q.	quaestio
resp.	respondeo
rub.	rubrica

Introduction

The role of prayer in medieval spirituality would be difficult to overestimate.[1] As so many of the great architectural and literary works of the period indicate, prayer was a vital element in both the private and public spheres of medieval spiritual life. The great cathedrals and monasteries in particular testify to a spirituality marked by a profound spirit of prayer.[2] In the medieval world, where the destiny of humanity was so often interpreted in the light of salvation history, prayer stands out as among the most significant, if not the most significant of all religious activities. Without prayer, humanity would be unable to overcome the alienating effects of sin, and, thereby, would be incapable of the spiritual pilgrimage back to God. Because of the important role of prayer in medieval spirituality, it is not surprising to see that it was the object of sustained theological reflection. One theologian whose works reflect the medieval interest in prayer is the Franciscan friar, Saint Bonaventure. The purpose of this dissertation is to examine the theme of prayer in the writings of Saint Bonaventure.

---

[1] On prayer in medieval spirituality, see: Jean Châtillon, "Prière III. Dans la tradition chrétienne C. moyen âge" in vol. 12 of *DS*, 2271-2288, esp. 2271-2272 for the anthropological and theological foundations of prayer in medieval culture. See also: Isnard W. Frank, "Gebet VI. Mittelalter" in vol. 12 of *TRE*, 65-71 and Jean Leclercq, "Ways of Prayer and Contemplation II. Western" in *Christian Spirituality 1*, vol. 16 of *WS*, 415-426. On the medieval vocabulary of prayer, see: Jean Leclercq, *Études sur le vocabulaire monastique du moyen âge* (Romae: Pontificium Institutum S. Anselmi, 1961) 80-144, esp. 128-139.

[2] On cathedrals, monasteries and other places of worship as sources for the study of public and private prayer in the Middle Ages, see: Jean Châtillon, "Prière," 2274-2275.

Bonaventure's theology lends itself to the study of prayer because he reflects on the mystery of God from the standpoint of the human person as pilgrim longing to return home; for him, prayer becomes the first step[3] as well as the culmination of the long journey back to God.[4] It is not surprising, therefore, to find the theme of prayer woven throughout his writings.[5] Although he did not dedicate any work exclusively to the subject of prayer,[6] it is

[3] *Brev,* prol. (V, 201a- 202b) and *Itin,* c. 1, n. 1 (V, 296a-297a). All references to Bonaventure's works are to the critical edition: *S. Bonaventura Opera Omnia,* ed. PP. Collegii a S. Bonaventura. 10 vols. (Quaracchi: Collegium S. Bonaventurae, 1882-1902). When referring to a text from the *Opera Omnia,* the volume number is indicated in parentheses by a Roman numeral, and the page number by an Arabic number. The letters a and b indicate the respective column of the page. On the authenticity of the different works in the *Opera Omnia,* see: Ignatius Brady, "The Opera Omnia of St. Bonaventure revisited," *Proceedings of the Seventh Centenary Celebration of the Death of Saint Bonaventure,* ed. Pascal F. Foley (St. Bonaventure, N. Y.: The Franciscan Institute, 1975): 47-54; "The Writings of Saint Bonaventure regarding the Franciscan Order," *SBM,* 89-112; and "The Edition of the <<Opera Omnia>> (1882-1902) of Saint Bonaventure," *AFH* 70 (1977): 367-376.

[4] *Itin* c. 7, n. 6 (V, 313b). According to Romano Guardini, one feature of Bonaventure's theology is its origin in his spirit of prayer: "Er ist kein unpersönlicher Denker. Seine Werke, selbst der auf den ersten Blick so streng sachliche Sentenzenkommentar, tragen alle den Stempel seiner milden, innigen Art. Die Theologie hat für ihn ihren Ursprung im Gebet." Guardini then goes on to point out that Bonaventure's theology also culminates in prayer: "Und das Ende der Theologie ist wiederum das Gebet." See: *Die Lehre des hl. Bonaventura von der Erlösung* (Düsseldorf: L. Schwann, 1921) 188.

[5] For an introduction into the writings of Bonaventure, see: Jacques Guy Bougerol, *Introduction to the Works of Bonaventure,* trans. José de Vinck (Paterson, N.J.: St. Anthony Guild Press, 1964). For a bibliography on Bonaventure's writings, see: *SB,* vol. 5.

[6] One text, entitled *De oratione* in MS Codex Vatic. Palat. lat. 612, Rome: Vatican Library, fol. 43c-46c, has been attributed by some scholars to Bonaventure. An early study of the text did not reach any conclusion as to authorship; see: Victorinus Doucet, "De quaestionibus S. Bonaventurae adscriptis in Cod. Vaticano Palatino Lat. 612," *AFH* 26 (1933): 490-491. Bougerol, in *Introduction,* 180, says the work is Bonaventure's but does not say why he holds that opinion. Balduinus Distelbrink in *Bonaventurae scripta, authentica dubia vel spuria critice recensita* (Roma: Istituto Storico Cappuccini, 1975) 14, maintains that *De oratione* is from Bonaventure's hand because it is ascribed to "bo" [onaventurae?] and found with other authentic questions (*Scien Chr* and *Myst Trin*) in the same codex. On the other hand, Brady, in "The Opera Omnia revisited," 56, notes that the inscription "bo," which is faded, may be in that condition because someone tried to erase it. Because of the Latin in *De oratione,* he says it may belong to John of La Rochelle. Given the various opinions concerning *De oratione,* the question of its authorship should be considered still open.

a topic that appears in his academic writings as well as in his practical writings.[7] Whether addressing a gathering of academics at the University of Paris or writing to a group of contemplative sisters, he insists on prayer as the way to union with God.[8] When writing to his confreres in the Franciscan Order, he does not hesitate to remind them of the importance of prayer in their lives as religious.[9] When commenting on scripture in the classroom or in the pulpit, he repeatedly speaks of prayer.[10] These references reveal his deep appreciation of the biblical teaching on prayer and his desire to educate others in this crucial facet of the evangelical life. Not to be forgotten are his prayers, which both give evidence to his own spirit of prayer and teach

---

[7] On this two-fold division of Bonaventure's writings, see: Zachary Hayes, *The Hidden Center. Spirituality and Speculative Christology in St. Bonaventure* (New York: Paulist Press, 1981) 8.

[8] *Hex,* coll. 2, n. 32 (V, 342a) and *Perf vitae,* c. 5, n. 5 (VIII, 119a), respectively.

[9] *Ep off I,* n. 3 (VIII, 469a-b); *Ep off II,* n. 4 (VIII, 470b); and *Reg nov,* c. 1-2 (VIII, 475a-479b).

[10] Bonaventure's development of the theme of prayer is particulary evident in the *Comm Lc* where he mirrors Luke's own interest in the subject. For a bibliogaphy on the subject of prayer in Luke's Gospel, see: Pierre Grelot, "Prière II. La prière dans la Bible," vol. 12 of *DS,* 2246-2247. For the texts on prayer in *Comm Lc,* as well as *Comm Jn* and *Coll Jn,* see the index of vol. 7 of the *Opera Omnia.* On the backround of the *Comm Lc,* see: Dominic Monti, *Bonaventure's Interpretation of Scripture in his Exegetical Works,* diss., The University of Chicago, 1979, 149-204. In Bonaventure's own homilies, which were given to a variety of audiences, he returns time and time again to the topic of prayer. (For the different texts on prayer, see the index of vol. 10 of the *Opera Omnia.*) The structure of the medieval sermon itself served to teach the theory and practice of prayer. As Bougerol notes in *Introduction,* 149, the *prothema,* which is an integral part of a medieval sermon, serves: ". . . to instruct the audience on the neccesity of prayer." After the *prothema,* an example of prayer was offered by the preacher who prayed that God would help him and/or the congregation. Bougeroul gives an example of how Bonaventure employed this method in *Introduction,* 137-138. On preaching and prayer in Bonaventure's theology, see: Erwin Eilers, *Gottes Wort. Eine Theologie der Predigt nach Bonaventura* (Freiburg: Herder, 1941) 76-79. On Bonaventure as preacher, see: Sophronius Clasen, "Der hl. Bonaventura als Prediger," *WW* 24 (1961): 85-113, esp. 101-105 in regard to the various groups of people who heard his preaching.

others the art of prayer.[11]

Despite the fact that prayer is a frequent theme in Bonaventure's writings, it has not attracted as much attention from scholars as would be expected.[12] Although many have examined his teaching on contemplation,[13] contemplation is only one aspect of medieval prayer. Another aspect is petitionary prayer; in fact, it is the most common and predominant expression of medieval prayer.[14] In a certain sense, it is also the most important because it corresponds to the ancient understanding of prayer.[15] Since

---

[11] These prayers include Bonaventure's personal prayers as well as biblical prayers. In his writings, he also makes use of prayers of other theologians. On personal prayers as the prime source for the study of prayer, see: Friedrich Heiler, *Das Gebet* (München: Verlag von Ernst Reinhardt, 1923) 27-34. See also the English translation of this work: *Prayer*, trans. Samuel McComb and J. Edgar Park (London: Oxford Univesity Press, 1932) xviii-xxiv. Reference is made in this study to the German original because the English translation mentioned lacks the critical apparatus of the original.

[12] The only major study of prayer in Bonaventure's writings is that of Thomas Villanova Gerster a Zeil, *Das Gebet nach der Lehre des. hl. Bonaventura* (Bolzano: 1931). This work is a helpful study of many of Bonaventure's texts on prayer; yet, it is limited by the fact that Bonaventure's teaching on prayer is not seen in light of the rest of his theology. In addition, the author makes no attempt to examine Bonaventure's thought against the background of the early and medieval Christian teaching on prayer. See also: F. Imle, *Das geistliche Leben nach der Lehre des. hl. Bonaventura* (Werl/Westfalen: Franziskus Druckerei, 1939) 413-449. For other references to Bonaventure and prayer, see the entry "oratio" in vol. 5 of *SB*, 689.

[13] On Bonaventure's teaching on contemplation, see the entry "contemplatio" in vol. 5 of *SB*, 672. Of particular worth is the study by Ephrem Longpré, "Bonaventure" in vol. 1 of *DS*, 1814-1840.

[14] Frank, "Gebet VI," 69, says: "In Theorie und Praxis der mittelalterlichen Frömmigkeit steht der deprekatorische Aspekt des Gebetes im Vordergrund." See also: Hans-Martin Barth, *Wohin - woher mein Ruf. Zur Theologie des Bittgebets* (München: Chr. Kaiser Verlag, 1981) 13. Bonaventure himself says: ". . . oratio est per modum *deprecativum." IV Sent*, d. 23, a. 1, q. 4, concl. (IV, 595a). "Deprecatio" has a two-fold meaning in the medieval vocabulary of prayer: ". . . *deprecatio* proprie est de malis amovendis, *oratio* vero de bonis adipiscendis, sed communiter ponitur unum pro altero." *Commentarium in Sapientiam*, c. 28 (VI, 226b). Concerning the authorship of this commentary, which should no longer be attributed to Bonaventure, see: Dominic Monti, "A Reconsideration of the Authorship of the Commentary of the Book of Wisdom attributed to St. Bonaventure," *AFH* 79 (1986): 359-391. On "deprecatio," see: *Dom 1 post Pent*, 2 (IX, 349b).

[15] Heiler speaks of petionary prayer as the most ancient form of prayer. It is the prototype and heart of all prayer; see: *Das Gebet,* 38, 60, and esp. 69, in reference to the Middle

in the Middle Ages prayer meant petition as well as contemplation,[16] it would be an impoverishment of Bonaventure's teaching on prayer to consider it exclusively from the perspective of contemplation. Petition and contemplation together form the pillars of his teaching on prayer and are inextricably bound to one another. As he points out in the *Journey of the Soul to God*, the contemplative ascent into God is impossible without asking for divine assistance:

> Since happiness is nothing other than the enjoyment of the highest good, and since the highest good is above us, no one is able to be happy unless one ascends above oneself, not with an ascent of the body, but of the heart. But we are unable to be raised above ourselves except through a superior power raising us. For regardless of how well the interior steps are ordered, nothing happens unless divine assistance accompanies [us]. Indeed, divine assistance accompanies those who ask humbly and devoutly from the heart; this means to sigh for it in this *valley of tears*, which

Ages. The Christian understanding of prayer as "oratio," at least up to the time of Bernard of Clairvaux, is a continuation of the ancient idea of prayer, inasmuch as it is conceived as asking something from God; see: Michael Dupuy, "Oraison," in vol. 11 of *DS*, 831-832. The ancient meaning of prayer corresponds to the predominant English undestanding of prayer; see the entries "pray" and "prayer" in *Webster's New Collegiate Dictionary* (Springfield, Mass.: G. & C. Meriam Co., 1975) 903-904. See also the list of synonyms for "pray" and "prayer" in *The New American Roget's College Thesaurus* (New York: The New American Library, Inc., 1962) 273. In the present study, some of the following synonyms of petition, which itself is a synonym of prayer, will be used: ask, address, plea, request, entreaty, supplication, appeal, beg, implore. For the entry "petition," see: *The New American Roget's*, 263.

[16] Dupy, "Oraison," 833 and Frank, "Gebet VI," 69-70. The two major streams of medieval prayer, supplication and contemplation, are noted by Heiler in: *Das Gebet*, 240-243. He describes the first as the Pauline prayer for pardon and the second as the Augustinian mystical ascent. Although these ways are distinct from each other, they are not mutually exclusive.

takes place through fervent prayer. Prayer, then, is the mother and origin of the ascent.[17]

Although Bonaventure considers the prayer of petition as fundamental to the soul's ascent into God, it has been generally neglected by scholars in favor of his teaching on contemplation.[18] The purpose of this study, therefore, is to approach the theme of prayer in Bonaventure's writings from the perspective of petitionary prayer. This methodological choice does not mean that the question of contemplation will be ignored, but, rather, that prayer will be considered, first of all, as a cry for divine assistance and only later as the union of the soul with God. Because of this emphasis on petitionary prayer, the present study considers this expression of prayer primarily as the supplication[19] of "the poor one in the desert;"[20] namely, the cry of the

---

[17] "Cum beatitudo nihil aliud sit, quam summi boni fruitio; et summum bonum sit supra nos: nullus potest effici beatus, nisi supra semetipsum ascendat, non ascensu corporali, sed cordiali. Sed supra nos levari non possumus nisi per virtutem superiorem nos elevantem. Quantumcumque enim gradus interiores disponantur, nihil fit, nisi divinum auxilium comitetur. Divinum autem auxilium comitatur eos qui petunt ex corde humiliter et devote; et hoc est ad ipsum suspirare in hac *lacrymarum valle*, quod fit per ferventem orationem. Oratio igitur est mater et origo sursum-actionis." *Itin*, c. 1, n. 1 (V, 296b-297a). All translations in this study are by the author. They are in most cases strict translations, although at times a more liberal translation is given when a strict translation was deemed to be unintelligible. At times, different translations of Bonaventure's works were consulted. These translations, which encompass a very limited number of the works found in the *Opera Omnia*, are listed in the bibliography. The fact that Bonaventure highly values prayer, and thus begins almost all of his mystical works with the call to prayer, is pointed out by Stanislaus Grünewald in: *Franziskanische Mystik: Versuch zu einer Darstellung mit besonderer Berücksichtigung des hl. Bonaventura* (München: Naturrechts-Verlag, 1932) 56. Grünewald also recognized the link between prayer and petition in Bonaventure's thought. He mentions (56) that when Bonaventure speaks of "oratio" in the *Perf vita*, c. 2 (VIII, 8a-11b), he means "hauptsächlich Bittgebet."

[18] The few authors who touch upon Bonaventure's teaching on petitionary prayer do so without taking into account the medieval emphasis on prayer as supplication; see: Gerster a Zeil, *Das Gebet*, 47 and Imle, *Das geistliche Leben*, 427-433.

[19] Among the various synonyms for prayer, "supplication" is especially fitting because it is generally understood as a humble and earnest request made to God; see: "supplicate" in *Webster's New Collegiate*, 1171. Other possible synonyms for prayer, such as "adoration," "praise" and "thanksgiving," denote a type of prayer that is touched upon only in passing in this study.

24

pilgrim, who, far from God, begs for the divine mercy that overcomes the alienation of sin and culminates in the contemplative encounter with God. This movement in prayer, from the cry for divine mercy to contemplative fulfillment, can be summed up in the words of the Psalmist quoted by Bonaventure in a homily in honor of Saint Anthony of Padua: "that poor man cried out, and the Lord heard him."[21]

The movement in prayer, from the cry for divine mercy to contemplative fulfillment in union with God, forms in four chapters the framework of this dissertation. The first chapter examines prayer in the light of Bonaventure's teaching on poverty, divine mercy and the advent of Christ. The second chapter looks at prayer as an act which, through the power of the

---

[20] Chapter One of the *Journey of the Soul into God* begins with the subtitle "Incipit speculatio pauperis in deserto" *Itin*, c. 1 (V, 296a-b) and then goes on to speak of the neccessity of prayer in the mystical ascent; see above, note 17. According to Philotheus Boehner, the poor one is symbolic of: "the man in need of union with God, the beggar in spirit who finds himself in the desert far from his Father and from his eternal home." See: Philotheus Boehner, introduction in *Works of St. Bonaventure*, vol. II: *St. Bonaventure's Itinerarium Mentis in Deum*, intro. trans. and comm. Philotheus Boehner (Saint Bonaventure, N.Y.: The Franciscan Institute, 1956) 109. This beggar should not be interpreted as a symbol of an isolated individual soul since the ascent of the individual soul is a participation in the ascent of the Church militant back to God. On the ascent of the soul and the Church spoken of in the *Itin*, see: Konrad Fischer, *De Deo trino et uno. Das Verhältnis von productio und reductio in seiner Bedeutung für die Gotteslehre Bonaventuras* (Göttingen: Vandenhoeck & Ruprecht, 1978) 27 ff.. On the significance and authenticity of the subtitle of Chapter One of the *Itin*, see: Hermann F. Schalück, *Armut und Heil. Eine Untersuchung über den Armutsgedanken in der Theologie Bonaventuras* (München: Verlag Ferdinand Schöningh, 1971) 4, note 11.

[21] "Iste pauper clamavit, et Dominus exaudivit eum." *De S. Antonio* (IX, 535a). The psalm quoted is Ps. 34: 6. This scriptural text also appears in *Comm Lc,* c. 7, n. 43 (VII, 176a). Unless otherwise noted, all biblical abbreviations are from *The New Oxford Annotated Bible with Apocrypha*, ed. Herbert G. May and Bruce M. Metzger (New York: Oxford University Press, 1977). In the translation of the biblical texts found in Bonaventure's works, reference was occasionally made to *The New Oxford* and the English translation of the Latin Vulgate in *New Catholic Edition of the Holy Bible,* ed. Catholic Scholars and others (New York: Catholic Book Publishing Company, 1949-1950). On the historical context and doctrinal content of Bonaventure's sermon on Saint Anthony, see: Francisco José Da Gama Caeiro, "L'interprétation du texte bonaventurien 'Sermo de S. Antonio.' Le problème historique et doctrinal," *EF* 18 (Supplément annuel 1968): 149-159.

Holy Spirit, conforms the poor to Christ and renders them adopted sons and daughters of God. The third chapter treats Bonaventure's understanding of the scriptural admonition to pray without ceasing by looking at vocal prayer, the desire for the good, and the struggle to live justly in the face of the forces of concupiscence. The fourth chapter situates contemplation within the context of prayer by considering it as the fulfillment of the prayer for mercy. This study closes by drawing some general conclusions concerning Bonaventure's teaching on prayer.

Chapter One: Poverty and Prayer

If the poor person in the desert is symbolic of everyone who calls out in prayer for divine assistance, why is it then that Bonaventure considers humanity to be poor?[1] The answer to this question plays a decisive role in determining the point of departure and subsequent development of his teaching on prayer. Bonaventure offers an insight into both the cause and nature of human poverty, and, thereby, an answer to the question concerning poverty and its relationship with prayer, when he speaks of the poor in the desert as those bent over and blinded by the effects of original sin:

> According to the original state of Creation, the human
> person was created fit for the quiet of contemplation and
> thus *God placed him in the paradise of pleasures.* But
> turning away from the true light to a changeable good, he
> and all who were to follow, were through his fault bent
> over by original sin which infected human nature in two
> ways; that is the mind by *ignorance* and the flesh with
> *concupiscence.* And so it is that the human person, *blinded*

---

[1] On the theological significance of poverty in Bonaventure's thought, see: Hermann Schalück, *Armut und Heil* and "Armut und Heil. Die theologischen Implikationen des Armutsgedankens bei Bonaventura" in vol. 4 of *SB*, 673-683. See also: Aidan Carr, "Poverty in perfection according to Saint Bonaventure," *FSt* 7 (1947): 313-323 and 415-425; Alexander Gerken, *Theologie des Wortes. Das Verhältnis von Schöpfung und Inkarnation bei Bonaventura* (Düsseldorf: Patmos Verlag, 1963) 175-181; 319-327 and 334; Wayne Hellmann, "Poverty: the Franciscan way to God," *TD* 22 (1974): 339-345; and Silvano Buscaroli, "La povertà francescana secondo S. Bonaventura," *MF* 78 (1978): 357-412.

and *bent over*, sits in darkness and does not see the light of

heaven ....[2]

Once bent over and blinded by the decision to turn away from the divine light, humanity lacks the gift of grace necessary for contemplation.[3] As a result of such poverty,[4] everyone must pray like a poor mendicant[5]; that is, as someone who begs from another.[6]

Prayer is the characteristic expression of the mendicant's begging, for what the poor need above all else is the divine grace sought in prayer.[7] Although the prayer of the mendicant is motivated by the necessity of poverty,[8] it is also encouraged by the conviction that the Lord hears the cry

---

[2] "Secundum enim primam naturae institutionem creatus fuit homo habilis ad contemplationis quietem, et ideo *posuit eum Deus in paradiso deliciarum.* Sed avertens se a vero lumine ad commutabile bonum, incurvatus est ipse per culpam propriam, et totum genus suum per originale peccatum, quod dupliciter infecit humanam naturam, scilicet *ignorantia* mentem et *concupiscentia* carnem; ita quod *excaecatus* homo et *incurvatus* in tenebris sedet et caeli lumen non videt ...." *Itin,* c. 1, n. 7 (V, 297b-298a). The image of one bent over by sin also appears in *Comm Lc,* c. 13, n. 24 (VII, 342b) and *Dom 18 post Pent,* 1 (IX, 423a). It was used earlier by Bernard of Clairvaux in *Sermo 80,* n. 4 in vol. 2 of *Sancti Bernardi Opera,* ed. Jean Leclercq, Henri Rochais and Charles Talbot (Rome: Editiones Cistercienses, 1958) 279-280.

[3] *Itin,* c. 1, n. 7 (V, 298a).

[4] According to Bonaventure, poverty is the lack of what is necessary: "... in *paupertate* intelligitur indigentia necessariorum." *Dom 2 Adventus,* 1 (IX, 48a).

[5] *Comm Lc,* c. 18, n. 58-66 (VII, 470a-472b).

[6] The work, *Evangelical Perfection,* describes a mendicant in the following terms: "*Mendicus* est qui ab alio petit." *Perf ev,* q. 2, a. 2, fund. 9 (V, 137b). See also, *Perf ev,* q. 2, a. 2 (V, 150b). On Bonaventure's idea of mendicancy and the mendicant controversy at the University of Paris, see: Sophronius Clasen, *Der hl. Bonaventura und das Mendikantentum* (Werl/Westfalen: Franziskus Druckerei, 1940).

[7] *Itin,* c. 1, n. 8 (V, 298a).

[8] The lack of what is necessary lies at the root of all petitionary prayer for "... omnis enim petitio praesupponit necessitatem et indigentiam in petente ...." *Dom 3 post Epiph,* 1 (IX, 183a). On meaning of "necessity" in Bonaventure's theology, see: *I Sent,* d. 6, au., q. 1, (I, 125a-126b) and *Myst Trin,* q. 7, a. 1 and 2 (V, 106a-112b).

of the poor.[9] This conviction is rooted in the generosity of the Lord, for as Bonaventure writes, God is most generous in sharing the gift of grace and desires that humanity ask for it in prayer.[10] The divine desire to share the gift of grace through prayer manifests itself in the call to conversion.[11] The response of the poor to the divine call reveals itself in the cry for mercy[12] and in the prayerful desire for Christ,[13] who himself entered into the world as a poor man so as to enrich the poor with spiritual gifts.[14] The relationship between poverty and prayer is the subject of the present chapter. In the first part of the chapter, the cause and nature of human poverty is studied. Then, the bond between poverty and prayer is pursued. Finally, the Christological dimensions of prayer are examined in light of the advent of Christ.

1. 1. Human Poverty

In the beginning, humanity was created poor inasmuch as from the moment of existence every ". . . creature depends essentially and totally on the Creator."[15] Yet in the Garden of Paradise,[16] humanity, unlike the poor in

---

[9] *Comm Lc*, c. 7, n. 43 (VII, 176a).

[10] *Brev*, p. 5, c. 10 (V, 263b).

[11] *II Sent*, d. 28, a. 2, q. 1, concl. and ad 1 (II, 682b-683a).

[12] *Comm Lc*, c. 15, n. 31 (VII, 394a).

[13] *Vig nat Domini*, 1 (IX, 88a-89a).

[14] *Epiph*, 1 (IX, 147b).

[15] ". . . creatura essentialiter et totaliter a Creatore dependet." *II Sent,* d. 1, p. 1, a. 3, q. 2, concl. (II, 35a). On this point, see: Hellmann, "Poverty: the Franciscan way to God," 340 and Schalück, "Armut und Heil. Die theologischen Implikationen," 675-676. This dependency on the Creator is poverty since the poor are those who lack the means of sustaining themselves. As the work *Perf ev* says: ". . . *pauper* est qui sibi non sufficit."

the desert, stood upright[17] and was able to contemplate without difficulty the light of divine wisdom reflected in the mirror of Creation. Although unable to gaze directly on the essence of God, humanity could discern, in the myriad creatures of Paradise, the unmistakable reflection of the Creator.[18] As Bonaventure writes in the *Breviloquium,*[19] all of the perceptible world was created as a book in which the wisdom of the Creator was revealed. By reading the Book of Creation, humanity was able to perceive the Triune God in a three-fold manner: first, in the divine traces of oneness, truth and goodness found in all creatures; then, in the divine image revealed in all ra-

---

Perf ev, q. 2, a. 2, fund. (V, 137b). See also: *Perf ev*, q. 2, a. 2 (V, 150b).

16 On the location of Paradise, Bonaventure says: "Unde secundum Sanctos paradisus terrestris est locus valde eminens et altus, quasi medium tenens inter hanc vallem miseriae et patriam caelestem . . . ." *Dom 12 post Pent,* 1 (IX, 399a).

17 *II Sent,* prooem. (II, 3b-4a). On humanity's original upright stance before God and this text, see: Hayes, *The Hidden Center,* 19-21. For a general treatment of the medieval teaching on humanity's original state, see: Heinrich Köster, *Urstand, Fall und Erbsünde in der Scholastik* in vol. 2 (Faszikel 3b) of *HDG,* 12-95. On the creation of humanity and the meaning of Paradise in Bonaventure's theology, see: *II Sent,* d. 17, dub. 2 (II, 426a-427b) and *Dom 12 post Pent,* 1 (IX, 399a).

18 *II Sent,* d. 23, a. 2, q. 3, concl. (II, 544b-545b). In this section of the *Commentary on the Sentences,* Bonaventure discusses the knowledge of God that Adam enjoyed in the Garden of Paradise. He refutes the opinion that Adam was able to contemplate the essence of God since this form of knowledge is available only in the state of glory. On the other hand, he points out that in the state of innocence, Adam was able to contemplate God without hindrance in the mirror of Creation because the mirror was not yet obscured by the effects of sin. For Bonaventure's treatment of the various opinions concerning Adam's knowledge of God, see: Marianne Schlosser, "Lux Inaccessibilis. Zur negativen Theologie bei Bonaventura," *FS* 68 (1986): 41-48. On the knowledge of God before and after the advent of sin, see also: *Dom 12 post Pent,* 1 (IX, 399a).

19 *Brev,* p. 2, c. 12 (V, 230b) and *Brev,* p. 2, c. 11 (V, 229a). On the concept of Creation as "book" in Bonaventure's theology, see: Winthir Rauch, *Das Buch Gottes. Eine systematische Untersuchung des Buchbegriffes bei Bonaventura* (München: Max Hueber Verlag, 1961) esp. 28-111. The book metaphor also appears in Hugh of St Victor's Theology, see: Grover A. Zinn Jr., "Book and Word. The Victorine Background of Bonaventure's Use of Symbols" in vol. 2 of *SB,* 151-164 and in Bernard of Clairvaux's theology, see: Ulrich Köpf, *Religiöse Erfahrung in der Theologie Bernhards von Clairvaux* (Tübingen: J.C.B. Mohr, 1980) 176-178. For a study on the symbolic understanding of "book" in classical and medieval literature, see: Ernst Robert Curtius, *Europäische Literatur und lateinisches Mittelalter* (Bern: A. Francke AG Verlag, 1948) 304-351.

tional creatures who possess a memory, intelligence and will; and finally, in the soul which has been transformed by the theological virtues of faith, hope and love into a divine similitude. These divine traces, images and similitudes served as the successive steps of a spiritual ladder upon which humanity returns to God in contemplation.[20]

Contemplation in the Garden of Paradise was possible as long as humanity remained faithful to its original nature.[21] Taken from the earth, formed in the image of God, and infused with divine grace, humanity stood upright in the presence of God as ruler and king of all of Creation. It continued to do so as long as it remained ordered to the Creator through the proper use of the intelligence, will and power. Thus, the original state of humanity included a fundamental orientation toward God and a continual call to be conformed to God. Both these elements are crucial for an understanding of what it means to stand upright in the presence of God. As Bonaventure points out in the *Commentary on the Sentences*, humanity was created not only with the possibility of standing upright inasmuch as it was made in the image of God, but, in fact, humanity already stood upright in the Garden because it was oriented toward God through the gift of grace. Humanity remains standing upright, however, only as long as it responds faithfully to the gift of divine grace.[22]

---

[20] *Brev*, p. 2, c. 12 (V, 230a-b). Bonaventure's teaching on contemplation and his use of the terms, divine traces (vestigii), image (imago) and similitude (similitudo) is treated in Chapter Four.

[21] *Itin*, c. 1, n. 7 (V, 297b-298a).

[22] *II Sent*, prooem. (II, 3a-5a). When speaking here of humanity's state in the Garden, Bonaventure uses various forms of the word "conversion" to indicate the original orientation of the soul toward God made possible through the gift of grace. The act of orienting, or "converting," the soul toward God is contemplation in a broad sense, for contemplation: ". . . consistit in conversione ad Deum . . . ." *II Sent*, d. 9, praenot. (II,

31

The gifts of grace were necessary in order to orient the soul toward God. They were also necessary because of human indigence: since men and women were created out of nothing, they were inherently weak and liable to fall into sin.[23] In addition to the two natural means of assistance, rectitude of conscience and synderesis,[24] the Creator also gave two gifts of grace enabling humanity to both avoid sin and seek after the divine good. The first gift of grace, which can be called preparatory grace or helping grace, enlightened the intellect, thereby revealing the eternal truth inscribed within human nature and the surrounding world. The second gift of grace is called sanctifying grace; it enabled men and women to love the Creator and each other in accordance with the divine will.[25] Through sanctifying grace they stood upright in the Garden, transformed, as it were, into the likeness of the Triune God.

240b) and, as such, is a form of prayer; see: *IV Sent,* d. 15, p. 2, a. 1, q. 4, concl. (IV, 368a).

[23] *Brev*, p. 2, c. 11 (V, 229b). On Bonaventure's understanding of grace, with a bibliography on the subject, see: Jean Pierre Rezette, "Gratia," *LSB*, 74-77.

[24] *Brev*, p. 2, c. 11 (V, 229b). The synderesis is identified with the will insomuch as it is inclined toward the good. It also struggles against evil. The rectitude of conscience, on the other hand, concerns proper judgment. On both meanings of the term "synderesis" in Bonaventure's theology, see: Jacques Guy Bougerol, "Synderesis," *LSB*, 125.

[25] "Duplicem etiam superaddidit perfectionem *gratiae*: unam gratiae *gratis datae*, quae fuit scientia illuminans intellectum ad cognoscendum se ipsum, Deum suum et mundum istum, qui factus fuerat propter ipsum; aliam gratiae *gratum facientis*, quae fuit caritas habilitans affectum ad diligendum Deum super omnia et proximum sicut se ipsum." *Brev*, p. 2, c. 11 (V, 229b-230a). The term "gratia gratis data" is sometimes translated as "actual grace," but it will be referred to here as preparatory, or helping grace. This is done to avoid any confusion between Bonaventure's understanding of the term and the more contemporary understanding of actual grace. The two should not be identified strictly with each other. On this point, see: Franz Mitzka, "Die Lehre des hl. Bonaventura von der Vorbereitung auf die heiligmachende Gnade," *ZKT* 50 (1926): 30; Johann Auer, *Die Entwicklung der Gnadenlehre in der Hochscholastik. Das Wesen der Gnade* (Freiburg: Herder, 1942) 348 and René Charles Dhont, *Le problème de la préparation à la grâce: débuts de l'école franciscaine* (Paris: Éditions Franciscaines, 1946) 218. The term "gratia gratum faciens" will be translated as "sanctifying grace."

1. 1. 1. The Poverty of Being

Even though humanity stood upright and was able to contemplate the Creator in the Book of Creation, it was, nevertheless, from the beginning poor, for it had been created out of nothing by another. It is, thereby, indebted to another for its very being. This ontological dependence on the Creator reveals the poverty of Creation in general and the poverty of humanity in particular. According to Bonaventure, all creatures are said to be indigent because, as creatures, they are dependent on God as the original source of being. Furthermore, they remain poor in that they remain dependent on the continual generosity of the Creator:

> . . . the first principle, by its omnipotent power and most
> kind generosity, brought every creature into *being* out of
> nothing. Because of this, the creature has of itself *non-
> being* and receives all *being* from another source. Thus,
> the creature was made, so that according to its indigence,
> it might always be in need of its principle, and this
> principle, in keeping with its generosity, might never
> cease to exercise an influence [on the creature].[26]

All creatures are poor because they are dependent on God for their eventual

---

[26] ". . . primum principium sua omnipotenti virtute et benignissima largitate creaturam omnem de nihilo produxerit ad *esse*; ac per hoc creatura de se habeat *non-esse*, totum *esse* habeat aliunde: sic facta fuit, ut ipsa pro sua defectibilitate semper suo principio indigeret et primum principium pro sua benignitate influere non cessaret." *Brev*, p. 5, c. 2 (V, 253b). See also: *I Sent*, d. 37, p. 1, a. 1, q. 1, concl. (I, 639a) and *II Sent*, 3d. 7, a. 1, q. 2, concl. (II, 865b).

fulfillment as well as for their origin and continued existence.[27] Rational creatures manifest a particular poverty of dependence, since the soul was meant from the beginning to find enjoyment in the Creator;[28] they experience ultimate happiness or beatitude only when the soul reaches this preordained end.[29]

1. 1. 2. The Poverty of Sin

The choice of the Creator to bring creatures into being out of nothing, as Bonaventure teaches, was a free act of grace in no way attributable to something that was lacking in God. The Creator was not forced to create, but, rather, chose to bring all things into existence as a gift.[30] While the gift of existence contained a call to turn toward God as the source of support and fulfillment, it also carried with it the eventual possibility of sin. According to

---

[27] *Myst Trin,* q. 1, a. 1, concl. (V, 49a).

[28] *I Sent,* d. 1, a. 3, q. 1, concl. and ad 1 (I, 38b-39a). See also: *I Sent,* d. 1, a. 3, q. 2, concl. (I, 41a); *I Sent,* d. 1, dub. 12 (I, 44b) and *II Sent,* d. 19, a. 1, q. 2, concl. (II, 463a). In all these texts, the verb *frui* is employed to describe the enjoyment of the Creator by the soul. On Bonaventure's understanding of "frui," see: Jacques Guy Bougerol, "Frui" in *LSB,* 73; Ludger Meier, "Zwei Grundbegriffe augustinischer Theologie in der mittelalterlichen Franziskanerschule" in *Fünfte Lektorenkonferenz der deutschen Franziskaner für Philosophie und Theologie* (Werl/Westfalen: Franziskus Druckerei, 1930): 59-64; and also: George Tavard, "La structure de l'expérience fruitive," *EF* 34 (1952): 205-211.

[29] *Itin,* c. 1, n. 1 (V, 296b). On the beatitude of the soul, see: Joanne Hartnett, *Doctrina Sancti Bonaventurae de deiformitate* (Mundelein, Illinois: Seminarii Sanctae Mariae ad Lacum, 1936); Ignatius Brady, "Beatitude and Psychology. A Problem in the Philosophy of St. Bonaventure," *FSt* 2 (1942): 411-425; Antonio Briva Mirabent, *La Gloria y su relación con la Gracia según las Obras de San Buenaventura* (Barcelona: Editorial Casulleras, 1957); and Atanasio Matanic, "'Beatitudo est in unione.' La felicità dell'uomo alla luce del magistero bonaventuriano," in Supplement II of *SBM,* 269-280.

[30] *I Sent,* d. 44, a. 1, q. 2, concl. ad 4 (I, 783b). See also: *II Sent,* d. 1, p. 2, a. 2, q. 1, concl. (II, 44b).

Bonaventure, this possibility of sin was engraved in the depths of human nature because it was created out of nothingness.[31] That which comes from nothing bears within the structure of its being an inclination to turn toward the nothingness from which it was created.[32] This turning toward nothingness is characteristic of evil[33] and is manifested in sin, that is to say, in the free choice of a corruptible good over the eternal good of the Creator.[34] In the Garden of Paradise, the possibility of sin embedded in human nature became a reality; for humanity, in the persons of Adam and Eve, opted to sin by turning away from the Creator to the nothingness of corruptible goods.[35]

The advent of sin rendered humanity poor in a new way for ". . . in turning away from God the human person is made poor on account of [his or her own] fault."[36] This second dimension of human poverty found in Bonaventure's theology can be termed the "poverty of sin" or "moral poverty."[37] As such, it designates the existential condition of all who suffer

---

[31] *Brev*, p. 3, c. 1 (V, 231a-b). On the possibility of sin according to Bonaventure, see: Maurits de Wachter, *Le péché actuel selon saint Bonaventure* (Paris: Éditions Franciscaines, 1967) 28-44.

[32] *Brev*, p. 5, c. 2 (V, 254a) and *II Sent*, d. 19, a. 1. q. 1, concl. ad 2 (II, 460b).

[33] ". . . semper malum facit tendere ad *non-esse* . . . ." *I Sent*, d. 46, dub. 7 (I, 836b).

[34] Bonaventure teaches that sin is the free choice of a changeable good over the eternal good of the Creator. As a result, sin is the privation, or corruption, of good; it is an option for the nothingness equated with corruptible beings, see: *Brev*, p. 3, c. 1 (V, 231a-b) and c. 5 (234b).

[35] On the sin of Adam and Eve as the choice of a changeable good over the eternal good, see: *Brev*, p. 3, c. 3 (V, 232b-233a). On original sin in Bonaventure's theology; see: Philippe Delhaye, "Peccatum originale," *LSB*, 106-107.

[36] ". . . homo in aversione a Deo efficitur: *pauper* propter culpam . . . ." *Dom 18 post Pent*, 2 (IX, 425b).

[37] In the *Perf ev* Bonaventure identifies two levels of being and two levels of nothingness (poverty): ". . . cum duplex sit *esse*, scilicet naturae et gratiae, duplex est nihilitas: uno modo per oppositionem ad *esse naturae*, alio modo per oppositionem ad *esse moris et*

35

under the consequences of sin, and like the poor one in the desert, stand in need of sanctifying grace. The poverty of sin is linked to the poverty of being; it is the result of humanity's refusal to accept the creaturely dependency proper to the poverty of being.[38]

Since rational creatures are created out of nothing, they should constitute God as principle, exemplar and end of their actions.[39] They do this by living with the help of grace according to the divine image etched into their nature. By nature, they are obliged to seek ultimate happiness in God alone because only an infinite good is able to satisfy the soul.[40] The reality of sin, however, is an attempt to deny dependence on God because it represents the attempt to make a created good into a final end.[41] Instead of freeing humanity from its ontological deficiency, sin results in a further deficiency, or poverty, on the moral level. Thus, humanity is a mendicant because it has lost the grace which previously oriented it toward God.[42]

---

gratiae." Perf ev, q. 1, concl. (V, 122a). This second level of nothingness, or poverty, which concerns moral behavior and grace, is "moral poverty." On these two levels of poverty, see: Hayes, *The Hidden Center,* 22. The nothingness of moral poverty can be attributed to sin and the subsequent loss of grace, see: *Brev,* p. 5, c. 3 (V, 255a). This poverty, which arises through human sinfulness, is spoken of as: "die Armut der Sünde" by Schalück, in the chapter "Der 'Pauper in Deserto' als Mensch in der Sünde;" see: *Armut und Heil,* 69-108.

[38] On this point, see: Schalück, *Armut und Heil,* 91-92 and Hellman, "Poverty. The Franciscan Way to God," 340-341.

[39] *De regno Dei,* n. 43 (V, 552a).

[40] *I Sent,* d. 1, a. 3, q. 2, concl. (I, 40b-41a); *Scien Chr,* q. 6, concl. (V, 35a-b); and ad 15 (V, 36b).

[41] *II Sent,* d. 42, a. 2, q, 1, concl. (II, 965a).

[42] "... genus humanum ... est ... *mendicans* per defectum gratiae et iustitiae ...." *Comm Lc,* c. 18, n. 58 (VII, 470a). On the relation between original justice and grace, see: Berard Marthaler, "Original Justice according to St. Bonaventure" in *Franciscan Approach to Theology,* ed. Sebastian Miklas (Washington, D.C.: The Franciscan Educational Conference, 1958): 166-175.

With the loss of sanctifying grace, humanity lost the ability to stand upright in God's presence; however, it can never forget this rectitude it possessed in the Garden, for not even sin can erase the image of God within the soul. As Bonaventure teaches in the *Commentary on the Sentences*, rational creatures after the Fall still retain the desire for rectitude despite their crippled stature.[43] Although they no longer stand upright, oriented as it were toward God as a divine similitude, rational creatures still reflect the divine image in their natural faculties. They long, albeit in a confused manner, to stand up straight; that is to say, they long for the rectitude found through the proper use of their faculties. Yet, they are helpless to do so because they are poor; they have lost the help of sanctifying grace which turned them toward God and fashioned them into a divine similitude. Without the assistance of grace, humanity is reduced from being a similitude to a wounded image of the divine.

Bonaventure considers this reality in his exegesis of the parable of the good Samaritan:

> Another [teaching] can even be drawn out according to the spiritual meaning [of the parable] such that the *person who is needy* on account of misery may be interpreted as the *human race*, which sinning in Adam, *went down from Jerusalem to Jericho*, that is to say, from paradise into the world, and *fell among robbers*; namely, into the power of demons who *robbed* him of the gifts of grace and *wounded* him in [his] natural powers. They *left him half-dead* in that after the *similitude* had been taken away only

---

[43] *II Sent,* prooem. (II, 5b-6b).

37

the *image* remained . . . . That image, nevertheless, was despoiled because of a turning away [from God] and wounded because of a turning around [to temporal goods] . . . .[44]

The loss of sanctifying grace and the wounding of the natural powers left humanity a beggar; a miserable caricature of the creature who originally stood upright in the Garden of Paradise.[45] The original rectitude, which was determined by justice and grace, was replaced with a state of anxious mendicancy. After the loss of sanctifying grace, humanity could no longer be conformed to the divine exemplar through the proper use of the faculties of intellect, will and power. Instead of looking to God as the source of truth, the intellect now searches elsewhere out of curiosity and is plunged into ignorance, misery and doubt. Like the intellect, the will also manifests the damage wrought by sin, for it no longer seeks to be conformed to the highest good through love. Driven by concupiscence, the will turns from the divine good to commutable goods but is continually unsatisfied by them. Finally, the faculty of power is impotent because it is no longer exercised in harmony with the source of all power. Once the king and ruler of all of Creation, humanity is now reduced to a fruitless begging for peace in the midst of a world

---

[44] "Alia etiam potest elici secundum *sensum spiritualem*, ut *persona indigens* ex miseria intelligatur *genus humanum*, quod in Adam peccante descendit *ab Ierusalem in Iericho*, id est a paradiso in mundum, et *incidit in latrones*, id est in potestatem daemonum, qui *spoliaverunt* eum gratuitis et *vulneraverunt* in naturalibus. Et *reliquerunt semivivum*, quia, subtracta *similitudine*, remansit sola imago . . . Illa tamen *imago* est *exspoliata* propter aversionem et *vulnerata* propter conversionem . . . ." *Comm Lc*, c. 10, n. 62 (VII, 271a-b). On the place of spiritual interpretation in Bonaventure's method of exegesis, see: Helmut Riedlinger, "Zur buchstäblichen und mystischen Schriftauslegung Bonaventuras" in *Grundfragen christlicher Mystik*, ed. Margot Schmidt and Dieter R. Bauer (Stuttgart-Bad Cannstatt: Friedrich Frommann Verlag, 1987): 139-156, esp. 150-156.

[45] *II Sent,* prooem. (II, 3a-6b). On Bonaventure's understanding of sin and this text, see: Hayes, *The Hidden Center*, 21-23.

alienated from the Creator.

The ignorance of the intellect and the concupiscence of the will are two primary expressions of moral poverty. Both mark the poverty of the poor in the desert. Both can be traced back to humanity's attempted rejection of its ontological poverty and the subsequent loss of grace. Bonaventure says that humanity was blinded when it turned from the divine light to seek another good.[46] The crippling action of concupiscence, which is evident in the way it deforms human nature by pulling it downwards toward temporal goods, blinds humanity to spiritual truths. As Bonaventure point outs in the *Commentary on Luke*, once humanity is bent over by concupiscence, it is incapable of looking upwards into the divine light.[47] Without this light of grace, humanity finds itself in the darkness of spiritual exile and is unable to find the way back to the divine good.[48]

Concupiscence of the will is one of the most bitter manifestations of the suffering associated with the poverty of sin. As the anxious searching for some finite good to replace the infinite one it lost, concupiscence is doomed to failure for ". . . nothing created is able to compensate for the good which

---

[46] *Itin*, c. 1, n. 7 (V, 297b-298a). On the question of concupiscence and poverty in Bonaventure's theology, see: Schalück, *Armut und Heil,* 76-78 and 86-95. See also: Berthold Schlachmuylders, "Concupiscentia," *LSB*, 37-38. Concupiscence is both the cause of original sin and a punishment of that sin in Bonaventure's theology. Concupiscence has a positive connotation, however, when understood as the desire for wisdom; see: *Hex*, coll. 2, n. 2 (V, 336a-b). For a general theological understanding of concupiscence, see: Karl Rahner, "Zum theologischen Begriff der Konkupiszenz" in vol. 1 of *Schriften zur Theologie* (Einsiedeln: Benziger Verlag, 1954): 377-414.

[47] *Comm Lc*, c. 18, n. 58 (VII, 470a-b). Bonaventure also pinpoints cupidity and avarice as the causes of this "spiritual kyphosis" in his spiritual interpetation of the woman in Luke's Gospel who was bent over for 18 years: "Potest autem per hanc *incurvationem longaevam* intelligi morbus *avaritiae* et cupiditatis, quae incurvat cor ad temporalia . . . ." *Comm Lc,* c. 13, n. 24 (VII, 342b). See also: *Dom 2 Adventus*, 1 (IX, 46a).

[48] *Dom 16 post Pent,* 1 (IX, 415b).

has been lost since it is infinite; therefore, [humanity] grasps, seeks and never rests."[49] This anxious, futile search for a finite good causes manifold sufferings according to the *Collations on John*. Here, Bonaventure identifies three specific areas where concupiscence seeks a finite good and three forms of sickness resulting from it.[50] The first area where concupiscence emerges is in the desire for carnal delights, which leads to bodily infirmity; the second is in the seeking of riches, which produces cupidity; and finally the third area is in the longing for honors, which causes ambitiousness.

Another manifestation of the poverty of sin appears in the intellect where the loss of divine grace produces a spiritual blindness. This blindness, which is sometimes referred to as ignorance, supplanted the contemplative vision of God which humanity enjoyed in the Garden of Paradise. Although the corporal eye is still able to perceive the physical world after the Fall, the rational eye has been dimmed and the contemplative eye has been blinded;[51] therefore, the divine reflection is obscured in the mirror of Creation:

> . . . to know God *in an effect* is to see by means of a
> mirror and this [takes place] in two ways: either by means
> of a clear mirror and eye, and thus the first person used to
> see before the Fall; or by means of a *darkened* mirror,
> and this is the way we see just now because on account of

---

[49] ". . . nihil creatum recompensare potest bonum amissum, cum sit infinitum, ideo appetit, quaerit et nunquam quiescit . . . ." *II Sent,* prooem. (II, 5b).

[50] *Coll Jn,* coll. 79, n. 8 (VI, 629a).

[51] *Hex,* coll. 5, n. 24 (V, 358a). See also: *Epiph,* 3 (IX, 159b). Bonaventure makes use in both of these texts of Hugh of St. Victor's teaching on the "three eyes" found in *De sacramentis, PL* 176, 329. See also: *Brev,* p. 2, c. 12 (V, 230a). On this theme in Bonaventure's theology, see: Adelhard Epping, "Zur Bonaventuras Schrift De reductione artium ad theologiam," *WW* 27 (1964): 114-115. For a comparison of Hugh's teaching with Bonaventure's, see: Zinn, "Book and Word." 164.

sin both our eyes have been darkened and all creatures
have been enveloped in darkness . . . .[52]

Because of its darkened vision, humanity is no longer able to discern
the divine presence in Creation, and the contemplative ascent up the ladder of
creatures back to the Creator is rendered impossible.[53] In the *Collations on
the Six Days,* Bonaventure describes this crippling inability to perceive the
divine presence in terms of spiritual illiteracy: when humanity peers into the
Book of Creation, it finds itself before a text written in a foreign language;
creatures appear merely as things; objects without symbolic significance or
transcendent reference to the divine author.[54]

In addition to concupiscence and spiritual blindness, the present state
of poverty or misery[55] is marked by manifold suffering, both spiritual and
corporal. In an Advent homily dealing with the imprisonment of John the
Baptist, Bonaventure interprets John's chains to be symbolic of the three-fold
state of human misery.[56] His exegesis does not ignore the existence of
concupiscence and spiritual ignorance: John's chains represent the pull of

---

[52] ". . . cognoscere Deum *in effectu,* hoc est videre *per speculum,* et hoc dupliciter; aut per
speculum *lucidum* et oculum, et sic videbat primus homo ante lapsum; aut per speculum
obscuratum, et sic videmus nos modo, quia propter peccatum et oculi nostri caligaverunt, et
omnes creaturae obtenebratae sunt . . . ." *Comm Jn,* c. 1, n. 43 (VI, 255b-256a). See also:
II Sent, d. 23, a. 2, q. 3 concl. (II, 545a) and *Dom 12 post Pent,* 1 (IX, 399a).

[53] *Hex,* coll. 13, n. 12 (V, 390a). Concerning the difficulty in seeing the reflection of the
divine in Creation after the Fall, see: Ulrich Gottfried Leinsle, *Res et Signum. Das
Verständnis zeichenhafter Wirklichkeit in der Theologie Bonaventuras* (München: Verlag
Ferdinand Schöningh, 1976) 177-188.

[54] *Hex,* coll. 2, n. 20 (V, 340a).

[55] Bonaventure observes in the *Brev* that in sinning humanity fell from the state of
innocence to the state of misery; see: *Brev,* p. 3, c. 3 (V, 233a).

[56] *Dom 2 Adventus,* 1 (IX, 45b-46a). On corporal misery, see also: *Dom 15 post Pent,* 1
(IX, 411b).

41

concuppiscence which binds the soul to worldly goods as well as the lack of spiritual vision. They also represent, however, the burden of corporal misery which weighs so heavily that humanity is unable to stand up and breathe. These chains of corporal misery are: hunger, thirst, nudity, and sickness. The weather is also a source of corporal misery because winter is too cold and summer too hot, autumn too dry and spring too humid. Even within the psychological realm there is misery, for the will is divided against itself, while at the same time it fights with reason.

The final aspects of the poverty of sin are spiritual, physical and eternal death.[57] Death is indicative of moral poverty in that it is nothing other than the tendency toward nothingness common to sin.[58] Humanity alone is directly responsible for these manifestations of misery. It bears the onus of spiritual death because it alone stripped the soul of divine life when it sinned and deprived it of grace.[59] In the aftermath of sin, humanity is spiritually dead.[60] Humanity is also responsible for physical death because it originally possessed the gift of grace which assured that the human body would never suffer the corruption of physical death. Only the advent of sin assured the advent of physical death.[61] The violent separation of the soul from the body at the moment of physical death, which itself is the result of sin, heralds the

---

[57] In Bonaventure's thought, death is the ultimate revelation of human poverty: ". . . in morte est summa privatio . . . . " *IV Sent,* d. 43, a. 1, q. 5, fund. 1 (IV, 891a). On death and poverty in Bonaventure's theology, see: Schalück, *Armut und Heil,* 100-108.

[58] *II Sent,* d. 19, dub. 3 (II, 474a).

[59] *Brev,* p. 5, c. 3 (V, 255a).

[60] *Coll Jn,* coll. 25, n. 2 (VI, 563b).

[61] *II Sent,* d. 19, a. 3, q. 1, concl. ad 2 (II, 470b). See also: *Dom 15 post Pent,* 1 (IX, 411b).

eternal suffering of those condemned to lose forever the vision of God.[62] This everlasting exile from the Creator is the final punishment of sin; it is eternal death.[63]

Sin brings the poor to the gates of death from which no one returns without divine intervention; only the gift of grace can open the gates of life.[64] Divine grace, understood as the continuous spiritual influence of God on the soul,[65] is the very life of the soul.[66] When the soul turns away from God, it turns away from the source of life and dies. In this dynamic of spiritual life and death, Bonaventure sees an analogy between the life of the soul and the life of the body: just as the body depends on the soul for life and remains alive as long as it is united to the soul, so too, the soul enjoys life as long as it is united to God.[67] Through sin, the poor have ruptured this vitalizing union with God; unless the gift of grace is restored, they will die in exile.

---

[62] *Brev*, p. 3, c. 5 (V, 234a-b).

[63] *Trip via,* c. 2, n. 2 (VIII, 8b) and *Perf vitae*, c. 5, n. 2 (VIII, 117b).

[64] Bonaventure equates sin with the gates of death and grace (along with the virtues) with the gates of life; see: *Coll Jn*, coll. 47, n. 2 (VI, 595b). On sin and the gates of death, see also: *Dom 20 post Pent*, 1 (IX, 432a).

[65] *I Sent*, d. 9, au., q. 4, concl. (I, 186b); *II Sent*, d. 26, au., q. 4, concl. ad 5 (II, 641a-b); and *II Sent*, d. 26, au., q. 6, concl. (II, 646a). Bonaventure often describes grace in terms of "influentia;" see: Jacques Guy Bougerol "Le rôle de l'influentia dans la théologie de la grâce chez S. Bonaventure," *RTL* 5 (1974): 273-300.

[66] *II Sent*, d. 26, au., q. 2, concl. (II, 636a); *II Sent*, d. 27, a. 1, q. 2, fund. 3 (II, 656b); and *II Sent,* d. 27, a. 1, q. 3, fund. 5 (II, 660a).

[67] *IV Sent*, d. 17, p. 1, dub. 3 (IV, 433a).

1. 2.   Mercy and the Call to Conversion and Prayer

The poor cry out in prayer for mercy in the midst of misery.[68] In the
final analysis, their supplication is the only alternative to spiritual death;[69] it
is the only road leading out of the desert of misery and back to union with
God.[70] Yet despite the importance of divine assistance and the corresponding
need to pray for it, there are many among the poor who refuse to turn to God
in prayer. In a sermon based on Mat. 8: 20, "Lord, save us, we are
perishing," Bonaventure notes that the present state of misery provides an
opportunity to experience the grace of God.[71] Many people, however, are
foolish and refuse to turn to God in the time of need. Instead of praying
patiently until God comes to their assistance, they become absorbed in their
misery. The experience of misery, which initially offered an occasion of
grace, becomes in the case of those who refuse to pray a road leading to

---

[68] *Comm Lc*, c. 18, n. 61 (VII, 471a).

[69] On the intrinsic link between petitionary prayer and death, see: Gisbert Greshake,
"Theologische Grundlagen des Bittgebets," *ThQ* 157 (1977): 36-38. On prayer for those
facing sickness or death, see: *IV Sent*, d. 23, a. 1, q. 4, concl. (IV, 595b) and *Dom 20
post Pent*, 1 (IX, 432a).

[70] Regarding this point in Bonaventure's theology, Etienne Gilson writes: "Man has turned
by a free act from the supreme God who is at once his beginning and his end; a new free
act in the reverse direction can never be sufficient to re-unite him with God, but such an act
is necessary all the same. We must begin by asking God to restore to us that of which we
are rightly deprived yet whose lack presses on us so cruelly; . . . But it should instantly be
added that if we have at our disposal the first act that may help us on the way back to God,
we have no other of any efficacy. Prayer first of all, more prayer, prayer unceasing: so
much man must do: more he can not do: the rest can come only come from God . . . . "
See: Etienne Gilson, *The Philosophy of St. Bonaventure,* trans. Dom Illtyd Trethowan and
Frank J. Sheed (Paterson, N.J.: St. Anthony Guild Press, 1965) 398-399.

[71] *Dom 4 post Epiph*, 1 (IX, 189a-b).

further misery. Without divine assistance, they perish in iniquity – overwhelmed, as it were, by the oppressive power of their poverty.

The decision of the poor to pray or not to pray for mercy is a free choice made in response to the divine call to conversion.[72] As a free choice, it can be understood only in reference to the gift of preparatory grace by which God moves the free will to turn back from the gates of death. This preparation is absolutely necessary if the sinner is to answer the call to conversion.[73] Bonaventure's insistence on the necessity of grace in the conversion process reflects his assimilation of the Augustinian tradition. Following this tradition, he maintains that the initial phase of conversion is dependent on the gratuitous intervention of God: "We have the beginning of our salvation when God has mercy."[74] In the same section from the *Commentary on*

---

[72] As can be surmised from the English, the word "conversion" comes from the Latin "conversio." It should be noted that Bonaventure does not always speak of "conversio" in the positive sense as a turning toward God. It can also signify the turning toward, and attachment to, temporal goods which follows upon the "aversio" of the rational creature away from God. In as much as the "conversio" is a turning back toward God, it is the foundation for contemplation; see note 22 above. On the dynamic of "aversio" and "conversio" in the context of sin, see: de Wachter, *Le péché actuel*, 207-221.

[73] *II Sent*, d. 28, a. 2, a. 1, q. 1, concl. and ad 1 (II, 682a-683a). On the question of preparatory or helping grace in Bonaventure's theology, see: Dhont, *Le problème de la préparation à la grâce*, 187-223 and Mitzka, "Die Lehre des hl. Bonaventura von der Vorbereitung auf die heiligmachende Gnade," 27-72.

[74] "Initium salutis nostrae Deo miserante habemus." *II Sent*, d. 28, a. 2, q. 1, concl. ad 1 (II, 683a). This quote, which Bonaventure attributes to Augustine, is actually from the *De ecclesiasticis dogmatibus, PL* 42, 1217 of Gennadius of Marseille as Dhont points out in *Le problème de la préparation à la grâce*, 215. The link between the Augustinian tradition and Bonaventure's teaching on grace and conversion is mentioned by Wolf Dieter Hauschild. Hauschild sees Bonaventure's reliance on the Augustinian conception of grace as a continuation of the early Franciscan teaching represented by Alexander of Hales: "Eine dogmengeschichtlich bedeutsame Systematisierung bringt nach 1235 die sog. ältere -> Franziskanerschule um -> Alexander von Hales in der ersten großen *Summa theologiae* mit speziellem Gnadentraktat (III, 61-69); auch -> Bonaventura trägt in seinen Schriften diese in der Augustintradition stehende Konzeption vor. Charakteristisch für sie ist die *Verbindung von Metaphysik und Psychologie*, die auf die Analyse der innermenschlichen Wandlungen im Zusammenhang von Bekehrung und Heiligung bezogen wird." See: Hauschild, "Gnade IV" in vol 13 of *TRE*, 486. On Augustine's theology of grace and

Sentences, he goes on to describe the entire dynamic of conversion and salvation: ". . . there are those four elements in the work of salvation; namely, *to invite, to assent, to assist* and *to persevere*: the first belongs to God's inspiration, the second belongs to free will, the third belongs to a divine gift and the fourth belongs to our solicitude as well as to divine assistance."[75]

The first step in the conversion process, the inspiration of God, falls under the broad category of preparatory grace. Preparatory grace includes any number of interior or exterior ways God chooses to invite the soul to conversion. Thus, natural habits, instilled virtues and interior illuminations assist the will in responding in an affirmative manner to the divine invitation.[76] A primary effect of preparatory grace is insight into the nature of

conversion, see: J. Patout Burns, "Grace: The Augustinian Foundation," in vol. 16 of *WS*, 345-348.

[75] ". . . sint in salutis opere ista quatuor, videlicet *invitare, acquiescere, adiuvare* et *permanere*; primum est inspirationis Dei, secundum libertatis arbitrii, tertium muneris divini, quartum sollicitudinis nostrae et divini pariter adiutorii." *II Sent*, d. 28, a. 2, q. 1, concl. ad 1 (II, 683a).

[76] ". . . quoniam nomine *gratiae gratis datae* non solummodo intelligimus illa quae enumerat Apostolus primae ad Corinthios duodecimo: *Alii datur per Spiritum* etc., sed etiam vocatur hic *gratia gratis data*, quidquid illud sit, quod superadditum est naturalibus, adiuvans aliquo modo et praeparans voluntatem ad habitum vel usum gratiae, sive illud gratis datum sit *habitus*, sicut timor servilis, vel pietas aliquorum visceribus inserta ab infantia, sive sit etiam aliquis *actus*, sicut aliqua vocatio vel locutio, qua Deus excitat animam hominis, ut se requirat." *II Sent*, d. 28, a. 2, q. 1, concl. (II, 682a-b). The interior illuminations of preparatory grace are particularly characteristic of the Franciscan school according to Auer: "Allgemein läßt sich feststellen, daß Thomas und seine Anhänger mehr die durch Gottes Vorsehung geschaffene äußere Situation (misericordia Dei) mit der helfenden Gnade meinen, während die Franziskaner mehr die innerseelischen Einwirkungen (illuminatio, excitatio, vocatio, directio) Gottes darunter verstehen." Auer, *Die Entwicklung. Das Wesen der Gnade*, 347. Despite the Franciscan emphasis on the interior action of preparatory grace, it should be noted that Bonaventure speaks of various external ways in which God moves sinners to conversion. The word *locutio*, for example, could denote an external, as well as an internal, call to conversion. In the *Coll Jn* Bonaventure says: "Nota, quod Dominus loquitur nobis aliquando per *signa creaturae;* aliquando per *litteras Scripturae*; aliquando quasi *per nuntios*, et hoc in praedicatione; aliquando quasi *voce viva*, et hoc interna inspiratione." *Coll Jn*, coll. 35 (an. 35) n. 1 (VI, 577a). Another way is through affliction and tribulation, see: *Comm Lc*, c. 15, n. 28 (VII, 393a) and *Dom 4 post Epiph*, 1 (IX, 189a-b).

good and evil. Without such knowledge, the will cannot make a free choice to turn from sin and return to God.[77] In the midst of moral poverty, the poor are in fact oblivious even to the possibility of choice. Although they are aware of goodness and search for it, they cannot come to a knowledge of God, the source of all goodness. Although their nature longs for perfection, they are unaware that perfection is found in God, who alone is the end of all Creation. Though they may even detest evil; they do so only because it has brought temporal suffering in its wake, not because it is an offense against God.[78]

Preparatory grace, understood in this context as spiritual insight into the nature of good and evil, is the foundation of the call to conversion in general, and of prayer, in particular. According to Bonaventure, the knowledge of divine goodness is a salient factor in the conversion process when coupled with a recognition of sin as an offense against that goodness. As such, sin is an evil which stands in opposition to God's goodness; it displeases God and requires an appropriate punishment.[79] The only thing the poor can do, other than suffer under the just punishment of God, is to acknowledge their sinfulness[80] and call out for mercy. The prayer for mercy is determined by preparatory grace since this grace reveals the reality of sin, facilitates the

---

[77] *II Sent*, d. 28, a. 2, q. 1, concl. (II, 682b).

[78] *II Sent*, d. 28, a. 2, q. 1, concl. ad 2, 3, and 6 (II, 683a-b).

[79] *IV Sent*, d. 14, p. 1, a. 2, q. 2, concl. (IV, 327a).

[80] Bonaventure terms the acknowledgment or recognition of sinfulness as "*Mentalis* confessio." He says: "Intelligendum est igitur, quod confessio peccati est *mentalis* et *vocalis. Mentalis* confessio est recognitio peccati et offensae . . . ." *IV Sent*, d. 17, p. 2, a. 1, q. 1, concl. (IV, 436b). He describes "*Vocalis* confessio" as the vocal confession of sin to God or another human being; see: *IV Sent*, d. 17, p. 2, a. 1, q. 1, concl. and ad 5 (IV, 436b-437a).

request for forgiveness[81] and makes known the availability of divine mercy.[82] Without the spiritual knowledge proper to preparatory grace, the poor would not only be ignorant to the nature of good and evil, they would also be unaware that God was merciful and ready to forgive those who humbly acknowledge their sinfulness and need for grace.

1. 2. 1. The Prayer for Mercy

The reality of human poverty and divine mercy points to the importance of praying for mercy. Although the theme of God's mercy appears throughout Bonaventure's writings, it takes on particular prominence within the context of his teaching on prayer. Mercy and prayer are inseparable: in the *Breviloquium,* he defines God as "most merciful" and then goes on to say that grace moves and directs the faithful to approach this most merciful God in trusting prayer.[83] They should confidently ask for mercy and not justice, for no one can claim to be worthy of God's grace.

---

[81] ". . . cognitio *offensae divinae* est de dictamine naturae adiutae aliquo modo per fidem. Quomodo enim scit homo, se *offendere Deum, quem non videt,* nisi per aliquem radium fidei hoc cognosceret? Cum autem hoc cognoscit, quod *Deum per praevaricationem inhonorat*; natura dictat, quod ab ipso est misericordia humiliter petenda; et hoc nunquam est, nisi recognoscatur culpa." *IV Sent,* d. 27, p. 2, a. 1, q. 1, concl. (IV, 436b). According to Bonaventure, faith is a form of preparatory grace; see: *II Sent,* d. 28, a. 1, q. 3, concl. (II, 680a).

[82] Preparatory grace moves the will in such a way that it comes to know of grace and ask for it; see: *II Sent,* d. 28, a. 2, q. 1, concl. (II, 682b). To ask for grace is to ask for mercy; see: *Trip via,* c. 2, n. 3 (VIII, 8b).

[83] ". . . cum primum principium in se ipso sit summe *verum* et *bonum,* in opere vero suo sit summe *iustum* et *misericors*; et summe *vero* debeatur firma assensio, summe *bono* fervens dilectio, summe *iusto* universalis subiectio, summe *misericordi* fiducialis invocatio; et gratia sit ordinativa mentis nostrae ad primi principii culturam debitam: hinc est, quod ipsa dirigit et regulat ad debita et meritoria exercitia in *credendis, amandis, exsequendis* et *postulandis,* secundum quod requirit summa veritas, bonitas, iustitia et misericordia in Trinitate beata." *Brev,* p. 5, c. 7 (V, 260b).

Those who trust in their own justice will be cursed, but those who trust in divine mercy will assuredly receive a blessing from the Lord.[84] Bonaventure makes this point while commenting on the *prothema* of a homily: "deal with your servant according to your mercy:"

> The *servant*, who in many matters offends his lord, asks incorrectly if he asks justice for himself from the lord because he requests punishment for himself; but when he humbles himself before his lord and asks for mercy, he quickly turns the lord to mercy. Thus, in the proposed text, the Psalm says: *deal with your servant [according to your] mercy*, not justice, because every day we act unjustly against the Lord. Therefore, let us ask mercy from him and he will not deny us, *because he is merciful and gracious*.[85]

Divine mercy is crucial, for it cleanses the poor from sin and liberates them from misery.[86] There can be no cleansing from sin without mercy

---

[84] *De annun B.V.M.*, 6 (IX, 686b).

[85] "*Servus*, qui in multis offendit dominum suum, si petit a domino iustitiam de se, male petit, quia petit de se ipso vindictam; sed quando humiliat se coram domino suo et petit misericordiam, citius flectit dominum ad misericordiam. Ita dicit Psalmus in verbo proposito: *Fac cum servo tuo misericiordiam*, non iustitiam, quia inique agimus quotidie contra Dominum. Petamus ergo ab eo misericordiam, et non negabit nobis, *quia misericors est et praestabilis super malitia*." *Dom 1 post Pent*, 2 (IX, 349a-b). Bonaventure goes on to say: "... et quia verbum sacrae praedicationis ab eo petere habemus, in humilitate cordis petamus, quia *humilium et mansuetorum semper* ei *placuit deprecatio*. Rogemus primo Deum." (IX, 349b). The psalm text, which serves as the *prothema*, is Ps. 119: 124. As was already mentioned in the Introduction (note 10), it was standard practice to use the *prothema* to teach the necessity of prayer. Here Bonaventure goes from the necessity of prayer in general: all are in need of the mercy which is received through prayer; to the necessity of prayer in particular: the homily depends on divine inspiration. The introduction then ends with a invocation to prayer (Rogemus primo Deum). Thus, the theoretical teaching on prayer finds immediate application in the situation at hand and the theory and praxis of prayer are linked within the context of the homily.

because in sinning against an infinite God, humanity has committed an offense which only the mercy of God can remit. The infusion of grace is the way the mercy of God relinquishes this offense;[87] yet grace does not drive out sin unless the free will assents to its purifying action.[88] Against the background of grace and free will, the supplication of mercy can be interpreted as the sign of assent to the workings of grace. As the parable of the prodigal son indicates, a prayer for mercy denotes an openness to divine inspiration; it brings about the remission of sin through the infusion of the gifts of grace.[89] This manifestation of divine mercy in the life of the prodigal son is assured to all those who do not let the fear of punishment keep them from asking for forgiveness. As Bonaventure says, God's mercy goes far beyond any offense which the sinner has committed.[90]

The prayer for mercy takes on added importance given the precarious situation of those who stand at the gates of death: they are more assured of obtaining divine mercy in this life than in the next. As Bonaventure writes in the *Commentary on the Sentences*, God has divided time in such a way that there is a time for mercy and a time for justice. This division is necessary since God is most merciful as well as most just.[91] In the present time of salvation history, mercy prevails over justice; mercy is available in

---

[86] *IV Sent,* d. 46, c. 4 (IV, 955b).

[87] *IV Sent,* d. 15, p. 1, au., q. 1, concl. (IV, 350b).

[88] *Brev,* p. 5, c. 3 (V, 254b).

[89] *Comm Lc,* c. 15, n. 34 (VII, 395a-b). This section describes the meeting of the father and son on the road back to home which, Bonaventure says, concerns the remission of sins; see: *Comm Lc,* c. 15, n. 40 (VII, 397b).

[90] *Dom 20 post Pent,* 1 (IX, 431b).

[91] *IV Sent,* d. 18, p. 1, a. 3, q. 2, dub. 2 (IV, 482b); *IV Sent,* d. 44, p. 2, a. 1, q. 1, concl. ad 6 (IV, 923a-b) and *IV Sent,* d. 46, a. 1, q. 3, concl. (IV, 960b).

abundance to all those who want to answer the call to conversion. While justice still demands that sinners in some way offer works of satisfaction, God is prepared to wash away the guilt proper to their infinite offense[92] and alleviate to some degree the suffering caused by moral poverty. This will not be the case after death, as those who have not accepted God's mercy in this life face the prospect of God's judgment. Given the gravity of the offense, the just punishment can be nothing less than eternal suffering.[93]

The forgiveness of sins is not the only end of the prayer for mercy; it also looks to the gift of sanctifying grace and eventual glorification. According to Bonaventure, the origin of grace lies in God's mercy,[94] and the imploring of mercy in prayer is ordered to the reception of the gifts of grace.[95] These gifts of grace are the manifestations of divine mercy which are poured into the hearts of those who approach God in prayer.[96] Thus, while prayer begins by asking for forgiveness, it also opens the door to the infusion of sanctifying grace. This reception of sanctifying grace posits glorification since there is no essential difference in Bonaventure's theology between the state of grace and glory.[97] The prayer which seeks mercy can be said to be or-

---

[92] *IV Sent*, d. 15, p. 1, au., q. 1, concl. (IV, 350b).

[93] *IV Sent*, d. 46, a. 2, q. 3, concl. (IV, 965b).

[94] *Trip via*, c. 2, n. 12 (VIII, 11b).

[95] *Trip via*, c. 2, n. 3 (VIII, 8b).

[96] *Brev*, p. 5, c. 10 (V, 263b).

[97] The link between prayer and glory is determined to a great degree by Bonaventure's theology of grace. He sees no essential difference between grace and glory. Thus, a prayer for mercy in general, or for a specific gift of grace in particular, is also (at least implicitly) a prayer for the glorification or deification of the soul. On grace and glory, see: *II Sent*, d. 27, a. 1, q. 3 (II, 659a-661b). See also: Mirabent, *La gloria y su relación con la gracia*, 245-273. According to Auer, Bonaventure is the first to take up the question of the relationship between grace and glory; see: *Die Entwicklung. Das Wesen der Gnade*, 166-167.

dered to sanctifying grace and glory as well as forgiveness. It can be considered the most fundamental and comprehensive of prayer forms since it seeks the three things which should be sought in prayer. As Bonaventure writes in the *Commentary on Luke*: ". . . prayer . . . ought to be for the sake of *obtaining a three-fold good*, that is forgiveness, grace and glory . . . . "[98]

1. 2. 2. The Decision to Pray

The decision to pray for mercy in general, or for any particular grace in particular, is not something Bonaventure takes for granted. Although the knowledge of good and evil indicates the appropriateness of prayer, there are many who do not act on it. Bonaventure illustrates this point in a homily where he distinguishes between the good and bad servants of God.[99] Mirroring the teaching of Francis of Assisi,[100] he underlines the radical nature of human poverty by reminding the congregation that the only thing they possess is sin. Any good which they have comes from God, who alone is the source of all good. Thus they will be lifted up out of their misery into a full knowledge of the Lord only when they humbly recognize the basic truth of their innate weakness and God's goodness.[101] Those who do are the "good

---

[98] ". . . oratio . . . debet esse propter *triplex bonum assequendum*, scilicet veniam, gratiam et gloriam . . . ." *Comm Lc*, c. 22, n. 58 (VII, 558b).

[99] *Dom 21 post Pent*, 2 (IX, 438a-440a).

[100] In the *Regula non bullata*, Francis of Assisi writes: "Et firmiter sciamus, quia non pertinent ad nos nisi vitia et peccata." *Regula non bullata*, c. 17, n. 6 in Kajetan Eßer, *Die Opuscula des hl. Franziskus von Assisi. Neue textkritische Edition* (Grottaferrata: Editiones Collegii S. Bonaventura, 1976) 392. On this text and poverty in Francis' spirituality, see: Kajetan Eßer, "Mysterium paupertatis. Die Armutsauffassung des hl. Franziskus von Assisi," *WW* 14 (1951): 181.

[101] "De primo dicit Isaias quinquagesimo secundo: *Ecce, intelliget servus meus, exaltabitur*

servants of the Lord." Those who do not are what the Scriptures call "evil servants." Despite their poverty and God's desire to save them, they act as if they were rich and without the need of salvation. According to the Book of Job: *"They have said to God: Depart from us, we do not want the knowledge of your ways. Who is the Almighty One that we should serve him? And what gain is it to us if we pray to him?"*[102]

The refusal of the evil servants to recognize their poverty and need for salvation is inseparable from their decision not to pray. They consider prayer to be meaningless because they believe they do not need to ask for anything

---

et elevabitur et sublimis erit valde. Dicit primo: *intelliget,* hoc est, plenam intelligentiam a Deo accipiet; quando enim homo cognoscit humiliter propriam infirmitatem suam, eo quod nihil boni habet a se ipso, immo a Deo habet, quidquid boni habet, a se tantum peccata sua; tunc accipit plenam intelligentiam divinae bonitatis. Et tunc *elevatur,* per gratiae Dei affluentiam, *et sublimis erit,* per visionis Dei plenariam fruitionem." *Dom 21 post Pent,* 2 (IX, 439a). As this text indicates, humility is an integral aspect in the acknowledgment of personal infirmity and divine goodness. In the work *Perf ev,* Bonaventure says humility arises from the consideration of both the ontological poverty and moral poverty marking human existence; see: *Perf ev,* q. 1, concl. (V, 122a). Such a consideration of human poverty, which also includes the recognition of God as the first principle and, thus, source of all, is the doorway to the experiential knowledge of God equated with wisdom, see: *Perf ev,* q. 1, concl. (V, 120b-121a). In regard to ontological and moral poverty, it should also be noted that the humble recognition of poverty and divine goodness, and with it the need for the prayer for mercy, often appears in relationship with moral poverty. This does not mean, however, that there is no relationship between ontological poverty and prayer. The reality of human weakness, which needs to be humbly acknowledged by the poor if they are to pray, is manifested in the poverty of sin. Yet as was previously explained, the very possiblity of moral poverty is rooted in the ontological truth of humanity's creation "ex nihilo." In similar fashion, the reality of divine goodness, which also needs to be acknowledged by the poor if they are to ask for the gifts of grace in the prayer for mercy, is rooted in the ontological truth of God's own being. As Bonaventure writes in the *Brev,* God, who is: ". . . summe . . . bonum in se ipso . . . ." wants to share generously the divine goodness through the infusion of the gifts of grace in prayer; see: *Brev* c. 5, n. 10 (V, 263b). Bonaventure holds that God is good and most generous because God is the greatest good, and consequently, most diffusive (This point is discussed in Chapter Two). In a Lenten homily he indicates that the knowledge of God's generosity as well as human poverty form the framework out of which prayer emerges: "Idcirco, carissimi, cognoscentes nostrae defectibilitatis *indigentiam* et divinae liberalitatis *affluentiam,* recurramus cum devota precum *instantia* ad Deum, Patrem luminum et datorem sapientiae . . . ." *Dom 1 in Quad,* 1 (IX, 204b).

[102] *"Qui dixerunt Deo: Recede a nobis, et scientiam viarum tuarum nolumus. Quis est Omnipotens, ut serviamus ei? Et quid nobis prodest, si oraverimus illum." Dom 21 post Pent,* 2 (IX, 439a). The text is from Job 21: 14.

53

that the Almighty could provide. They are similar to those who are approaching death and refuse to accept the true implications of their illness. The word of God, which can be considered a form of preparatory grace, enlightens the sick to their situation and to the means of recovery.[103] Yet, even when God has enlightened them to the reality of their situation, there is no assurance that they will act on such knowledge. If they, like the evil servants, decide to reject the truth of divine inspiration, they will also refuse to pray, for as Bonaventure says: "No one ardently *asks* unless one believes that one has need of the thing one is asking and trusts in a hearing."[104]

The invitation to conversion and prayer remains unanswered as long as the poor refuse to assent to the action of grace. Assent to divine inspiration is the second step in the dynamic of salvation. In the first step, where God invites the soul to conversion, the light of grace illumines the eyes of those in the shadows of death. Like the column of fire which guided the Israelites through the darkness of the desert to the Promised Land, God's grace guides

---

[103] Bonaventure describes the state of the unrepentant and the effect of the word of God in the following way: ". . . quando homo abominatur omnem cibum, ut non valeat comedere, de proximo imminet sibi mors, nisi per remedium medicinale adiuvetur; sic anima, quando *abominatur* caelestem *escam* divini verbi, prae nimia delectatione peccati ita absorbetur et obcaecatur, ut tanquam devia et infirma *appropinquet usque ad portas mortis* aeternae, nisi virtute divini verbi sanetur et dulcedine reficiatur et eius lumine dirigatur, ut possit discernere bonum a malo, inter statum culpae et gratiae et differentiam mortis et vitae." *Dom 20 post Pent,* 1 (IX, 432a). On the word of God in medieval theology, see: Zoltan Alszeghy, "Die Theologie des Wortes Gottes bei den mittelalterlichen Theologen" *GR* 39 (1958): 685-705.

[104] "Nullus enim ardenter *petit*, nisi credat, se rei, quam petit, indigentiam habere et fiduciam de exauditione." *De modo vivendi* (IX, 724a). The importance of realizing one's need for God's assistance is crucial for the birth of prayer, since as Bonaventure says: ". . . nullus autem orat pro eo quod iam habet . . . ." *IV Sent*, d. 45, dub. 5 (IV, 952a). See also: *Comm Jn,* c. 14, n. 35 (VI, 442b) and: "Nemo petit ab alio quod ipse potest per se implere." *III Sent,* d. 17, a. 2, q. 1, concl. ad 1 (III, 372a). Both these axioms appear to be based on Augustine's statement: "Nam quid stultius, quam orare ut facias quod in postestate habeas?" *De natura et gratia,* c. 18, n. 20 *PL* 44, 256. On this teaching, see: *III Sent,* d. 17, a. 2, q. 1, note 3 (III, 371a).

sinners out of the darkness of misery to the eternal homeland.[105] This grace reveals to the will the existence of the gifts of grace and moves it to ask for them in prayer. As Bonaventure points out: "Therefore the will never rises up either to know of grace or to ask [for it] unless it be moved in some manner from above and through some gift of preparatory grace . . . ."[106] Preparatory grace, however, never forces the will to assent to its promptings. The decision to pray for mercy always remains a free choice. This choice is safeguarded by God, who offers the gifts of grace to those in misery but does not force the poor to ask for them.[107] In the end, the free decision of the poor determines if they will assent to the invitation to conversion by praying for the gifts of grace.

Those who do not accept the divine invitation cut themselves off from God's life. By their refusal to assent to divine inspiration, they cannot hope to reach the third step in the dynamic of conversion and salvation, which is the reception of God's gifts. The fact that the poor are by nature weak, and through sin, infirm, does not obligate God to share with them the gifts of sanctifying grace. In the *Collations on John*, Bonaventure states that God's grace is given in proportion to the soul's disposition for it, not according to the gravity of the need itself.[108] Just as God freely decides to call men and women to conversion, so, too, they must decide freely to turn back to the Almighty in prayer and, thereby, prepare themselves for the reception of

---

[105] *In Pent*, 9 (IX, 341b).

[106] "Ideo liberum arbitrium nunquam assurgit nec ad cognoscendam gratiam nec ad petendam, nisi aliquo modo a sursum excitetur et per aliquod donum gratiae gratis datae . . . ." *II Sent*, d. 28, a. 2, q. 1, concl. (II, 682b).

[107] *Brev*, p. 5, c. 10 (V, 263b).

[108] *Comm Jn*, c. 5, n. 17 (VI, 306a).

sanctifying grace. Preparatory grace moves the will in that direction by inviting it to cry out for a share in God's goodness and life.[109] Within this dynamic of salvation, prayer emerges as the privileged way to respond to God's inspiration because it uniquely disposes the soul to receive the gift of grace: "There is no better preparation for receiving divine grace than the petition of devout prayer."[110]

The reception of sanctifying grace neither marks the end of God's salvific action nor does it render prayer superfluous. Consequently, the fourth step in the conversion process outlined by Bonaventure is perseverance in the state of grace. This perseverance, which is marked by prayer, requires a continuous effort on the part of the poor to remain faithful to the Lord. It also requires God's continual assistance until the work of salvation is fulfilled. Conversion cannot be reduced to one single act by which the soul turns back to God. The initial prayer for mercy signals only the beginning of a long journey back to God. The journey also entails a concerted effort to lead a holy life. Since this effort itself is dependent on divine grace,[111] prayer must be a continual, integral part of the spiritual journey of the poor. Prayer seeks the grace which will bring the soul to the point

---

[109] *III Sent*, d. 28, a. 2, q. 1, concl. (III, 682b). This same section notes that preparatory grace is not in itself a disposition for the reception of sanctfying grace but, rather, an aid to help the soul dispose itself for the reception of sanctifying grace. Preparatory grace does this by alerting the will to the existence of sanctifying grace. Without such knowledge, the will would remain ignorant to the existence of sanctifying grace and, thus, incapable of praying for the gift of grace.

[110] "Nulla enim melior praeparatio ad impetrandam divinam gratiam quam petitio devotae orationis." *Dom 5 post Pascha*, 1 (IX, 312a). On prayer as a disposition for receiving the gift of grace, see also: *Brev*, p. 5, c. 10 (V, 263b) and *Dom 4 post Pascha*, 1 (IX, 309b-310a).

[111] *Itin*, c. 1, n. 8 (V, 298a).

where it is reoriented completely toward God.[112] While prayer begins with the admission of poverty and the request for God's mercy, it culminates in the glorification of the repentant poor.[113]

The call of the poor to conversion and prayer is summed up in Bonaventure's exegesis of the parable of the prodigal son.[114] All four elements of conversion appear to some degree in this parable; namely, divine invitation, human assent, the reception of God's gifts and perseverance in grace. The prodigal son is a mendicant by choice. He made himself poor by turning away from the Highest Good and squandering his inheritance of grace in a foreign land, yet, God does not abandon him in his misery; instead God invites him to conversion through the misery proper to poverty. The prodigal assents to divine inspiration by considering his own indigence, remembering his father's goodness, and by deciding to pray for mercy. He then sets out for his father's home by abandoning sin in favor of good works. While on the road he is met by his father, who mercifully bestows different gifts of grace upon him. As a penitent, however, the prodigal is ever mindful of his indigence and continues to ask that he might know the fullness of the father's love.[115] Bonaventure likens his prayer to the humble supplication of

---

[112] *Circum Domini*, 1 (IX, 137a).

[113] The link between prayer, grace, and the glorification of the poor is evident in Bonaventure's sermons on Francis of Assisi; see: *De S.P.N. Franc*, 5 (IX, 597b) and the *Sermon on the Feast of the Transferral of the Body of St. Francis* in *The Disciple and the Master. St. Bonaventure's Sermons on Francis of Assisi*. trans., ed., and intro. Eric Doyle (Chicago: Franciscan Herald Press, 1983) 138-141. On the sources used by Doyle for his translation, see: Doyle, *The Disciple and the Master*, 24-25 and 29. Bonaventure concludes both sermons (Doyle's translation, 141) and in *De S.P.N. Franc*, 5 (IX, 597b) by inviting those present to pray for the gift of grace so they, too, may join Francis in glory.

[114] *Comm Lc*, c. 15, n. 21-52 (VII, 389b-402b).

[115] Bonaventure's exegisis of the parable of the prodigal son distinguishes two moments of prayer in the conversion process. The first begins when the prodigal realizes his poverty

57

King Manasseh:

Calling upon your goodness, I now bend my knee before you. I have sinned Lord, and I acknowledge my iniquity. I beg Lord, asking: forgive me, that you may neither destroy me together with my iniquities nor at the same time save up evils for me forever, because you will save me, [who am] unworthy, according to your great mercy. And I will praise you at all times on all the days of my life, because the power of the heavens praises you and to you is glory for ever and ever.[116]

---

and his father's goodness. At this point, the prodigal prays that he be treated like one of the father's servants because he does not consider himself worthy enough to be called a son. This first prayer is motivated by hope. The second prayer appears when the prodigal is met by his father. He no longer asks to be treated like a servant, but simply states once again that he is not worthy to be called a son. This prayer is different from the first because the son has already been infused with grace and, thereby, reoriented to God. The prodigal is still a penitient, however, so he continues to admit his unworthiness. This admission of need is itself a prayer for the fullness of grace; that is, for the fullness of God's merciful love. On the first moment of prayer, see: *Comm Lc*, c. 15, n. 31 (VII, 394a) and on the second, see: *Comm Lc*, c. 15, n. 36 (VII, 396a-b).

[116] "'Nunc flecto genua mea coram te, precans bonitatem tuam. Peccavi, Domine, et iniquitatem meam agnosco; peto rogans: Domine, remitte mihi, ne simul perdas me cum iniquitatibus meis neque in aeternum reserves mala mihi, quia indignum salvabis me secundum magnam misericordiam tuam, et laudabo te semper omnibus diebus vitae meae; quoniam te laudat virtus caelorum, et tibi est gloria in saecula saeculorum.'" *Comm Lc*, c. 15, n. 36 (VII, 396a-b). Although Bonaventure says this prayer is from the *Book of Chronicles*, it is actually from the *Prayer of Manasseh*; see: *Comm Lc*, c. 15, n. 36, note 6 (VII, 396a).

1. 3. The Advent of Christ

The conversion of the prodigal son demonstrates the importance of
praying for mercy. His prayer for mercy, like that of all the poor, finds its
point of convergence in Jesus Christ. Bonaventure develops this
Christological dimension of mercy and prayer with particular force and
beauty in his Advent and Christmas homilies.[117] In a homily of the *First
Sunday of Advent*, he interprets the text "the one desired by all the nations
will come" in the context of prayer and the desire for the coming of Christ.[118]
The advent of Christ was something desired and prayed for by the holy men
and women of the Old Testament period; desolate and afflicted by the
seeming delay of the awaited Saviour, they called out to the God of mercy for
the fulfillment of the promise of salvation. Their prayer was not without
cause, since mercy was what originally moved God to make the promise of
salvation to Abraham and the descendents of Israel.[119] Encouraged by the

---

[117] In many of these homilies, Bonaventure speaks of the prayer of the patriarchs and
prophets who called out for mercy. Although their prayer was answered in the coming of
the Saviour, that does not mean that prayer is no longer necessary. On the contrary, during
Advent Bonaventure reminds his listeners of the importance of praying in the present so
that Christ through grace might come into their lives; see: *Dom 1 Adventus*, 14 (IX, 38a);
Dom 2 Adventus, 3 (IX, 49b) and *Dom 2 Adventus*, 4 (IX, 51a). This coming in grace is
the third of four "advents" mentioned by Bonaventure: the first is "in carnem," the second
"ad iudicium," the third is "in *mentem* per gratiam novam," and the fourth is "ad *mortem*
per aeternam gloriam;" see: *Dom 1 Adventus*, 6 (IX, 32a).

[118] *Dom 1 Adventus*, 2 (IX, 27a-b). The text "*veniet desideratus cunctis gentibus*" is from
Hag. 2: 8 and is found in the Vulgate, see: *Bibliorum sacrorum iuxta vulgatam
Clementinam*, ed. Aloisius Gramatica (Cologne: Benziger, 1914) 870. The text is not
found, however, in the post conciliar Vulgate; see: *Nova vulgata bibliorum sacrorum*,
editio. The Second Vatican Council (Roma: Liberia Editrice Vaticana, 1979) 1668.

[119] *Comm Lc*, c. 1, n. 99 (VII, 33b) and *Comm Lc*, c. 1, n. 128 (VII, 40a).

generous mercy of God and moved by their own poverty, the patriarchs and saints of old desired and prayed for nothing less than the coming of the Son of God.[120]

The people of the Old Covenant prayed with sincere longing for the coming of the Son of God because he is in himself most desirable.[121] According to Bonaventure, something is desirable if it is beautiful to see, useful in effect and sweet to taste. These three qualities are found in a most excellent manner in Christ: he is beautiful to gaze upon, of help to those who receive him and a source of spiritual sweetness to the soul. The Son of God is beautiful to gaze upon because he is without any blemish of original or actual sin: the vision of such innocence brings delight to those who behold it. He is also of assistance to those who receive him: the possession of his illuminating grace aids the soul searching for God in the darkness of ignorance. Nothing in Creation can offer such clarity of vision to the soul since creatures are mere shadows and similitudes of the truth, while the Son of God is the fullness of truth. Finally, he is the one desired by the nations because his wisdom brings spiritual sweetness to the soul which turns to him instead of clinging to temporal goods.

The prayerful desire for Christ is also rooted in humanity's fallen nature.[122] As Bonaventure points out in his *Christmas Eve* homily, the divine

---

[120] *Dom 1 Adventus*, 2 (IX, 28b); *Dom 1 Adventus*, 22 (IX, 43a-45b); *Dom 2 Adventus*, 4 (IX, 50a); *Dom 2 Adventus,* 9 (IX, 56a-b); *Vig nat Domini*, 1 (IX, 88a-89a) and *De purif B.V.M*, 4 (IX, 651b).

[121] *Dom 1 Adventus*, 2 (IX, 28b-29a).

[122] In one advent homily, Bonaventure speaks of a four-fold state of human misery which gave rise to a four-fold desire for a four-fold coming of Christ. Each one of these states of misery was represented by an Old Testament figure: "Circa primum nota, quod adventum hunc sancti Patres desideraverunt ex quadruplici consideratione, scilicet ex consideratione miseriae *iniquitatis*, quae est pronitas ad malum, et tali modo desiderabat David, *in iniqui-*

image and likeness were etched into the soul by the Creator. Marked by such excellence, rational creatures stood at the summit of visible Creation and all other creatures were subject to them. Although they eventually forfeited their original excellence through sin, rational creatures still retained the desire to return to the former state of grace.[123] After the Fall, the light of faith illuminated some to the need for the humble Incarnation of the Son of God; they understood that he would humble himself because humanity had exalted itself through sin.[124] Through this advent of the Son, the soul would be restored to its former excellence. Thus, they began to love the Son of God

---

tatibus conceptus: Quemadmodum desiderat cervus ad fontes aquarum, ita desiderat anima mea ad te, Deus. - Miseriae *infirmitatis*, quae est difficultas ad bonum, et hoc modo desiderabat Iob: *Quis mihi tribuat auditorem ut desiderium meum audiat Omnipotens?* - Miseriae *caecitatis*, quae est ineptitudo ad cognoscendum verum, et hoc modo desiderabat Tobia: *Quale gaudium mihi erit, qui in tenebris sedeo et lumen caeli non video?* et tertii Regum decimo: *Universa terra desiderabat vultum Salomonis, ut audiret sapientiam eius* etc. - Miseriae *captivitatis*, quae est impedimentum ad aeternum regnum, et hoc modo fuit desiderium in Daniele; Danielis decimo: *Daniel, vir desideriorum, intellige verba, quae ego loquor ad te, et sta in gradu tuo.* Desiderabat enim, ut Christus veniret sicut *iustificatio* contra miseriam iniquitatis, sicut *corroboratio* contra miseriam infirmitatis, sicut *illuminatio* contra miseriam caecitatis et sicut *liberatio* contra miseriam captivitatis." *Dom 2 Adventus*, 9 (IX, 56a-b).

[123] "*Quis mihi det te fratrem meum sugentem ubera matris meae, ut inveniam te foris et deosculer te et iam me nemo despiciat?* Canticorum octavo. In verbo proposito desiderium animae devotae desiderantis Nativitatem Christi in proximo futuram describitur ordinate. Ordo autem et ratio huius desiderii talis fuit: anima rationalis, cum creata est, Dei imagine est insignita et cunctis visibilibus praeposita, et *omnia subiecta sunt pedibus eius*, secundum illud Genesis primo: *Faciamus hominem ad imaginem et similitudinem nostram, et praesit piscibus maris*, etc. Sed hanc excellentiam perdidit, cum peccavit; remansit tamen in ea sublimitatis et excellentiae *appetitus*." *Vig nat Domini*, 1 (IX, 88a). Along somewhat the same lines, see: *II Sent,* prooem. (II, 5a-6b).

[124] "Videns igitur anima lumine fidei illustrata, se non posse in pristinam excellentiam restitui, nisi tantum se humiliaret Dei Filius, quantum se exaltaverat homo superbus . . . ." *Vig nat Domini*, 1 (IX, 88a). Those who preceded Christ's birth in time were able to be illuminated by grace because the merit of Christ's passion was already at work by virtue of God's promise of salvation. Even though they were illuminated by grace, those who lived in the period of the Law and the Prophets were in a period of darkness as compared to those who live after the historical revelation of the Son of God. On the different periods of grace and types of knowledge associated with faith and the Scriptures, see: *III Sent*, d. 13, a. 2, q. 3, concl. ad 6 (III, 290b); *Christus mag*, n. 3-5 (V, 568a-b) and *Epiph*, 1 (Collatio) (IX, 150a). See also: Hayes, *The Hidden Center*, 101-102. On the humility of God in the Incarnation, see: Gerken, *Theologie des Wortes*, 315-334.

and yearn for union with him. No union other than that with the incarnate Christ could ultimately satisfy the desire of their souls because one who loves desires to be joined to the beloved. The fulfillment of this desire necessitates the visible presence of the beloved since no one can be united in a satisfying manner with a lover who is absent or hidden.[125]

Bonaventure unfolds his thought on prayer and union with the incarnate Christ in the context of a sermon for Christmas Eve on the Song of Songs. The particular text on which he was preaching reads: "Who will give you to me as a brother, sucking my mother's breasts, so that I may find you outside, and kiss you, and no one would despise me." According to Bonaventure's exegesis, this text expresses the prayer of a devout soul, who, looking into the future, longs to be united with the coming Christ. It is a radical prayer because it asks for nothing less than the open manifestation of God in the flesh:

> This devout soul, therefore, asks for the *manifest ap-*
> *pearance* of the Son of God, because it does not only ask
> that he be given to it *in the mind* like that devout soul in
> the ninth chapter of Book of Wisdom, *"Give me*, O Lord,
> *the wisdom that sits by your throne*, etc.," but it was
> asking that he be given in the flesh: *"Who will give you as*
> *a brother to me."* It was not asking that he be given
> *secretly* in the flesh, as in the womb of the Virgin, but
> *openly*, as in the lap or in the manger. Whence it adds:
> *sucking my mother's breasts*," as if he says: I do not only

---

[125] "Et quia amans amato desiderat copulari, desideravit gratam copulam; et quia copulari non poterat gratanter absenti et latenti, ideo desiderat eius praesentiam et apparentiam." *Vig nat Domini*, 1 (IX, 88a).

ask that you be given to me as God in the soul, nor so much as a brother in the womb, but that you be given openly as a child in the lap. And this was brought to fulfillment in the nativity . . . ."[126]

The radical nature of this prayer is seen not only in the fact that it sought the Incarnation of Christ, but even more in that it sought the immediate coming of Christ in the flesh.[127] It did not ask that Christ be given at some later date, but, rather, prayed that Christ be given at once lest the promise of salvation be delayed any longer.[128] Bonaventure sees three good reasons behind this prayer. First, God had already promised, and even sworn to Abraham, that the Saviour would be given to the people. Trusting in the promise, the people of the covenant, ". . . dared to address and insistently ask their God: *show to us your mercy O Lord*."[129] Second, the people dared to petition God for help because they were faced on all sides by tribulation. They prayed for the coming of the Son of God because they realized that no human being could rescue them from the death of sin; only the Son of God could redeem them. Third, they dared to call out for the fulfillment of the

---

[126] "Petit igitur haec anima devota Filii Dei *manifestam apparentiam*, quia non tantum petit, sibi dari *in mente*, sicut illa anima devota, Sapientiae nono: *Da mihi*, Domine, *sedium tuarum assistricem sapientiam* etc.; sed petebat, dari in *carne: Quis mihi det te fratrem meum*. Nec petebat, dari in carne *latenter*, sicut in Virginis utero, sed *apparenter*, sicut in gremio vel in praesepio; unde addit: *sugentem ubera matris meae*, quasi dicat: non tantum peto, te mihi dari ut Deum in anima, nec tantum fratrem in utero, sed manifeste dari ut parvulum in gremio; et hoc est in nativitate completum . . . ." *Vig nat Domini*, 1 (IX, 88a-b). The text from the *Book of Wisdom* is Wis. 9:4 and from the *Song of Solomon* (*Canticle of Canticles*), S. of S. 8:1.

[127] *Vig nat Domini*, 1 (IX, 88b-89a).

[128] On this theme, see also: *Dom 1 Adventus*, 2 (IX, 27a).

[129] ". . . ausae sunt . . . Deum suum alloqui et petere instanter: *Ostende nobis, Domine, misericordiam tuam*." *Vig nat Domini*, 1 (IX, 88b).

63

divine promise because they were weary and afraid of not seeing the coming of the Lord which had been foretold by the Prophets.

In the fullness of time, the God of mercies generously responded to the cry of the people by fulfilling the long awaited promise of salvation: he embodied his mercy[130] by giving his only begotten Son to the world in the mystery of the Incarnation.[131] In doing so Bonaventure says: "God offered the greater of the alms which can be offered: he gave his Son to us and in this he gave us everything that he possessed . . . ."[132] The alms which the Father offered by giving the Son expressed his great generosity because the poor were not given money, but a person; not a servant, but the Son.[133] In the gift of the Son, the generosity of the Father was complete: in the Son he gave all he was because he and the Son are of the same nature; in the Son he gave all he possessed because he and the Son are equal; and in the Son he gave all he could because he gave his only begotten Son. In these three ways, the gift of the Son reveals the richness of the Father's merciful love and fills the poor with an abundance of spiritual gifts.

---

[130] "*Suscepimus, Deus, misericordiam tuam in medio templi tui. Haec misericordia* Christus est, quam omnes Sancti desiderabant, clamantes: *Ostende nobis, Domine, misericordiam tuam et salutare tuum da nobis,* id est, Iesum tuum da nobis. Hanc misericordiam *suscepit* hodie Simeon *in ulnas suas in medio templi,* quem Virgo Maria prius susceperat in medio ventris sui." *De purif B.V.M.,* 4 (IX, 651b).

[131] *Vig nat Domini,* 1 (IX, 89a-b). On the timing of the Incarnation, see: *Brev,* p. 4, c. 4 (V, 244a-245a).

[132] "Deus maiorem eleemosynam fecit, quae fieri potest; dedit Filium suum nobis et in hoc dedit nobis totum, quod habuit . . . ." *De purif B.V.M.,* 1 (IX, 636a). The image of God as almsgiver is also found in the legends of Saint Francis; see: *Leg maj,* c. 7, n. 9-10 (VIII, 525a-b) and Thomas de Celano, *Vita secunda S. Francisci Assisiensis,* n. 77 in vol. 10 of *Analecta Franciscana,* ed. PP. Collegii S. Bonaventurae (Quaracchi: Collegium S. Bonaventurae, 1927) 177.

[133] *Vig nat Domini,* 1 (IX, 89a-b). It was also an act of generosity on the part of the Son because he came personally and did not send anyone in his place; see: *Dom 1 Adventus,* 2 (IX, 27b).

64

The gift of the Son was the most useful gift that could ever be given to the poor. As the perfect gift which descends from the Father, it " . . . relieves all of our needs and our multiple indigence . . . ."[134] and, thereby, enables the poor to stand upright once again before God. This gift of the only begotten Son of God, who as a child was openly manifested to the world in a manger, brings strength, illumination and liberation to the human race. Although God was the strength of the poor before the Incarnation, it is fitting that the most powerful God should become a weak infant so that humanity could be strengthened in such an exchange.[135] In the Incarnation, the Son of God became the true bread of life offered for the sustenance of the poor and infirm. While all stand in need of divine nourishment, Bonaventure points out that religious and priests in particular should long for the bread from heaven:

> We ought to always desire this fortifying bread according
> to that which the Jews said: *Give us always this bread.*
> Nevertheless religious and priests, namely they who ask
> during the whole day *give to us our daily bread,* should

---

[134] " . . . omnem nostram relevet necessitatem et multiplicem indigentiam . . . ." *Vig nat Domini,* 1 (IX, 90a). Bonaventure's use of the verb "relevare" is significant because it means "to raise up" as well as "to relieve;" see: "Relevo," in Charlton T. Lewis and Charles Short, *A Latin Dictionary* (Oxford: The Clarendon Press, 1975) 1555-1556. See also: "Relevo" in Albert Blaise, *Lexicon latinitatis medii aevi* (Turnholt: Brepols, 1975) 785. Although the text cited above uses "relevare" in the sense of relieving a need, "relevare" can also convey the idea in Bonaventure's writings of raising or lifting up. When reflecting on the raising to life of the widow of Nain's son (Lk. 7: 11-17), he says, for example: "Est enim reverenter magnificandus Deus de opere recreationis, eo quod est . . . secundo, *manifestativum sapientiae* in relevatione hominis prostrati . . . ." *Dom 15 post Pent,* 1 (IX, 412b). Thus, it can be said that God's mercy revealed in Christ relieves the misery of the poor who are bent over by sin and, in doing so, helps them to stand upright once again. In regard to Christ and the return of the poor to the state of rectitude symbolized by standing upright, see also: *Dom 18 post Pent,* 1 (IX, 423a-424a).On Bonaventure's use of "relevare" and the question whether the incarnation was "decens" (fitting or proper) on the part of God and humanity, see: *III Sent,* d. 20, au., q. 1, concl. (III, 418a).

[135] *Vig nat Domini,* 1 (IX, 90a).

desire [this bread] most of all. And we ask [for this bread] both in the morning and evening, in the night and during the day, because we ought to always be hungry in accord with that text from the twenty-fourth Chapter of Ecclesiasticus: *they who eat me will still hunger* etc..[136]

The gift of the child also brought the light of salvation to those who had been blinded by their ignorance of God.[137] This coming of Christ as the light of the world is paradoxical in that the Son of God illuminates humanity by shrouding the brilliance of his eternal light in the mantle of temporal flesh. As Bonaventure states: "And therefore it was necessary that [the true light] be cloaked in flesh so that people might be able to see and imitate [it]."[138] Although the Son was from all eternity the true light, he was inaccessible to the poor before the Incarnation because they could not comprehend him.[139] In the Incarnation, however, the flesh serves as a filtering material, like a cloud covering the sun, thereby allowing humanity to gaze upon the splendor of the Son.[140] Once the radiance of his light was

---

[136] "Hunc panem fortificantem semper debemus desiderare, secundum quod Iudaei dixerunt: *Domine, semper da nobis panem hunc.* Maxime tamen debent desiderare Religiosi et sacerdotes, qui tota die petunt: *Panem nostrum quotidianum da nobis hodie*; et mane et sero et nocte et die petimus, quia semper esurire debemus, secundum illud Ecclesiastici vigesimo quarto: *Qui edunt me adhuc esurient* etc.." *Vig nat Domini,* 1 (IX, 90a). The text from *Ecclesiasticus* is from Sir. 24:21.

[137] *Dom 2 Adventus,* 4 (IX, 50b-51a) and *Dom 4 post Epiph,* 1 (IX, 189b).

[138] "Et ideo necesse fuit, carne obumbrari, ut homines possent videre et imitari." *Vig nat Domini,* 1 (IX, 90b). The use of "necesse fuit" evokes the question of the necessity of the Incarnation. On this question in Bonaventure's theology, see: Gerken, *Theologie des Wortes,* 193 ff. and Hayes, *The Hidden Center,* 153-191. In regard to the above text and the question of poverty and necessity, see: Gerken, 175-181.

[139] *Vig nat Domini,* 1 (IX, 90b).

[140] *III Sent,* d. 3, p. 1, dub. 2 (III, 79a-b); *Comm Jn,* c. 8, n. 18 (VI, 358a); *Comm Lc,* c. 9, n. 64 (VII, 237b); *Vig nat Domini,* 1 (IX, 90b); and *In nat Dom,* 4 (IX, 113a). The

tempered for human eyes, he who was previously inconceivable and beyond reach, appeared to the world as one both visible and approachable. As a result, men and women can look upon the Son, and illuminated by his witness to the truth, they can imitate his example of virtue.[141]

The truth of the Son's advent in the flesh cannot be perceived, however, unless there is a corresponding advent in the mind.[142] While Christ came into the world as a poor and humble child,[143] he also comes to the faithful in prayer as a penetrating light enlightening the mind.[144] This coming of divine light illuminates the mind to spiritual truths hidden in the shadows of sin; it is like a fire which illuminates the faithful with the splendor of

theme of "obumbratio Christi" also appears in Bernard of Clairvaux; see: n. 7, *Sermo 20* in vol. 1 of *Sancti Bernardi Opera*, 119 and n. 6, *Sermo 48* in vol. 2 of *Sancti Bernardi Opera*, 70. The question of illumination in Bonaventure's theology is discussed at greater length in Chapter Four.

[141] *Vig nat Domini*, 1 (IX, 90b); *Epiph*, 1 (IX, 147a-b); *Dom 2 post Pascha*, 1 (IX, 295b); and *Dom 2 post Pascha*, 2 (IX, 297b-299a; 301a).

[142] In the work *Christus mag*, Bonaventure writes there are two ways in which the believer knows something in faith. The first is when the light of Christ comes into the mind as divine wisdom and reveals the mysteries of faith. The second is when Christ comes in the flesh as witness and gives indisputable authority to the doctrine of faith found in the Scriptures; see: *Christus mag*, n. 2-5 (V, 568a-b). Gerken identifies the coming of Christ in the mind spoken of in *Christus mag*, n. 3 (V, 568a-b) with the "uncreated Word;" see: *Theologie des Wortes*, 116, while Winfried Schachten speaks of it in relation to the "inspired Word," see: *Intellectus Verbi. Die Erkenntnis im Mitvollzug des Wortes nach Bonaventura* (Freiburg: Verlag Karl Alber, 1973) 157. On theme of revelation and authority in Bonaventure's theology with reference to *Christus mag*, see: Renato Russo, *La metodologia del sapere nel sermone "Unus est magister vester Christus"* (Grottaferrata: Editiones Collegii S. Bonaventurae, 1982) 38-48. On Bonaventure's understanding of revelation and the medieval tradition, see: Joseph Ratzinger, *The Theology of History in St. Bonaventure*, trans. Zachary Hayes (Chicago: Franciscan Herald Press, 1971) 56-75.

[143] *Comm Lc*, c. 2, n. 16 (VII, 48a); *Vig nat Domini*, 2 (IX, 93a); *Vig nat Domini*, 6 (IX, 95a); *In nat Dom*, 28 (IX, 128b-129a); *Dom infra octavam nat Dom*, 1 (IX, 130a); *Epiph*, 1 (IX, 146b-147a) and *Epiph*, 3 (IX, 159a). On the salvific nature of Christ's poverty in Franciscan theology in general and in Bonaventure's theology in particular, see: Schalück, *Armut und Heil*, 148-172.

[144] *Dom 20 post Pent*, 1 (IX, 432b-433a). See also: *Epiph*, 6 (IX, 165a-b).

truth.[145] As the true and eternal light, the Son is a gift of the Father offered to the blind lest they forever walk in darkness.[146] Without the assistance of such a gift, it would be impossible for anyone to perceive the truth of divine revelation.[147] Once illuminated by the divine light, the faithful can perceive and assent to the truth of Christ's Incarnation,[148] as well as grow in their understanding of this salvific advent by imitating his example.[149]

In addition to bringing illumination and strength to the poor, the Father's gift of the Son heralds the dawn of liberation for those held captive by the power of the Devil.[150] Although the Almighty could have conceivably liberated men and women without the Incarnation,[151] it is, nevertheless, fitting that it was accomplished through the incarnate Son. As the appropriate medium between the extremes of human and divine nature, he is the perfect mediator of reconciliation.[152] As mediator, the Son forged peace between God and humanity by means of his total gift of self: in the nativity he offered

---

[145] *Dom 20 post Pent*, 1 (IX, 432b-433a).

[146] *Dom 4 post Epiph*, 1 (IX, 189b).

[147] *Christus mag*, n. 3 (V, 568a-b).

[148] *Epiph*, 3 (IX, 157b).

[149] According to Bonaventure, the imitation of Christ leads to a greater revelation of truth; see: *Perf vita*, c. 3, n. 3 (VIII, 12b-13a).

[150] *Vig nat Domini*, 1 (IX, 90b-91a). On Christ's passion and humanity's liberation from the power of the Devil, as well as from the penalties of sin, see: *III Sent*, d. 19, a. 1, q. 3 and q. 4 (III, 405a-408b). The fact that humanity is under the power of the Devil is due to its own free choice to give this power to the Devil; see: *Comm Lc*, c. 15, n. 27 (VII, 392a).

[151] *Vig nat Domini*, 1 (IX, 90b) and *III Sent*, d. 20, au., q. 4, concl. (III, 431a-b). On this point, see: Hayes, *The Hidden Center*, 174.

[152] *Vig nat Domini*, 1 (IX, 90a-91b). On Christ as the medium between humanity and God and as the mediator of humanity's reconciliation with God, see: *III Sent*, d. 19, a. 2, q. 2 (III, 409a-411b).

himself to humanity, and in the passion he offers himself back to God for the sake of humanity.[153] This reconciliation between sinner and God, which is effected in Christ's flesh, opened the door to the liberation of the soul from the power of evil. Bonaventure equates this advent experience to the liberation of the chosen people from Egypt:

> ... he descended in the *flesh* as a *most potent power* for the sake of strengthening [us]; whence it is said in the third chapter of Exodus: *I descended into Egypt so that I might liberate my people from the hands of the Egyptians. - He descended* at that time *into Egypt* when he assumed the state of punishment of human misery, so that by patiently suffering the evils of the penalty, he might delete the evils of guilt in us; so that by handing himself over to the hands of the Jews, *he might liberate* us *from the hands of the Egyptians*, that is of the demons; and so that by undergoing temporal death he might destroy eternal death.[154]

---

[153] *Vig nat Domini*, 1 (IX, 91a). See also: *Dom 1 Adventus*, 2 (IX, 27a).

[154] ". . . descendit in *carnem* ut *virtus potentissima* ad roborandum; unde dicitur Exodi tertio: *Descendi in Aegyptum, ut liberem populum meum de manibus Aegyptiorum.* – Tunc *descendit in Aegyptum*, quando poenalitatem humanae miseriae assumsit, ut, patienter sustinendo mala poenae, in nobis deleret mala culpae; et tradendo se manibus Iudaeorum, nos *liberaret de manu Aegyptiorum*, id est daemoniorum; et suscipiendo mortem temporalem, destrueret mortem aeternalem." *Dom 20 post Pent,* 1 (IX, 432b). The text from Exodus is Ex. 5: 8. For other texts concerning liberation and the paschal mystery, see: *Dom 1 Adventus*, 14 (IX, 38b); *Feria sexta in Paras*, 2 (IX, 265b); *In Resurrec*, 1 (IX, 274a-275a); *Dom 2 post Pascha*, 1 (IX, 295a-296a); and *In Ascen*, 7 (IX, 322a). It should be noted that Bonaventure speaks of the Incarnation in terms of "condescensio"and "descensio" in his reflection on the advent of Christ; see: *Dom 1 Adventus*, 22 (IX, 44a-b); *Dom 2 Adventus*, 4 (IX, 50b-51a); *In nat Domini*, 4 (IX, 113a); and *Dom 20 post Pent,* 1 (IX, 432b). On the theme of condescension in Bonaventure's theology with special reference to the Incarnation, see: Gerken, *Theologie des Wortes*, 327-329; Hayes, *The Hidden Center*, 135-137; and Schalück, *Armut und Heil*, 131-138.

Bonaventure speaks of the liberation of the poor in somewhat the same terms in a homily on the Resurrection. He states that Christ liberates the poor from the poverty of sin in three specific ways. First, the offense of sin is offset by the infusion of grace. Second, the obligation of punishment is removed by the merits of Christ's death. Third, the adversity of corporal misery is eradicated in the reception of glory in the resurrection.[155] The Father offsets the indigence of the poor by justifying them through the merits of the Son's passion. This justification is characterized as a new life in Christ made possible by the Father's merciful infusion of grace into the souls of the spiritually dead. The obligation of punishment is removed when Christ fulfills the Father's promise of salvation: he frees the poor from the just penalty of sin by offering himself in his passion to the Father as the price of liberation. The liberating power of the Son's passion descends to the depths of limbo to unbind the poor awaiting salvation. The adversity of corporal misery is eradicated in the promised future advent of the Son: when the Son comes at the time of the resurrection, he will glorify the servants of God by transforming their bodies into a likeness of his own.

The advent of the Son, which brings about the liberation of the poor from the poverty of sin, does not, however, signal the end of prayer. On the contrary, it elicits from the poor a response of devout prayer. In devout prayer, they seek to be united with the Son in love through a remembrance of the many benefits of his advent. According to Bonaventure, devotion is: ". . . the affection of grateful love arising from the remembrance of the benefits of Christ."[156] As a response of grateful love, it is preceded by the servile de-

---

[155] *In Resurrec*, 1 (IX, 274a-275b). See also: *Dom 1 Adventus*, 2 (IX, 29a-b).

[156] ". . . devotio est affectio amoris suavis proveniens ex memoria beneficiorum Christi."

votion commonly shown by servants to their masters and culminates in the amorous devotion characteristic of union with Christ.[157] For Bonaventure, the time set aside for prayer is a privileged time for the cultivation and expression of devotion. In the *Rule of Novices*, for example, he urges newcomers to religious life to cultivate devotion by pondering the manifold benefits of Christ's redemptive love and to express that devotion in prayer.[158] This devout prayer is of great import for the novices who are longing to encounter and enjoy the presence of Christ during prayer:

> Nevertheless pay attention to this, so that in the prayer
>
> which you offer you may be more zealous as to devotion
>
> then to consummation, so that as soon as you will have
>
> found Christ, you may not prolong the prayer any
>
> further, but, rather, enjoy him whom you were seeking,
>
> saying with the spouse: *I have found him whom my soul*

De S. M. Magdalena, 3 (IX, 561a). In this homily, Bonaventure draws an analogy between devotion and the scent of the perfume used by Mary to anoint the feet of Jesus. He says (IX, 561a): "Sicut enim unguentum ex variis odoriferis rebus fit, sic ex multis, quae Dominus fecit propter nostram redemptionem, fecit hoc unguentum devotionis consurgere." In a similar vein Bonaventure writes in the *Comm Lc*: "Unguentum *devotionis* conficitur ex speciebus *pretiosissimis*, id est omnibus Christi beneficiis, quae crescunt in horto dominico." *Comm Lc*, c. 23, n. 72 (VII, 586b). On devotion in the Middle Ages, see: Jean Châtillon, "Devotio," *DS* 3, 710-716, esp. 713 in regard to Bonaventure. On devotion to Christ and Bonaventure's work, the *Tree of Life*, see: Patrick Francis O'Connell, *The "Lignum Vitae" of Saint Bonaventure and the Medieval Devotional Tradition*, diss., U Fordham (Ann Arbor: UMI, 1985).

[157] *De S. M. Magdalena*, 1 (IX, 557b-558a). This homily speaks of devotion as "devotio subiectiva," "devotio gratifica" and "devotio amorosa." Each one of these levels of devotion are equated with the act of kissing: "devotio subiectiva" with the kissing of the feet; "devotio gratifica" with the kissing of the hands; and "devotio amorosa" with the kissing of the lips. For Bonaventure, the kissing of the lips is symbolic of the union brought about between humanity and God through the power of love. In his explanation of unitive love, he relies on the teaching of Pseudo-Dionysius. Bonaventure's use of the Areopagite's teaching on the unitve power of love is treated in Chapter Four.

[158] *Reg nov*, c. 2, n. 4 (VIII, 477b-478a).

loves, I have seized him and will not let him go.[159]

The cultivation and expression of devotion in prayer directed toward union with Christ is also treated in the *Tree of Life*. Given the decidedly Christological orientation of devotion in Bonaventure's theology,[160] it is not surprising that the stated intent of the work is the cultivation of devotion to Christ by means of reflection on his life.[161] In particular, the *Tree of Life* intends to further devotion by preposing a series of meditations on specific historical events in the life of Christ. This is done first of all by drawing the poor into affective contact with the individual events through an imaginative and moving depiction of the historical scene.[162] Once they have been engaged affectively by the historical event, they are moved to respond by entering more fully into its spiritual meaning. This response is not a mere sentimental reaction to the examples of love witnessed in the life of Christ. It is rather the expression of the devout desire to be united with Christ, the Son of God. This desire is summarized in a prayer found in the last meditation of the *Tree of Life*:

> Believing, hoping and loving *with all [my] heart, with all [my] mind and with all [my] strength,* may I be carried

---

[159] "Hoc tamen attende, ut in oratione, quam facis, magis studeas ad devotionem quam consummationem, ut statim, cum inveneris Christum, orationem ulterius non protendas, sed eo fruere, quem quaerebas, dicens cum sponsa: *Inveni quem diligit anima mea, tenui eum nec dimittam* . . . ." *Reg nov*, c. 2, n. 5 (VIII, 478a). The Scripture is S. of S. 3: 4.

[160] On the Christological orientation of devotion in Bonaventure's theology, see: Châtillon, "Devotio," 713.

[161] *Lig vit*, prol. 1-2 (VIII, 68a-b).

[162] On this method of meditative prayer, which Ewert Cousins describes as the "mysticism of the historical event," see: Ewert Cousins, "Francis of Assisi: Christian Mysticism at the Crossroads," in *Mysticism and Religious Traditions*, ed. Steven T. Katz (New York: Oxford University Press, 1983) 166-168.

into you, beloved Jesus, as to the goal of all things, because you alone satisfy, you alone save, you alone are good and pleasing to those who seek you and *love your name*. 'For you, my good Jesus, are the redeemer of the lost, the saviour of the redeemed, the hope of exiles, the fortitude of laborers, the sweet consolation of anguished spirits, the crown and imperial dignity of the triumphant, the singular reward and joy of all the citizens of heaven, the glorious offspring of the most high God, and the sublime fruit of the virgin womb, the most abundant fountain of grace *of whose fullness we have all received.*'[163]

1. 4. Summary

The present chapter began by asking why Bonaventure considers humanity to be poor and then sought to examine his teaching on prayer in light of his response to that question. According to Bonaventure, poverty is a comprehensive theological category comprising the poverty of being and the poverty of sin. Both levels of poverty are expressions of human dependency on the Creator: the first stems from God's free creative act which brings

---

[163] "In te igitur ut finem omnium credens, sperans et amans *ex toto corde, ex tota mente, ex tota anima, ex omni virtute* ferar, desiderate Iesu, quia tu solus sufficis, tu solus salvas, tu solus bonus et suavis es te requirentibus et *diligentibus nomen tuum*. 'Tu enim, mi bone Iesu, redemptor es perditorum, salvator redemptorum, spes exsulum, laborantium fortitudo, anxiatorum spirituum dulce solatium, triumphantium corona et imperiale fastigium, unica merces et laetitia omnium civium supernorum, inclyta proles summi Dei et fructus sublimis uteri virginalis, uberrimus quoque fons gratiarum omnium, *de cuius plenitudine nos omnes accepimus.*'" *Lig vit,* fr. 12, n. 48 (VIII, 85b).

human beings into existence; the second is the result of sin which strips men and women of the gift of sanctifying grace, thereby rendering them mendicants. The first level is the reality of all created beings who look to the Creator as the source of being, while the second reflects humanity's choice to turn away from the Creator into the nothingness of lesser goods. This free choice, which is already embedded in the ontological level of being by nature of its creation out of nothingness, brings about a state of misery symbolized in Bonaventure's theology by a blind, bent-over, poor person. The hallmarks of this person's misery are: the damaged faculties of the soul, corporal suffering and the onus of physical, spiritual and eternal death.

Bonaventure's teaching on poverty and prayer focuses on the relation between human misery and divine mercy: he stresses that the misery of the poor can be relieved by divine mercy if and when they call out for it in prayer. The possibility of the prayer for mercy is revealed within the dynamic of God's call to conversion. Through the action of preparatory grace, the poor come to realize the nature and implications of their misery; they are, likewise, made aware of God's desire to forgive them and share with them the gift of sanctifying grace and eventual glory. This enables them to know what should be sought for in prayer: divine mercy. Their prayer for mercy emerges as a privileged way of responding to the call to conversion, for it seeks the forgiveness of sins, the infusion of sanctifying grace and glory. It is grounded in God's merciful desire to come to the help of those suffering under the burden of misery. Thus, only after the divine initiative has been acknowledged, can the prayer for mercy be spoken of as a human response arising out of the experience of misery.

The interplay between divine initiative and human response within the context of the prayer for mercy is manifested with striking clarity in the gradual unfolding of salvation history. In the midst of the darkness of misery, God revealed to the patriarchs and prophets that a Saviour would be given to the nations who would set them free from the chains of death. Once enlightened as to the coming of the Saviour, the patriarchs and prophets began to desire that he would come quickly, and as a brother, to take flesh among them. Their desire was translated into the cry for mercy which was satisfied eventually in the Incarnation of the Son of God. This entrance of the Son into history as the gift of the Father reveals the depths of divine concern for the poor. According to Bonaventure, the Father gave everything that he could possibly give when he offered his only begotten Son as an alms to the poor.

As the gift which descends from the Father of mercies, the Son is the divine response to the the poor's cry for mercy: he strengthens, illuminates and liberates those who find themselves before the gates of death. As the embodiment of divine mercy, he enters into human history as a poor man who shared in the fragility of mortality. This advent of the Son in history enables humanity to stand upright before God. The coming of the Son of God does not render further prayer useless, for the poor of every age are called to pray that the Son will enter into their lives in an advent of grace. As Bonaventure points out, their devout prayer is a continual necessity if they wish to be united with Christ and experience in their own lives the divine riches which the Father gives to the faithful in his only begotten Son.

Chapter Two: Spiritual Adoption

The advent of the Son of God, which the poor seek in their prayer for mercy, offers them the opportunity of entering into the Kingdom of God as adopted sons and daughters of the Father.[1] While sin had alienated them from the Father and left them prey to the power of Satan, the coming of the Son reconciled them to the Father and liberated them from the grip of Satan. Once freed from servitude to the forces of corruption and death, they could become adopted sons and daughters of God through the regenerative power of the Holy Spirit.[2] The Holy Spirit, present in the world by means of grace, transforms the poor into the image of the natural Son[3] and leads them as adopted sons and daughters into the Kingdom of God.[4] This gift of the Spirit, which the Father sends together with the Son,[5] renders the poor rich in grace[6] and gives testimony that they are the sons and daughters of the Father, for it moves them to cry out in prayer "Abba, Father!"[7]

---

[1] *Comm Jn*, c. 1, n. 27 (VI, 252a-b) and *Comm Jn*, c. 1, n. 33, resp. (VI, 253b).

[2] *III Sent*, d. 1, a. 2, q. 3, concl. ad 5 (III, 30b-31b); *Coll Jn*, c. 3, coll. 11, n. 4 (VI, 551a-b); and *Circum Domini*, 1 (IX, 137a).

[3] *III Sent*, d. 10, a. 2, q. 2, concl. ad 4 (III, 237a-b).

[4] *Coll Jn*, c. 3, coll. 11, n. 4 (VI, 551b).

[5] *III Sent*, d. 1, a. 2, q. 3, concl. ad 5 (III, 31a-b).

[6] *Dom 4 post Pascha*, 1 (IX, 309b-310a).

[7] *Circum Domini*, 1 (IX, 137a) and *In Pent*, 2 (IX, 334b). On the meaning of the term "Abba," or "Father," in the Scriptures, see: W. Marchel, *Abba, Père! La prière du Christ et des chrétiens* (Rome: Biblical Institute Press, 1971) and Joachim Jeremias, *The Prayers of*

The purpose of this second chapter is to examine the prayer of the poor by considering it within the context of the spiritual adoption[8] initiated by the Father in the advent of the Son of God and brought to completion in the outpouring of the Holy Spirit.[9] Since the adoption of the sons and daughters of God is tied to their degree of conformity to the natural Son of God,[10] the prayer of the poor will be examined first of all in light of Bonaventure's teaching on prayer and the imitation of Christ. Although prayer in imitation of Christ is a distinctive mark of the adopted son or daughter of God,[11] it should not be forgotten that it is the gift of the Holy Spirit which transforms the poor into sons and daughters of God.[12] Since prayer is one of the ways the gift of the Holy Spirit is sought,[13] it is of crucial value for those wishing to be

---

Jesus, trans. John Bowden, Christoph Burchard and John Reumann (Norwich: SCM Press, 1967). On the testimony of the Spirit to the spiritual adoption of believers, see: Marchel, 224-225 and Jeremias, 65.

[8] The thematic of prayer and spiritual adoption is developed extensively in the Pauline theology of prayer; see: David Stanley, *Boasting in the Lord. The Phenomenon of Prayer in Saint Paul* (New York: Paulist Press, 1973) 115-130. Stanley speaks of this thematic (115) as: ". . . the dominant motif in Paul's conception of Christian prayer." It is also a concern of other New Testament writers; see: David Stanley, *Jesus in Gethsemane. The Early Church Reflects on the Suffering of Jesus* (New York: Paulist Press, 1980) 103-104; 136; 162; 164-165; 171; 185; 193; 232-233; and 242.

[9] According to Bonaventure, the entire Trinity is involved in the adoption of the sons and daughters of God, see: *III Sent,* d. 1, a. 2, q. 3, concl. ad 5 (III, 30b-31b); *III Sent,* d. 10, a. 2, q. 2, concl. and ad 4 (III, 236a-237b); *III Sent,* d. 10, a. 2, q. 3, concl. and ad 1-4 (III, 238a-b); *Comm Jn,* c. 17, n. 45 (VI, 477a); *Trip via,* c. 1, n. 13 (VIII, 6b); and *Vig nat Domini,* 1 (IX, 89b).

[10] *III Sent,* d. 1, a. 2, q. 3, concl. (III, 29b-30a); *III Sent,* d. 10, a. 2, q. 2, concl. ad 4 (III, 237a-b); *III Sent,* d. 10, dub. 5 (III, 240b); *Dom infra octavam nat Domini,* 2 (IX, 132b-133a); and *Dom 22 post Pent,* 5 (IX, 446a-b). On this point, see: Hayes, *The Hidden Center,* 183-187 and Gerken, *Theologie des Wortes,* 41-42.

[11] *Comm Lc,* c. 11, n. 1-4 (VII, 277a-278b) and *Dom 22 post Pent,* 5 (IX, 446a-b).

[12] *Brev,* p. 5, c. 1 (V, 252a-253a) and *Coll Jn,* c. 3, coll. 11, n. 4 (VI, 551a-b).

[13] Among many texts, see: *IV Sent,* d. 45, a. 3, q. 1, concl. ad 3 (IV, 949b); *Brev,* p. 4, c. 10 (V, 251b); *Brev,* p. 5, n. 10 (V, 263b-264b); *Comm Jn,* c. 14, n. 35 (VI, 442b); *Coll Jn,* c. 1, coll. 5, n. 5 (VI, 543a); *Comm Lc,* c. 11, n. 35 (VII, 288a); *Perf vit,* c. 5, n. 5

78

numbered among the children of God. Thus, this chapter considers prayer as the request for the gift of the Holy Spirit, as well as an expression of conformity to the Son of God. To arrive at a better understanding of these dimensions of prayer in Bonaventure's theology, special attention is given to his exegesis of the "Our Father."

2. 1. The Imitation of Christ

Bonaventure writes in the *Commentary on the Sentences* that in the Incarnation the Son liberates the poor from the servitude of sin, thereby, freeing them to become children of God.[14] This spiritual adoption is not a by-product of the Incarnation, but, rather, the fundamental reason why the Son took on flesh: ". . . the Incarnation is ordered to this end that we may be sons of God."[15] The work of spiritual adoption is undertaken in the Incarnation by the Son because he is the natural son of the Father through whom others may be led into an analogous filial relationship with the Father.[16] While the filiation of those adopted is not identical with that of the only begotten Son, it can be compared to it in so far as the filiation of the Son of God is the cause and model for all other filiations:

It must be said that we and Christ are spoken of as sons of

(VIII, 119a); *Epiph*, 1 (IX, 145b); *Dom 4 post Pascha*, 1 (IX, 309b-310a); *In Ascen*, 1 (IX, 314b); *Dom infra octavam Ascen*, 2 (IX, 329b); *In Pent*, 5 (IX, 336a); *In Pent*, 10 (IX, 346b); and *De annun B.V.M*, 6 (IX, 686b).

[14] *III Sent*, d. 1, a. 2, q. 3, concl. ad 5 (III, 30b-31b).

[15] ". . . incarnatio ad hoc ordinatur, ut simus filii Dei." *III Sent* d. 1, a. 2, q. 3, concl. (III, 30a).

[16] *III Sent*, d. 1, a. 2, q. 3, concl. and ad 2 (III, 29b-30b); *III Sent*, d. 10, dub. 5 (III, 240b-241b); and *Brev*, p. 4, c. 2 (V, 242b-243a).

God in a way which is neither completely *equivocal* nor completely *univocal*. It is not *univocal* because one filiation is temporal and gratuitous while the other is natural and eternal. It is not *equivocal* because by the mediation of that filiation and through conformity to it, we are rendered adoptive sons. Just as *all paternity in heaven and earth is named* from the Father, so too all filiation from the Son.[17]

As the above text suggests, the reality of spiritual adoption, which is accomplished in the work of redemption proper to the Son, needs to be appropriated through conformity to Christ. This conformity is appropriated by the poor through their imitation of the life and death of Christ.[18] In his human nature: "Christ was the example of virtue and of all Christian perfection . . . ."[19] which should be imitated.[20] Those who imitate his example walk in his footsteps along the same path he took back to heaven.[21]

---

[17] "Dicendum, quod nos et Christus dicimur *filii Dei*, nec omnino *aequivoce*, nec omnino *univoce*; non *univoce*, quia una est filiatio temporalis et gratuita, alia naturalis et aeterna; non *aequivoce*, quia mediante illa filiatione et per conformationem ad illam filii efficimur adoptivi. Sicut enim a Patre *omnis paternitas in caelo et in terra nominatur*, sic a Filio omnis filiatio," *III Sent*, d. 10, dub. 5 (III, 240b).

[18] *Apol paup*, c. 2, n. 12-13 (VIII, 242b-243b); *Dom 2 post Pascha*, 2 (IX, 297b-300b); and *Dom 22 post Pent*, 5 (IX, 446a-b). See also: *Brev*, p. 4, c. 1 (V, 241b). On the imitation of Christ in Bonaventure's theology, see: Ignatius Brady, "St. Bonaventure's Theology of the Imitation of Christ" in *Proceedings*, 61-72; Clasen, *Der hl. Bonaventura und das Mendikantentum*, 89-94; Hayes, *The Hidden Center*, 25-48; 59-61; 130-135; 144-146; Bonifatius Strack, *Christusleid im Christenleben* (Werl/Westfalen: Dietrich Coelde Verlag, 1960) 71 ff.; and Regis J. Armstrong, *The Spiritual Theology of the "Legenda Major" of Saint Bonaventure*, diss., U Fordham (Ann Arbor: UMI, 1978) 116-124.

[19] "Christus enim secundum humanam naturam fuit exemplum virtutis et totius christianae perfectionis . . . ." *Perf ev*, q. 3, a. 3, fund. 2 (V, 175a). See also: *III Sent*, d. 35, a. u., q. 2, concl. (III, 776b) and *Apol paup*, c. 2, n. 12 (VIII, 242b-243a).

[20] *Apol paup*, c. 2, n. 12-13 (VIII, 242b-243a) and *De purif B.V.M.*, 1 (IX, 639b).

Since Christ himself often turned to the Father in prayer and urged his disciples to do the same, it is not surprising to see that prayer emerges in Bonaventure's theology as a distinctive way of being conformed to Christ.[22] As he points out in the *Commentary on the Sentences*, one of the reasons Christ prayed in the flesh was to offer his followers an example of virtue[23] to be imitated in their own lives. He became an example of prayer so that: ". . . he might invite his disciples, and consequently others, to the endeavor of prayer . . . ."[24]

---

[21] *Dom 2 post Pascha*, 2 (IX, 299b). The image Bonaventure employs here to describe the imitation of Christ is that of walking in his vestiges or footsteps. The examples of poverty, chastity, and obedience left by Christ are the footprints he left on the road as he was going back to heaven. Francis of Assisi uses the same imagery of walking in the footsteps of Christ when describing the evangelical calling of the friars; see: *Regula non bullata*, c. 1, n. 1 in *Die Opuscula*, 377. On the idea of following Christ in the Franciscan sources, see: Giovanni Iammarrone, "La 'Sequela di Cristo' nelle Fonti Francescane," *MF* 82 (1982): 417-461, esp. 421-429 for Francis' writings and 438-444 for Bonaventure's treatment of Francis and the imitation of Christ. On Francis and the imitation of Christ in Bonaventure's writings, see also: Armstrong, *The Spiritual Theology*, 120-124.

[22] Among many texts, see: *III Sent*, d. 17, a. 2, q. 1, concl. (III, 371a-b); *Comm Jn*, c. 17, n. 2 (VI, 467a-b); *Comm Lc*, c. 3, n. 50-51 (VII, 82b); *Comm Lc*, c. 11, n. 1-2 (VII, 277a-278a); *Comm Lc*, c. 11, n. 15 (VII, 282a); *Comm Lc*, c. 22, n. 51-58 (VII, 555b-558b); *Lig vit*, fr. 3, n. 10 (VIII, 73b); *Apol paup*, c. 2, n. 13 (VIII, 243a); and *Dom 22 post Pent*, 5 (IX, 446b).

[23] "Dicendum, quod absque dubio decens fuit, Christum orare, maxime *in diebus carnis suae*. - Ratio autem huius condecentiae potest quadruplex assignari, videlicet propter *meritum*, propter *virtutis exemplum*, propter *veritatis argumentum* et propter *officium explendum*." *III Sent*, d. 17, a. 2, q. 1, concl. (III, 371a-b). See also: *Comm Lc*, c. 11, n. 2 (VII, 277b).

[24] " . . . discipulos suos, et per consequens alios invitaret ad orationis studium . . . ." *III Sent*, d. 17, a. 2, q. 1, concl. (III, 371b).

2. 1. 1. Exemplarism and Perfection

The linking of prayer with the imitation of Christ is grounded in Bonaventure's teaching on divine exemplarism and perfection.[25] This teaching focuses on the Son of God, who as the Word, proceeds from the Father by reason of exemplarity.[26] Since the Son, as Word, is the perfect expression of the Father, he is the similitude, or exemplar, of the Father.[27] He is also the exemplar of Creation,[28] for all things were created though him and are called to return to the Father with him.[29] As the Uncreated Word, the Son is the eternal exemplar of the Father.[30] All creatures derive their perfection from the eternal exemplar according to their participation in the goodness of God and shine forth in the mirror of the Uncreated Word.

As the Incarnate Word, the Son is the temporal exemplar and mirror of all graces, virtues, and merits. The perfection of the Incarnate Word is seen in the Church in accord with the state and the respective gifts of the

---

[25] On the theme of exemplarism in Bonaventure's theology, see: Jean-Marie Bissen, *L'exemplarisme divin selon saint Bonaventure* (Paris: J. Vrin, 1929); Gerken, *Die Theologie des Wortes*, 54 ff.; and Zachary Hayes, intro., *St Bonaventure's Disputed Questions on the Mystery of the Trinity*, intro. and trans. Zachary Hayes (St. Bonaventure, N.Y.: The Franciscan University, 1979) 47-54. Exemplarism and the imitation of Christ is treated in the secondary literature listed above in note 18.

[26] *I Sent*, d. 6, au., q. 3 (I, 129a-130b).

[27] *Hex*, coll. 1, n. 16 (V, 332a); *I Sent,* d. 31, p. 2, a. 1, q. 2, concl. (I, 542a-b); and *I Sent*, d. 31, p. 2, a. 1, q. 3, concl. (I, 544a).

[28] *I Sent*, d. 27, p. 2, au., q. 2, concl. (I, 485b).

[29] *Hex*, coll. 1, n. 16-17 (V, 332a).

[30] *Apol paup*, c. 2, n. 12 (VIII, 242b-243a).

individual members. Just as creatures do not reflect the total perfection of the eternal exemplar, the members of the Church do not reflect the total perfection of the temporal exemplar. The members reflect, however, the perfection of the Incarnate Word according to the degree they have been empowered by grace to imitate his example of holiness in the context of their lives.

While every action of Christ offers an insight into the way of salvation, not every one is meant to be imitated.[31] Bonaventure clearly distinguishes in the *Defense of the Mendicants* between those actions of Christ that are to be imitated and those that are not.[32] He divides the actions of Christ into six categories. The first two, which concern the power and wisdom of Christ, are not to be imitated unless one has received a special gift to do so. Otherwise, it would be presumptuous, for example, to try to imitate Christ's walking on the water and multiplying of the loaves. To want to imitate other actions of Christ, such as his ability to foresee the future and read the secrets of hearts, would be a sign of undue curiosity. The next two categories deal with the severity of Christ's judgment and the dignity of his priestly office. Actions such as driving the money changers from the temple, are to be imitated only by rulers, while sacramental actions, such as the celebration of the Eucharist and the forgiveness of sins, are to be imitated only by prelates.

The final two categories of Christ's actions concern his merciful condescension to the weak and those actions of perfection which are to be imitated by all. Both of these categories make reference to prayer as a way in which the disciple is to imitate Christ. Condescension to the weak is apparent in Christ's hiding from persecution, fear of death, and in the Garden of

---

[31] *IV Sent*, d. 3, p. 2, a. 3, q. 1, concl. ad 3 (IV, 84b).

[32] *Apol paup*, c. 2, n. 13 (VIII, 243a-b). See also: *Dom 2 post Pascha*, 2 (IX, 299a-b).

Gethsemane where he prayed for the removal of the chalice of suffering. While these actions are in themselves imperfect, they are perfected by Christ's decision to mercifully condescend to strengthen those suffering under the burden of human weakness. Inasmuch as they are imperfect acts directed toward the weak, they do not always have to be imitated. In fact, in certain circumstances, it is better not to imitate them.[33] On the other hand, no restrictions are placed on the imitation of those actions of Christ, such as prayer, which directly concern the perfection of life. Christ demonstrated these actions by:

> . . . observing poverty, maintaining virginity, subjecting
> himself to God and human beings, spending watchful
> nights in prayer, interceding for those crucifying him and
> offering himself to death out of the highest love even for
> his enemies.[34]

Prayer clearly holds a prominent place among the actions of Christ pertaining directly to the perfection of life. Since it falls under the category of the perfection of life, it is not a religious action intended for any one privileged group or class of people, but, rather, one meant to be practiced by all. All are called to reflect the perfection of Christ by conforming themselves to this essential aspect of his life.

Just as all people are called to prayer, so, too, are all aspects of life to be marked by prayer. In the *Commentary on Luke,* Bonaventure underscores

---

[33] *Apol paup,* c. 1, n. 10-11 (VIII, 238b-239b). On perfection and condescension, see: Clasen, *Der hl. Bonaventura und das Mendikantentum,* 92-94 and Hayes, *The Hidden Center,* 134-137.

[34] " . . . paupertatem servare, virginitatem custodire, Deo et hominibus se ipsum subiicere, noctes in oratione pervigiles ducere, pro crucifixoribus exorare et morti se summa caritate etiam pro inimicis offerre." *Apol paup,* c. 2, n. 13 (VIII, 243a-b).

the universal importance of Christ's example of prayer by pointing out that every dimension of his life was permeated by prayer: "In all situations the Lord is found *praying* . . . . "[35] By praying in all things, Christ left an example of how others can integrate prayer into the various dimensions of their own lives. Seven specific situations from his life serve as a model of prayer applicable in one way or another to all religious and social groups; they indicate that prayer is not to be restricted to any special aspect of life nor to any particular group of people:

> For he prayed in the reception of baptism, as here: *and it came to pass as Jesus had been baptized and was praying*, so that he might give a model of praying to those who are approaching baptism. - In the *solitude of the desert*; later in chapter five: "he used to withdraw into the desert and pray," so that he might give a model to those who are contemplating. - In *preaching*; later in chapter six: "it came to pass in those days, he went out to the mountain to pray," so that he might give a model to those who are preaching. - In the *working of miracles*; in chapter eleven of John: "Father I give thanks to you," etc., so that he might give a model to those who are working. - in the *passion*; chapter twenty-six of Matthew: "having gone further he fell upon his face," so that he might give a model to those who are undergoing struggle - In the *administration of the body;* later in chapter twenty-two: "when the chalice having been taken, he gave thanks to

---

[35] "In omnibus invenitur Dominus *orans* . . . ." *Comm Lc*, c. 3, n. 50 (VII, 82b).

God," so that he might give a model to priests. - In the *commending of the spirit;* later in chapter twenty-three: "Father, into your hands I commend my spirit; and saying these things he expired," so that he might give a model to those who are dying." [36]

2. 1. 2. The Passion of Gethsemane and Obedient Prayer

While all the examples of Christ at prayer are instructive for those called to imitate the Son of God, there is one example among them which Bonaventure singles out in several of his works for special treatment: Christ's obedient prayer in the Garden of Gethsemane. In addition to the *Commentary on Luke,*[37] he reflects on this example of prayer in the *Tree of*

---

[36] "Oravit enim in *baptismi susceptione,* sicut hic: *Et factum est, Iesu baptizato et orante,* ut daret formam orandi accedentibus ad baptisma. - In *deserti solitudine;* infra quinto: 'Ipse secedebat in desertum et orabat,' ut formam daret contemplantibus. - In *praedicatione;* infra sexto: 'Factum est autem in diebus illis, exiit in montem, ut oraret,' ut formam daret praedicatoribus. - In *miraculorum operatione;* Ioannis undecimo: 'Pater, gratias ago tibi' etc., ut daret formam operantibus. - In *passione;* Matthaei vigesimo sexto: 'Progressus cecidit in faciem suam,' ut formam daret sustinentibus. - In *corporis administratione;* infra vigesimo secundo: 'Accepto calice, gratias egit Deo,' ut formam daret sacerdotibus. - In *spiritus commendatione;* infra vigesimo tertio: 'Pater, in manus tuas commendo spiritum meum; et haec dicens exspiravit,' ut formam daret morientibus." *Comm Lc,* c. 3, n. 51 (VII, 82b). The Scripture quotes referred to are: Lk. 3: 21; Lk. 5: 16; Lk. 6: 12; Jn. 11: 41; Mt. 26: 39; Lk. 22: 17; and Lk: 23: 46. The text quoted above ends with the admonition: "Et sic omnibus est orandum" which should be translated normally as: "And so all must pray." In the previous section, (see note above) however, Bonaventure writes: "In omnibus invenitur Dominus *orans . . . .* " and goes on to list the same seven life situations found in the above text. This could indicate that the passage should be translated: "And so it is neccessary to pray in all situations." That the text may have presented interpretative problems already in the Middle Ages is suggested by the alternate reading listed by the Quaracchi editors, see: note 11 (VII, 82b). The alternate they give for: "Et sic omnibus" is: "Et in omnibus est orandum." Of the two translations given above, the first refers to the call to pray which Christ addresses to all people and the second to the idea of prayer as an intrinsic part of life. Both translations reflect different aspects of the same idea: the example of perfection revealed in Christ's prayer is relevant to all situations and people.

[37] *Comm Lc,* c. 22, n. 51-58 (VII, 555b-558b).

86

Life[38] and the *Commentary on the Sentences.*[39] When considered from the point of view of the Christian tradition, his choice to devote special attention to this example is not surprising. The mystery of the Son of God's prayerful struggle with the will of the Father in the Garden of Gethsemane has been the subject of continued reflection on the part of Christians from the very beginnings of the Church.[40]

The desire on the part of Christians to reflect on Christ's prayer in Gethsemane is amplified by Bonaventure's view of Christ's passion as an especially moving instance of exemplary perfection.[41] That the prayer in the Garden of Gethsemane is itself a cogent expression of Christ's passion is confirmed by a prayer found in a section of the *Tree of Life* entitled "On the Mystery of the Passion." After meditating on Christ's painful struggle in prayer, Bonaventure is moved to respond to this example with a prayer of his own:

> Ruler, Lord Jesus, from whence [come] such vehement
> anguish and anxious supplication to your soul? You did
> offer, did you not, a completely voluntary sacrifice to the
> Father? But still - so that we, believing you [share] in the
> true nature of our mortality, might be formed to *faith*, so
> that in similar suffering of tribulations we might be lifted
> up toward *hope*, and so we might have a greater *incentive*

[38] *Lig vit*, fr. 5, n. 18 (VIII, 75b-76a).

[39] *III Sent*, d. 17, a. 1, q. 3 (III, 367a-370b) and *III Sent,* d. 17, a. 2, q. 2-3 (III, 373a-375b). Much of this same material is also found in *Brev*, p. 4, c. 9 (V, 249a-b).

[40] On this theme, see: Stanley, *Jesus in Gethsemane.*

[41] *Dom 2 post Pascha*, 2 (IX, 296a-300b). On the imitation of the passion of Christ, see: Strack, *Christusleid im Christenleben,* 71 ff..

of love toward you — you expressed the natural weakness of the flesh in evident signs of this kind by which we might be taught that *you truly bore our sorrows* and that not without a sense of pain you tasted the bitterness of the passion.[42]

In contrast to the devotional interpretation found in the *Tree of Life*,[43] the *Commentary on Luke* interprets Christ's prayer in Gethsemane in view of its possible pastoral application by Franciscan preachers. According to Bonaventure's exegesis of Lk. 22: 39-45,[44] the example of Christ provides

---

[42] "'Dominator Domine Iesu, unde animae tuae tam vehemens anxietas et anxia supplicatio? Nonne voluntarium omnino Patri sacrificium obtulisti'? Verum ut, veram in te credentes nostrae mortalitatis naturam, formaremur ad *fidem* et in tribulationum perpessione consimili erigeremur ad *spem* et maiores erga te *amoris stimulos* haberemus, naturalem carnis infirmitatem huiusmodi expressisti evidentibus signis, quibus doceremur, quod *vere dolores nostros pertuleris* et non absque doloris sensu degustaveris amaritudines passionum." *Lig vit*, fr. 5, n. 18 (VIII, 75b-76a). The prayer above is an adaptation of a section of the ninth meditation once attributed to Anselm of Canterbury; see: *De humanitate Christi, PL* 158, 753. It is now ascribed to Abbot Ekbert of Schönau; see: André Wilmart, *Auteurs spirituels et textes dévots du moyen âge latin* (Paris: Études Augustiniennes, 1971) 194. On the text from Ekbert of Shönau and the *Lig vit*, see also: O'Connell, *The "Lignum Vitae" of Saint Bonaventure*, 162-164, esp. 163. Bonaventure's adaptation of Ekbert's text links Christ's prayer in Gethesemane with the theological virtues of faith, hope and love. He does much the same thing in *Lig vit*, fr. 12, n. 48 (VIII, 85b). This approach is consistent with his teaching on prayer, for he considers prayer to be an expression of the theological virtues; see: *III Sent*, d. 9, a. 2, q. 2, concl. ad 2 (III, 215b) and *Comm Lc*, c. 22, n. 58 (VII, 558b). It was the teaching of the Franciscan school of Bonaventure's day that prayer was an expression of faith, hope and love; see: *Quaestio 26, De oratione, satisfactionis parte*, membrum 1, a. 2, in vol. 4 of *Alexandri Alensis Universae Theologiae summa in quattour partes ab ipsomet authore distributa* (Cologne: 1622) 675a-678a. This text, which will be referred to as *De orat*, is a rich, untapped, source for the study of the nascent Franciscan theology of prayer. It, and some of the other questions found in Alexander's *Summa*, are the work of various Franciscan theologians; see: Bougerol, *Introduction*, 180. On prayer and the theological virtues in the Franciscan tradition, see: Timothy J. Johnson, "Contemplative Prayer and the 'Constitutions of the Order of Friars Minor Conventual.'" *MF* 87 (1987): 103-107. Prayer and the theological virutes are also treated in Chapter Four.

[43] On the *Lig vit* and devotion, see: O'Connell, *The "Lignum Vitae of Saint Bonaventure."* See also: Ewert Cousins, intro., Bonaventure, *The Soul's Journey into God. The Tree of Life. The Life of St. Francis*, trans. and intro. Ewert Cousin, pref. Ignatius Brady (New York: Paulist Press, 1978) 34-37.

them with a seven-fold compendium of advice on the art of prayer. It reveals that all prayer should be secret, solicitous, devout, discreet, vigorous, anxious and circumspect. Prayer is meant to be offered in secret because Christ sought out a remote place to pray when he ascended the Mount of Olives. It should be solicitous for the good of the soul because Christ admonished the disciples to pray lest they succumb to temptation. The fact that Christ prayed on his knees is a testimony to the devotion which is to accompany prayer. His petition that the cup be passed from him only if it be in accord with the Father's will is a sign of the discretion proper to prayer. The comfort Christ received in the Garden from the angel should also be a part of the prayer of those who follow his example. The anxious cry of Christ, which is indicative of his concern for the Church and his willingness to pour out his blood for her, is also to be part of prayer. Finally, Christ did not forget his disciples while praying; three times he returned to them,[45] thus revealing the circumspection needed in all prayer. His readiness to turn to God in prayer and to turn to encourage his followers distinguishes him as the best possible prelate.

Both the pastoral interpretation of Christ's prayer in Gethsemane found in the *Commentary of Luke*, and the devotional interpretation of the *Tree of Life*, stand at first glance in sharp contrast to the decidedly

---

[44] *Comm Lc*, c. 22, n. 51-57 (VII, 555b-558a). On the *Comm Lc* and the formation of Franciscan preachers, see: Monti, *Bonaventure's Interpretation of Scripture*, 149-204.

[45] *Comm Lc*, c. 22, n. 58 (VII, 558b). Christ's three-fold turning to God and to his disciples (Mt. 26:36-46) gives Bonaventure cause in this text to examine prayer and the divine influence on the soul in terms of triads. That Christ turned three times to God in prayer indicates prayer should be: against three kinds of temptation; an act of the three powers of the mind; in accord with the three theological virutes; and for the sake of obtaining the three-fold good. That Christ visited the apostles three times indicates that he visits the soul in three ways: by comforting the irascible power with zeal, the rational power with light and the concupiscible power with desire.

speculative treatment of the same prayer found in the *Commentary on the Sentences*. Here Bonaventure limits himself to an examination of the petition recorded in Mat. 26:39: "My Father, if it be possible, let this cup pass from me; nevertheless not as I will, but as you will".[46] Yet, despite the different methods employed in the respective works, all three recognize the exemplary nature of Christ's prayer in Gethsemane. With words reminiscent of the prayer cited above from the *Tree of Life*, Bonaventure writes in the *Commentary on the Sentences* that Christ's petition was directed toward a three-fold end: the teaching of faith in the humanity of Christ, the giving of hope to the suffering, and the encouragement of obedient love through the example of Christ's subjection to the will of the Father.[47] As a result, the

---

[46] *III Sent*, d. 17, a. 2, q. 3 (III, 374a-375b). The title of the question dealing with Christ's prayer in Gethsemane (III, 374a-b) is sufficient in itself to confirm Bonaventure's speculative approach to the petition. It reads: "Utrum oratio, qua Christus oravit in passione, ut calix transferretur, fuerit a ratione, an a sensualitate." Bonaventure answers the question by saying that the material of the petition came from the sensual will, while the form of its presentation was of the rational. In explaining the respective roles of the sensual and rational will, he employs a courtroom analogy (III, 375b): "Et attendendum est, quod ratio in petitione illa servavit formam prudentis et fidelis *advocati*, qui desiderium sensualitatis proponit, servata tamen forma *iuris*. Dictat enim *ius divinum*, quod omnis appetitus debet esse Deo subiectus." Much of the same kind of courtroom language is found in *Comm Jn*, c. 12, n. 42, resp. ad 3 (VI, 419b) where Bonaventure states that Christ's prayer in Jn. 12:27 was proposed by the rational will in response to the urging of the sensual will: "Quod obiicitur, quod *ratio* petiit; dicendum, quod sermo ille formatus est secundum imperium rationis, et ratio proposuit petitionem. Et sicut advocatus aliquando non petit pro se, nec quia illud velit, sed pro alio, et quia alius vult; sic et *ratio* pro *sensualitate* petebat; nec hoc volebat, immo potius mori pro salute nostra." Remaining in the realm of courtroom imagery, Bonaventure also speaks of the angels as advocates who intercede with God on behalf of humanity: "Dicendum, quod sicut videmus in causis terrenis, quod qui nescit loqui coram praetore conducit advocatum, qui loquatur et alleget pro ipso; sic in spiritualibus intelligendum, quod cum nos nec perorare, immo quasi nec balbutire sciamus coram Deo, quod Angelus tanquam advocatus et allegator magnus in illa superna curia assumit verbum et orationem nostram proponit." *IV Sent*, d. 45, dub. 7 (IV, 953a). The use of the courtroom analogy can be explained in terms of the classical influence on medieval prayer. Châtillon points out (following Thomas of Aquinas) that the "orationes" of classical times were often defense appeals made before a judge. This juridical sense behind the "orationes" was able to be carried over easily into the "orationes" of those who appeal with their petitions to God, the judge of human actions. See: "Prière," 2272.

90

Lord: ". . . prayed more for us in that prayer than he prayed for himself."[48]

The three-fold character of Christ's petition explains why Bonaventure describes his prayer in the Garden as less than perfect,[49] yet worthy of imitation by the poor.[50] When Christ prayed: "My Father, if it be possible, let this cup pass from me" he was frightened by the thought of his impending death. His reaction of fear before death confirms the truth of his humanity, for it is natural for human beings to be frightened by the prospect of death.[51] His willingness to enter into the poverty of human misery to the extent that he shared in fear is an imperfect action which does not need to be imitated in the pursuit of perfection.[52] Christ's willingness, however, to act

---

[47] *III Sent*, d. 17, a. 2, q. 3, concl. (III, 375b).

[48] ". . . magis oravit pro nobis in illa oratione, quam oraret pro se." *III Sent*, d. 17, a. 2, q. 3, concl. (III, 375b). Bonaventure goes beyond this position at times and interprets Christ's prayer in Gethsemane exclusively in terms of its pedagogical value for others. For example in the same commentary he writes: "Non enim petebat, ut exaudiretur, sed ut nos erudiremur; sicut petiit, calicem a se transferri . . . ." *III Sent*, d. 17, a. 2, q. 2, concl. (III, 374a-b). See also: *Comm Jn*, c. 12, n. 42, resp. ad 1 (VI, 419b). That Christ prayed to teach others is one way of explaining why he at times prayed when he knew that his prayer was not in conformity to the Father's will and, thus, would not be answered. Sometimes Christ's prayer originated from the sensual or pious will, which as opposed to the rational, is not always in conformity to the divine will. Any prayer arising from the rational will will be answered but not necessarily all those arising from the sensual. On this question, see: *III Sent*, d. 17, a. 2, q. 2-3 (III, 373a-375b) and *Comm Jn*, c. 12, n 42, resp. and ad 1 (VI, 419b).

[49] *Apol paup*, c. 2, n. 13 (VIII, 243a-b).

[50] *Comm Lc*, c. 22, n. 54 (VII, 556b-557a).

[51] *Brev*, p. 4, c. 8 (V, 249a-b). Bonaventure points out here that it is natural for the sensual will to want to avoid death. On the sensual will, as well as the pious and rational will in Christ, see: Hayes, *The Hidden Center*, 117-122, esp. 120-122 in reference to Christ's Gethsemane prayer.

[52] *Apol paup*, c. 2, n. 13-14 (VIII, 243a-b). Christ's fear in Gethsemane indicates he prayed as a poor person. His fear in prayer can be considered an expression of poverty inasmuch as fear is a dimension of human misery which Bonaventure maintains is a penalty of sin; see: *Brev*, p. 4, c. 8 (V, 248b). Although Christ prayed as a poor person in the sense just mentioned, he did not pray as a poor person in need of grace; see: *Perf ev*, q. 2, a. 2, fund. 9 (V, 137b); *Perf ev*, q. 2, a. 2 (V, 150b); and *Comm Lc*, c. 16, n. 6 (VII, 405b). This aspect of Christ's prayer was a point of contention in the poverty dispute

imperfectly by sharing in human fear, is an act of mercy meant to strengthen the hope of the poor as they struggle to live out the mystery of the passion in their own lives.[53] Although the fear Christ accepted for the sake of others need not be imitated, the loving obedience to the Father expressed in the same petition does. When he qualified his petition with the words: "nevertheless not as I will but as you will," he revealed that he had subordinated his will to that of the Father and that his followers should do the same. As Bonaventure writes, Christ prayed in such a manner:

> ... so that he might show that our *will* must be *subjected*
> to the divine will in all matters; which he showed in the
> added condition, *not as I wish, but as you* [*will*]; And in
> this he ordered *charity* in us which endeavors to subject
> our affection to the divine will in all things.[54]

Christ's subjection to the Father in Gethsemane is an example of obedient prayer grounded in the mystery of his eternal filiation. This conclusion can be supported by a brief examination of the meaning of sonship in Bonaventure's theology. He applies the title "Son" in a technical sense to the second person of the Trinity in order to define his relation to the Father.[55] The Son is the natural Son of the Father generated from all time by the Fa-

---

between the secular masters and the mendicants at the University of Paris; see: Clasen, *Der hl. Bonaventura und das Mendikantentum*, 103-104.

[53] *III Sent*, d. 15, a. 1, q. 1, concl. (III, 331a). See also: *III Sent*, d. 17, a. 2, q. 3, concl. (III, 375b) and *Lig vit*, fr. 5, n. 18 (VIII, 75b-76a).

[54] " ... ut ostenderet, *voluntatem* nostram divinae voluntati esse per omnia *subiiciendam*, quod ostendit in conditione apposita, non *sicut ego volo, sed sicut tu*; et in hoc ordinavit in nobis *caritatem*, quae affectum nostrum divinae voluntati per omnia conatur subiicere." *III Sent*, d. 17, a. 2, q. 3, concl. (III, 375b).

[55] *I Sent*, d. 31, p. 2, a. 1, q. 2, concl. (I, 542b). It should be noted that Bonaventure also speaks in a general way of the Son including within that term the specific contents of the titles "Son," "Image" and "Word." See: *III Sent*, d. 1, a. 2, q. 3, concl. (III, 29b).

ther.[56] In the generation of the Son, the Father actively communicates the whole of his substance to him resulting in another person, who, although distinct, is a perfect likeness of Father.[57]

An analysis of the generation of the Son in terms of the modalities of love indicates that the Father's love is completely active while the Son's is both passive and active; for the Son, who proceeds from the Father's gratuitous love as the beloved,[58] also loves the Father in return.[59] From this dynamic of love, the Holy Spirit proceeds as a distinct person whom the Father and Son breathe forth[60] in mutual love.[61] By reason of the Son's passive acceptance and active communication of love, the filiation of the Son of God, and in an analogous fashion the filiation of those who are conformed to him through imitation of him, can be defined in terms of the reception of, and response to, the love of the Father.[62] In this light, obedience in prayer can be said to be grounded in the mystery of filiation because it is one way in which the Son of God, and those who wish to conform themselves to him, respond in love to the Father.[63]

---

[56] *III Sent*, d. 1, a. 2, q. 3, concl. (III, 29b) and *III Sent,* d. 10, a. 2, q. 3, concl. ad 2 (III, 238b).

[57] *I Sent,* d. 5, a. 1, q. 2, concl. (I, 115b) and *I Sent,* d. 9, au., q. 1 (I, 181a-b).

[58] *I Sent,* d. 6, au., q. 2, concl. (I, 128a).

[59] *I Sent,* d. 2, au., q. 4, concl. (I, 57b); *Itin,* c. 6, n. 2 (V, 311a); and *Comm Jn,* c. 15, n. 18, resp. (VI, 450a). Bonaventure's use of the modalities of love in his analysis of the Trinity is dependent on Richard of St. Victor's *De Trinitate,* see: *PL* 196, Liber 5, c. 23, 965-966. See also: Hayes, *Disputed Questions,* 33-35 and 54-60.

[60] *I Sent,* d. 10, a. 2, q. 3, concl. (I, 204a-b).

[61] *I Sent,* d. 10, a. 2, q. 1, concl. (I, 201a).

[62] On the filiation of the Son of God as the ontological basis for all other relations, see: Hayes, intro., *St. Bonaventure's Disputed Questions,* 49.

For Bonaventure, this obedience of the Son in prayer is the historical concretization of his eternal love for the Father,[64] which, in addition to offering the poor an example of prayer worthy of imitation, renders them sons and daughters of God. As the Son of God who eternally receives and returns the love of the Father, Christ did not cease to respond in love to the Father when faced with the specter of death. Instead, he returned the love of the Father by subjecting himself to the will of the Father in an act of obedience culminating in his crucifixion. This obedience of Christ to the Father, which is ontologically grounded in their mutual love, is mirrored on the anthropological level in the relation common to sons and fathers. As Bonaventure notes, it is of the nature of sonship for sons to petition and obey their fathers. This anthropological dimension of sonship takes on added significance when viewed through the prism of salvation history: just as it is fitting for sons to petition and obey their fathers, it is fitting for the Son of God to take on flesh to bring about the redemption of humanity through supplicant prayer and obedience to the Father. Such supplication and obedience, exemplified as it is in the passion of Gethsemane, enables the poor to become the adoptive sons and daughters of God.[65]

---

[63] *III Sent,* d. 17, a. 2, q. 3, concl. (III, 375b).

[64] This point is developed by Hayes, *The Hidden Center,* 171.

[65] *"Rursus,* si consideremus *modum reparationis,* magis competit Filio. Reparati enim sumus per mediatoris obedientiam et supplicationem; et quia magis competit, filium supplicare patri et obedire: hinc est, quod magis competit personae Filii incarnari quam alii. Unde Anselmus in libro *Cur Deus homo*: 'Convenientius sonat, Filium supplicare Patri quam aliam personam.' - *Postremo,* si consideremus *reparationis fructum* vel effectum, magis competebat Filio incarnari; quia incarnatio ad hoc ordinatur, ut simus filii Dei." *III Sent,* d. 1, a. 2, q. 3, concl. (III, 30a). The text from Anselm is found in *Cur Deus homo,* Liber 2, c. 9, 105 of vol. 2 of *S. Anselmi Opera Omnia,* ed. Franciscus Schmitt (Rome: 1940).

2. 1. 3. The "Our Father"

As the passion in Gethsemane reveals, prayer was one way Christ
subjected himself in loving obedience to the will of the Father. It also
indicates his followers should conform themselves to him by following his
example of obedience. His obedience on the eve of his death was not an isolated expression of filial love; it summarizes, rather, the tenor of his entire
earthly pilgrimage.[66] His life was lived out from beginning to end in obedience to the Father; he came into the world to do the will of the Father and
remained obedient to him in his passion and death. In his obedience to the
Father, he left the poor an example of perfection to be imitated.[67] Christ's
example of obedience is reflected in those who show their love for him by
means of their obedience to the commandment of fraternal love he has given
them.[68] Through their loving obedience, they enter into a relationship of
friendship with him, which is indicative of their status as the sons and daughters of God. As adoptive sons and daughters, they can approach the Father
and ask him for anything that pertains to their salvation and know with assurance they will be heard.

One privileged way for the sons and daughters of God to approach the

---

[66] *Comm Jn*, c. 6, n. 59 (VI, 328b). On Christ's love for, and obedience to, the Father and
the imitation of his example by his followers, see: Strack, *Christusleid im Christenleben*,
51-54 and 120-125, respectively. On obedience in Bonaventure's theology, see also:
Bruno Marcucci, "La virtù dell'obbedienza nella perfezione secondo la dottrina di S.
Bonaventura," *StFr* 50 (1953): 3-30.

[67] *Comm Lc*, c. 6, n. 95 (VII, 161a) and *Apol paup*, c. 2, n. 13 (VIII, 243a-b).

[68] *Comm Jn*, c. 15, n. 19-23 (VI, 450b-451b).

Father in prayer is to avail themselves of the prayer Christ taught his disciples. This prayer, commonly referred to as the "Our Father,"[69] is the heritage of those wishing to imitate Christ. As Bonaventure points out in the *Commentary on Luke*, the teaching of the Our Father is based on Christ's example of prayer and the disciples' desire to imitate his example.[70] Instead of simply telling them how to pray, Christ sought to teach them first of all through his own practice of prayer. His example did not go unnoticed by the disciples; on observing him at prayer, they promptly asked to be taught how to pray so they could imitate him. It was fitting that they responded to Christ's example and asked him to teach them to pray. Otherwise, they might have asked in prayer for something which would be against God's will. Because of his divine nature, Christ was able to instruct them to pray in conformity to the will of God. The result of his instruction is the Our Father. According to the *Breviloquium*, the divine origin of this prayer leaves no doubt that it contains those things God wishes to be sought in prayer:

> And because, *we do not know what we should pray for as is necessary*, lest we wander astray uncertain, [God] gave us a formula in prayer, which he composed, in which is contained in a seven-fold number of petitions the totality of the things that ought to be asked.[71]

---

[69] The Our Father has been the object of intense study and reflection over the centuries. For a historical/exegetical study of the Our Father with an extensive bibliography (in the footnotes) of the research done on this prayer, see: Santos Sabugal, *Abba' . . . La oración del Señor* (Madrid: La Editorial Católica, 1985), esp. 49-51 and 117-124 on the medieval exegesis of this prayer.

[70] *Comm Lc*, c. 11, n. 1-3 (VII, 277a-278a).

[71] "Et quia, *quid oremus, secundum quod oportet, nescimus*, ne vagaremur incerti, formam nobis tradidit in oratione, quam composuit; in qua sub septenario petitionum numero universitas comprehenditur petendorum." *Brev*, p. 5, c. 10 (V, 263b).

The petitions of the Our Father are a summary of all prayer as well as a compendium of everything the poor need to request in prayer. Together they form a prayer singled out by Bonaventure for its nobility. As he says in the *Commentary on Luke*: "Furthermore the *nobility* of this prayer is evident. Although it is most brief, it contains in itself every prayer and all things which must be requested . . . ."[72] The nobility, or dignity, of this prayer is also apparent in the structure of its petitions. In reference to the five petitions of the Lucan text,[73] Bonaventure observes an order of dignity determined by the relative importance of what they request from the Father.[74] In his view, the consummation of glory is to be requested above everything else, then the preservation of grace, and finally the pardoning of sin. The consummation of glory is found in the perfect knowledge and reverence of God and is requested in the petitions: "May your name be sanctified" and "Your kingdom come." The preservation of grace, through continual divine assistance, is requested in the petition: "Give us this day our daily bread." The request for the pardoning of sin is expressed in the two-fold petition: "Forgive us our sins as

---

72 "Patet etiam huius orationis *nobilitas*. Quamquam sit brevissima, continet in se omnem orationem et omnia postulanda." *Comm Lc*, c. 11, n. 8 (VII, 279a-b).

73 It should be noted that Luke's version of the Our Father contains five petitions while Matthew's contains seven. In his writings, Bonaventure comments on both versions of the Our Father. He briefly treats Matthew's version (Mt. 6: 9-13) in *Brev*, p. 5, c. 10 (V, 263b-264b); *De donis*, coll. 2, n. 4-5 (V, 463a-b) and *Lig vit*, fr. 12, n. 49 (VIII, 86a-b). Luke's version of the Our Father (Lk. 11: 2-4) is treated in *Comm Lc*, c. 11, n. 1-17 (VII, 277a-282b). Bonaventure also touches on Matthew's text in the course of his exegesis of the Lucan text in the *Comm Lc*. Despite the different number of petitions found in the Lucan and Matthean versions of the Our Father, Bonaventure maintains there is harmony between them as far as content is concerned; see: *Comm Lc*, c. 11, n. 5-9 (VII, 278b-279b). The reason the two versions differ as to the number and wording of the petitions stems from the difference between the audiences Christ was addressing in each one of the Gospels. Luke's version is shorter than Matthew's version because it was intended for the larger group of disciples while Matthew's version was intended for the apostles. Despite the brevity of Luke's text, it contains implicitly everything found in Matthean text.

74 *Comm Lc*, c. 11, n. 7 and 9 (VII, 279a-b).

we forgive those indebted to us. And lead us not into temptations." This final request is formulated in two petitions since the pardoning of sin includes the remission of the evil committed along with the removal of its accompanying punishment.

2. 1. 3. 1. The Consummation of Glory and Sanctification

The first petition found in the Lucan text: "May your name be sanctified," seeks the consummation of glory through the sanctification of God's name in the intellect.[75] Although the divine name is holy in itself, it is still necessary for it to be sanctified in the intellect of the poor. The sanctification of God's name is a dynamic process leading to the perfect knowledge of God enjoyed by those who contemplate him in eternal glory; it is marked by an ever deepening knowledge of God which brings in its wake a corresponding growth in spiritual freedom. The first step on the way toward the perfect knowledge of God begins in the reception of grace. By means of grace, the existence of God is acknowledged, and the faithful are liberated from the foolishness of those who contend there is no God. The next step carries the poor beyond the knowledge of God provided by faith to the knowledge of what God is not. This knowledge fosters freedom from idolatry.[76] The final step toward sanctification is revealed in the perfect

---

[75] *Comm Lc,* c. 11, n. 10-11 (VII, 279b-280a).

[76] When Bonaventure speaks here of the knowledge of what God is not, he may be referring to the knowledge often identified with negative theology. This hypothesis is strengthened by an examination of the distinctions Bonaventure makes in regard to the knowledge of God in his exegesis of the first petition of the Our Father. At first he speaks of the knowledge of what God is, then of what God is not, and finally about the perfect knowledge of God. He identifies the perfect knowledge of God with the gift of wisdom which transforms the poor into a divine similitude and, thus, into a son or daughter of

knowledge of God proper to the gift of wisdom. The gift of wisdom liberates the poor from all misery and perfectly sanctifies God's name within them in the glory of heaven.

2. 1. 3. 2. The Consummation of Glory and Reverence

Whereas the first petition of the Our Father reported in Luke's Gospel requests the consummation of glory equated with perfect knowledge of God in the intellect, the second asks for the consummation of glory equated with perfect reverence of God in the affections.[77] According to Bonaventure, perfect reverence in the affections is manifested in the perfect obedience of the saints who dwell in the eternal kingdom of God. He teaches that to pray: "Your kingdom come," is to ask for the complete and universal obedience of the end of time when Christ will subject himself together with the entire universe to the Father. Only at that time will God be said to reign perfectly in all the saints. When all things have been given over to the Father, the saints will also become kings and reign with God in the eternal kingdom. This is the kingdom that must be begged for, and desired, by the poor in prayer. Although it is not present on earth in its fullness, it is, nevertheless, found among those who are obedient to God. Those who are not obedient to God, on the other hand, demonstrate that they instead belong to the kingdom of darkness.

God. This process of transformation, which begins with the knowledge of God in faith and progresses through the shedding of false concepts of God to the transformation of the soul into a similitude of the Son of God, is characteristic of Bonaventure's theology of contemplation examined in Chapter Four.

[77] *Comm Lc*, c. 11, n. 12 (VII, 280b).

2. 1. 3. 3. The Preservation of Grace

The third petition: "Give us this day our daily bread," moves the focus of the Lucan Our Father away from the eternal glory of God to the daily spiritual and material needs of the poor in the present life.[78] While Bonaventure notes in the *Commentary on Luke* that the preservation of grace is the goal of the third petition,[79] he does not hesitate to say that it also includes the request for daily material sustenance. In his commentary on this petition, Bonaventure follows the exegetical tradition of the Latin Fathers who tended to interpret the request for daily bread in both a material and spiritual sense.[80] His spiritual and material interpretations of the daily bread are based on the five breads Christ used to feed the crowd of five thousand in Jn. 6: 9 ff.. The first bread gives sustenance to the body and consists in food, drink and clothing. The second bread is the understanding of the Scriptures given to the poor who hunger for spiritual nourishment. The third bread is the sacrament of the Eucharist given by Christ for the life of the world. The fourth bread is the assistance of grace enjoyed by the members of the king-

---

[78] *Comm Lc,* c. 11, n. 13-14 (VII, 280b-281b).

[79] *Comm Lc*, c. 11, n. 7 (VII, 279a).

[80] On the various interpretations of the Lord's Prayer by the Latin Fathers, see: Klaus Bernhard Schnurr, *Hören und handeln. Lateinische Auslegungen des Vaterunsers in der Alten Kirche bis zum 5. Jahrhundert* (Freiburg: Herder, 1985), esp. 158-159 on the tendency of such Fathers as Tertullian, Cyprian, Jerome, Augustine, and Chromatius to interpret the third petition in both a material and spiritual fashion. On the third petition, see also: Walter Dürig, "Die Deutung der Brotbitte des Vaterunsers bei den lateinisches Vätern bis Hieronymus," *LitJ* 18 (1968): 72-86 and W. Rordorf, "Le 'pain quotidien' (Mt 6, 11) dans l'exégèse de Grégoire de Nysse," *Aug* 17 (1977): 193-199.

dom of God, while the fifth and final bread is the obedience to the will of the Father exemplified in the life of Christ.

2. 1. 3. 4. The Forgiveness of Sin and the Remission of Evil

The fourth petition of Luke's version of the Our Father concerns the forgiveness of sin. When the poor pray: "Forgive us our sins," they are asking the Father to mercifully pardon the offenses they have committed.[81] As Bonaventure indicates, Matthew's version of the same petition speaks of these offenses as debts. When Matthew (Mat. 6: 12) says: "Forgive us our debts," it is evident that those praying for forgiveness appeal as debtors who are unable to cancel the debt they have incurred through sin. Such an appeal for mercy is an essential dimension in the process of forgiveness for only the mercy of God revealed in Christ can cancel the accumulated debt of sin. The prayer for mercy is not sufficient of itself, however, to assure the reception of divine mercy. Turning once again to the Matthean text (Mt. 6: 12) to clarify Luke's petition, Bonaventure says the phrase: "as we forgive our debtors" is a condition for the forgiveness of sin. This condition forges a direct link between the mercy requested by debtors in prayer and the mercy they should show to those who are in debt to them because of sin. When those who pray for mercy also show mercy to others by forgiving their debt of sin, they can be assured of receiving the merciful cancelation of their own personal debt of sin.

---

[81] *Comm Lc,* c. 11, n. 15 (VII, 281b).

2. 1. 3. 5. The Forgiveness of Sin and the Removal of Punishment

The fifth petition of Luke's Our Father also concerns the forgiveness of sin. It approaches the dynamic of forgiveness, however, from a different perspective than the fourth petition. Here the forgiveness sought in prayer reaches beyond the cancelation of the unpayable debt of sin mentioned in the fourth petition to include the removal of the punishment provoked by sin.[82] Those who pray: "And lead us not into temptation" request the removal of the punishment of sin. Their petition is a prayer to resist those temptations provoked by concupiscence,[83] which is itself a punishment of sin.[84] From this perspective, the removal of the punishment of sin does not signify the elimination of the temptations arising from concupiscence, but, rather, the ability to overcome them. Thus, the prayer for the removal of the punishment of sin is an appeal to emerge victorious in the struggle against temptation. This prayer is predicated by the recognition of human infirmity, for it is impossible for the poor to resist unassisted the multitude of temptations assailing them. On the other hand, the prayer to overcome temptation should also be motivated by confidence in divine help since God never allows the forces of temptation to exceed the strength of those being tested.

---

[82] *Comm Lc*, c. 11, n. 7 (VII, 279a).

[83] *Comm Lc*, c. 11, n. 16 (VII, 282a).

[84] *II Sent,* d. 32, a. 1, q. 1, concl. ad 3 (II, 761b) and *II Sent,* d. 32, a. 2, q. 2, concl. (II, 768a-769b).

2. 2. The Advent of the Holy Spirit

Christ taught the disciples to turn confidently to the Father in prayer because the Father is the generous source of all good gifts. As Bonaventure's exegesis of Lk. 11: 11-13 indicates, if an earthly father knows how to share good gifts such as food with his son, so much more will the heavenly Father listen to the supplication of the poor and freely share with them the richness of his goodness.[85] Such goodness on the part of the Father is not an accidental quality, but, rather, of the very nature of God as the greatest Good. Following the teaching of Pseudo-Dionysius, Bonaventure repeats throughout his writings that God is the greatest Good and, consequently, most diffusive or communicative. This divine communication of the good, eternally present in the Trinity, is temporally manifested in the creation of the universe.[86] Creation stands foremost as a witness to the goodness of God,[87] who moved by love, desired from all eternity to share the abundance of divine goodness with rational creatures.[88]

---

[85] *Comm Lc*, c. 11, n. 29-35 (VII, 286a-288a).

[86] *Itin*, c. 6, n. 1-3 (V, 310b-311a). On Bonaventure's use of the Pseudo-Dionysian axiom, "Bonum diffusivum sui," see: Jacques Guy Bougerol, "Saint Bonaventure et le Pseudo-Denys l'Aréopagite," *EF* 18 (Supplément annuel 1968): 81-104. On the use of this axiom and Bonaventure's theology of God, see: Hayes, intro., *St Bonaventure's Disputed Questions* 32-33. Hayes points out here that Bonaventure's reflection on God as Good is characteristic of the early Franciscan theologians who appear to have been motivated in their research by Francis' own image of God as a good and loving Father. On Francis' image of God as Father, see: Kajetan Eßer, *Franziskus und die Seinen* (Werl/Westfalen: Dietrich Coelde Verlag, 1963), 34-40. On Francis' prayer to the Father, see: Oktavian Schmucki, "Die Stellung Christi im Beten des hl. Franziskus," *WW* 25 (1962): 134-145.

[87] *II Sent,* d. 1, p. 2, a. 2, q. 1, concl. (II, 44b).

Prayer is one specific way rational creatures are called to partake in that goodness. As Bonaventure notes in regard to the text from Jn. 16: 24: "Ask, and you will receive, so your joy may be full," Christ taught the disciples a way of prayer which by definition asks for a share in God's diffusive goodness:

> Although the divine goodness is of such generosity and diffusion that it invites others to accept its precious gifts, nevertheless, on account of the prudence of discretion which it has in addition to the affluence of the diffusion, it gives its precious gifts of grace to no one unless one diligently prepares oneself; therefore, for this purpose, so that his disciples be suitable to receiving the infusion of the diffusive goodness, our Lord Jesus Christ, in the proposed text, first of all moves them, and in them anyone of us, to the fitting opportuneness of the preparation which is required on our part. . . . the appropriateness of the preparation required on our part is noted when it is said: *Ask*. For certainly there is no better preparation for receiving divine grace than the petition of devout prayer.[89]

---

[88] *III Sent*, d. 32, au., q. 1, concl. (III, 698b). See also: *II Sent*, d. 16, a. 1, q. 1, concl. (II, 394b).

[89] "Licet tantae sit liberalitatis et diffusionis divina bonitas, ut alios ad accipienda sua pretiosa dona invitet, tamen, quia propter prudentiam discretionis, quam insuper habet cum affluentia diffusionis, nulli dat sua pretiosa dona gratiae, nisi diligenter se praeparet; ideo Dominus noster Iesus Christus ad hoc, ut discipuli sui idonei essent ad recipiendum influentiam diffusivae bonitatis, in verbo proposito eos et in eis quemlibet nostrum primo, inducit ad convenientem congruentiam *debitae praeparationis* ex parte nostri . . . *convenientia debitae praeparationis* ex parte nostri notatur, cum dicitur: *Petite*. Nulla enim melior praeparatio ad impetrandam divinam divinam gratiam quam petitio devotae orationis." *Dom 5 post Pascha*, 1 (IX, 311b-312a). Bonaventure goes on to explain (IX,

Those who follow Christ's teaching by asking to share in the divine goodness receive a definitive answer to their supplication in the advent of the gift of the Holy Spirit.[90] This gift of the Holy Spirit, which Christ promised to his disciples,[91] proceeds from the mutual, generous love of the Father and Son[92] and is: "the gift in whom all other gifts are given."[93] It is essential in the dynamic of spiritual filiation,[94] for it brings to completion the work undertaken by the Son by transforming those already liberated by the Son into

---

312a) the rest of the text from John in the following words: "Secundo notatur *affluentia supernae diffusionis* ex parte Dei, cum subditur: et *accipietis*; quasi diceret: tantae liberalitatis et diffusionis est divina bonitas, ut in nobis sit accipere. Tertio notatur *efficacia completae perfectionis* ex parte doni, cum subinfertur: *ut gaudium vestrum sit plenum.*" On prayer as a request for a share in the goodness of God, see also: *Brev*, p. 5, c. 10 (V, 263b-264b) and *Comm Lc*, c. 11, n. 8 (VII, 279a-b). Prayer should be loved greatly precisely because it enables those who pray to receive the good things which come from God; see: *Comm Lc*, c. 11, n. 3 (VII, 278a)

[90] On prayer, divine goodness, and the gift of the Holy Spirit, see also: *Brev*, p. 5, c. 10 (V, 263b-264b) and *Comm Lc*, c. 11, n. 35, (VII, 288a). On the Holy Spirit in Bonaventure's theology, see: Jean François Bonnefoy, *Le Saint-Esprit et ses dons selon Saint Bonaventure* (Paris: J. Vrin, 1929); Hayes, intro., *Saint Bonaventure's Disputed Questions*, 54-66; and Fanny Imle, *Die Theologie des heiligen Bonaventura* (Werl/Westfalen: Franziskus Druckerei, 1931) 158-180.

[91] *Dom 4 post Pascha*, 1 (IX, 310b).

[92] *I Sent*, d. 10, a. 2, q. 1, concl. (I, 201a). On this text and the Holy Spirit as gift, see: Renzo Lavatori, *Lo Spirito santo dono del Padre e del Figlio* (Bologna: Edizioni Dehoniane, 1987) 167-168.

[93] " . . . Spiritus sanctus est donum, in quo omnia alia dona donantur . . . ." *I Sent*, d. 18, au., q. 1, concl. (I, 323b). See also: *IV Sent*, d. 45, a. 3. q. 1, concl. ad 3 (IV, 949b) and *Comm Lc*, c. 11, n. 35 (VII, 288a). A proper understanding of the above text depends, according to Bonaventure, on the interpretation of the ablative "in quo." He maintains that the ablative here indicates both the idea of accompaniment and causality. While the gift of the Holy Spirit always accompanies the gift of sanctfying grace, it may not accompany other gifts such as prophesy. All gifts, however, are said to be given in the Holy Spirit in that the Holy Spirit is the exemplary cause of all giving; see: *I Sent*, d. 18, au., q. 1, concl. (I, 323b-324a). On this point, see also: *II Sent*, d. 26, au., q. 2, concl. ad 1 (II, 636a-b). On the Holy Spirit as "donum," see: Lavatori, *Lo Spirito santo dono del Padre e del Figlio*, esp. 165-172 in regard to Bonaventure's theology. See also: Hayes, intro., *Saint Bonaventure's Disputed Questions*, 61-62.

[94] *In Pent*, 7 (IX, 338a).

the adoptive sons and daughters of God.[95] The gift of the Holy Spirit, present in the soul by means of sanctifying grace,[96] renders those who receive it acceptable to God and, consequently, they become sons and daughters of God. Although the poor are already acceptable by reason of their status as creatures created from the goodness of God, they still require the gift of the Holy Spirit to be conformed to the image of God.[97] As they are conformed to the divine image, they are made acceptable to God[98] and adopted as sons and daughters.[99] The degree of their filiation can be judged in terms of their conformity to the natural Son, for as the *Commentary on the Sentences* states: ". . . we are sons of God inasmuch as we are in harmony with the image of the natural Son . . . ."[100]

The advent of the gift of the Holy Spirit enables the poor to become temporally through the influence of grace that which the Son is eternally by nature.[101] Formerly sons and daughters of perdition, they now become the sons and daughters of God as they receive the gifts of grace poured into the soul by the Trinity.[102] Although already sons and daughters of God by virtue

---

[95] *III Sent,* d. 10, a. 2, q. 2, concl. and ad 4 (III, 236a-237b).

[96] *Brev*, p. 5, c. 1 (V, 252a-253a).

[97] *II Sent,* d. 29, a. 1, q. 1, concl. (II, 695b-696a) and *Brev*, p. 5, c. 1 (V, 252a-253a).

[98] *II Sent,* d. 4, a. 1, q. 2, concl. ad 1, 2, and 3 (II, 134a).

[99] *II Sent,* d. 29, a. 1, q. 1, fund. 6 and concl. (II, 695b-696a). On this point, see: Romano Guardini, *Die Lehre des hl. Bonaventura*, 95-96.

[100] ". . . filii Dei sumus, in quantum sumus conformes imagini Filii naturalis . . . ." *III Sent*, d. 10, a. 2, q. 1, concl. ad 4 (III, 237a-b).

[101] *III Sent*, d. 4, a. 1, q. 3, concl. ad 2 (III, 103b) and *III Sent* d. 10, dub. 5 (III, 240b).

[102] *In Pent,* 7 (IX, 338a). Unless otherwise mentioned, the terms "gift of grace," "gifts of grace," "gift of the Holy Spirit," and "gifts of the Holy Spirit" will be used interchangeably throughout this work in reference to the gift of sanctifying grace. All these terms refer here

106

of creation, they are now transformed by grace into the adopted sons and daughters of God and recover the divine likeness, or similitude, previously lost through sin.[103] As adopted sons and daughters in grace, they are once again ordered to receive the inheritance of the kingdom of God.[104] The same cannot be said of those who are not conformed to the Son of God. They are also sons and daughters of God by virtue of creation; however, they are not adopted sons and daughters of God, but, rather, sons and daughters of the Devil because they have been disfigured by sin[105] and assimilated to the image of the Devil. They bear the likeness of their father, the Devil,[106] whom they imitate in their sinful actions and from whom they inherit Gehenna.[107]

The gift of grace, whose advent brings to completion the work of adoption begun by the Father in Christ, was merited by Christ as head of the Church. As Bonaventure writes in the *Commentary on the Sentences*: "He himself [Christ], as far as he is head of the Church, merited for us the grace by means of which we are adopted sons."[108] In addition to meriting the gift of

---

to the temporal procession of the Holy Spirit. While the eternal procession of the Spirit signifies the procession of the Holy Spirit as mutual love between the Father and the Son, the temporal procession signifies the reception of the Holy Spirit who accompanies the donation of sanctifying grace. On the eternal and temporal procession of the Holy Spirit, see: *I Sent*, d. 14, a. 1, q. 1, concl. (I, 245b-246a).

[103] *III Sent*, d. 10, dub. 4 (III, 240a) and *III Sent*, d. 10, a. 2, q. 1, concl. ad 4 (III, 234b).

[104] *III Sent*, d. 10, a. 2, q. 1, concl. (III, 234a).

[105] *III Sent*, d. 10, dub. 4 (III, 240a-b).

[106] *Dom 22 post Pent*, 5 (IX, 446a-b).

[107] *III Sent*, d. 4, dub. 3 (III, 117a-b).

[108] "Ipse enim nobis meruit gratiam, per quam sumus filii adoptivi, in quantum est caput Ecclesiae." *III Sent*, d. 10, a. 2, q. 2, concl. (III, 236a-b). On the question of the merit of Christ, see: Guardini, *Die Lehre des hl. Bonaventura*, 76-85, and esp. 95-96 in regard to the question of spiritual adoption.

grace as head of the Church, Christ also distributes, as head of the Church, this grace among the members of the Church.[109] It is because the Church receives the gift of grace from Christ as its head[110] that it concludes all prayers with the words: "Through our Lord Jesus Christ."[111] This gift of grace cleanses the poor in baptism from evil in the waters of regeneration, establishes them as sons and daughters of God,[112] and leads them to call out in prayer: "Abba Father."[113] It also reorients them toward the goodness of God by conforming their intellects and affections to Christ in faith and love; therefore, it can be said to further the participation of the poor in the mystery of divine filiation.[114]

---

[109] *III Sent,* d. 13, a. 2, q. 1, concl. (III, 284b); *Dom 13 post Pent,* 1 (IX, 404b); and *In Pent,* 7 (IX, 337b-338a). On the question of grace (in this context referred to as "gratia capitis") and the headship of Christ, see: Romano Guardini, *Systembildende Elemente in der Theologie Bonaventuras,* ed. Werner Dettloff (Leiden: E.J. Brill, 1964) 184-198 and Hayes, *The Hidden Center,* 98-102.

[110] *Dom 13 post Pent,* 1 (IX, 404b).

[111] "Nam omnis dulcedo gratiae est per Iesum. Et propter hoc Ecclesia omnes orationes terminat: Per Dominum nostrum Iesum Christum." *Dom 13 post Pent,* 1 (IX, 404b). See also: *De orat,* membrum 3, a. 5, 706b.

[112] *III Sent,* d. 10, a. 2, q. 2, concl. ad 4 (III, 237a-b); *De test Trin,* n. 6 (V, 536a-b); *De donis,* coll. 3, n. 13 (V, 471b) and *Circum Domini,* 1 (IX, 136b-137a). On this point, see: Imle, *Die Theologie des heiligen Bonaventura,* 195. On the sacrament of baptism, see: *Brev,* p. 6, c. 7 (V, 271b-272b).

[113] " . . . Christianus dicitur a Christo uncto; et ille verus Christianus est, qui habet *oleum gratiae in vasis suis.* Et talis potest clamare: *Abba, Pater;* et talis est, qui recipit *lavacrum regenerationis,* ut dicit Apostolus ad Titum, quia *secundum suam misericordiam salvos nos fecit per lavacrum regenerationis et renovationis Spiritus sanctus.* Et Spiritus sanctus in corde nostro facit nos vere clamare . . . . " *Circum Domini,* 1 (IX, 136b-137a).

[114] *III Sent,* d. 10, a. 2, q. 2, concl. ad 4 (III, 237b). As this text indicates, the intellect is conformed to Christ through faith and the affections through charity. This two-fold action of grace can be identified with the "gratia capitis" inasmuch as the grace of headship given by Christ encourages the growth of faith and love in those who receive it. On this point, see: *III Sent,* d. 13, a. 2, q. 3, concl. (III, 289b).

2. 2. 1. Prayer for Advent of the Holy Spirit

Given the decisive role of the Holy Spirit in the dynamic of spiritual filiation, it is not surprising to find Bonaventure underlining the need to pray for the advent of the Holy Spirit. In a homily from the Easter Season, for example, he links the promise made by Christ concerning the coming of the Holy Spirit to the necessity of prayer. He begins by reminding the congregation that the Holy Spirit is a "regal present" or "imperial gift" promised by Christ to his disciples,[115] which removes the indigence of the poor by enriching them with the gifts of grace.[116] In the course of the homily, he identifies some of the dispositions required of anyone wishing to receive this gift of the Holy Spirit; one of these dispositions is devout prayer.[117] The prayer of the disciples, marked as it was by devotion, prepared a fitting dwelling place among them for the Holy Spirit, thereby, encouraging the

---

[115] "*Cum venerit ille Spiritus veritatis, docebit vos omnem veritatem,* Ioannis decimo sexto. Videns Dominus noster Iesus Christus, discipulos suos desolari de recessu suo corporali, in remedium desolationis in verbo propositio promittit eis regale xenium, imperiale donum, scilicet Spiritum sanctum . . . ." *Dom 4 post Pascha,* 1 (IX, 309a). The text from John's Gospel is Jn. 16: 13. On Christ's promise of the Holy Spirit to the apostles, see: *Comm Jn,* c. 14, n. 25-27 (VI, 441a-b) and *Comm Jn,* c. 14, n. 34-36 (VI, 442b-443a).

[116] "Tertio venit ut *rex totius opulentiae* propter amotionem totius indigentiae; unde Actuum secundo: *Factus est repente de caelo sonus tanquam advenientis spiritus vehementis et replevit totam domum, ubi erant sedentes*; unde sequitur: *Repleti sunt omnes Spiritu sancto.* Ita enim Spiritus sanctus Apostolos virtutibus et donis et muneribus adimplevit et opulentavit, ut in nullo egerent, cum eos constituit heredes et reges regni caelorum et principes fidei christianae. Hic est enim, *qui suscitat de terra,* avaritiae, avarum et *inopem, et erigit de stercore,* immunditiae, peccatorem et *pauperum,* ut opulentatus veris divitiis gratiae, *sedeat cum* apostolicis *principibus et solium gloriae teneat,* in caelesti patria." *Dom 4 post Pascha,* 1 (IX, 310a).

[117] *Dom 4 post Pascha,* 1 (IX, 309b-310a). See also: *Dom infra octavam Ascen,* 2 (IX, 329b; 330b).

109

advent of the Holy Spirit.[118]

Desire in prayer is another disposition which facilitates the advent of of the Holy Spirit.[119] In the *Commentary on Luke,* Bonaventure links desire with prayer for the gift of the Holy Spirit when he writes: "That Spirit is given to those *petitioning* and desiring according to that saying of the Psalm: 'I opened my mouth, and panted.'"[120] He then goes on to convey the intensity of the desire for the Holy Spirit by mentioning an out of the ordinary, but effectively unique, example of desire: a wild ass in heat.[121] This example, found in Jer. 2: 24, was used by Jeremiah to chastise Israel for her infidelity; he compared Israel to a wild ass, who driven by lust, sniffs the wind of the desert looking for satisfaction from all who pass by. The linking of desire with prayer for the Holy Spirit is also found, albeit, in a more conventional fashion, in the *Breviloquium* where Bonaventure interprets the ten day period separating Ascension from Pentecost in terms of the Lord's intent to encourage the disciples to seek the coming of the Holy Spirit:

---

[118] "Nota ergo, quod tria loca frequentare solet et visitare adventu suo Spiritus sanctus, videlicet locum *orationis,* locum *praedicationis* et locum sanctae *congregationis.* In loco orationis attrahunt eum Sanctorum *desideria* . . . Solet ergo Spiritus sanctus familiarius advenire ad locum *orationis.* Libenter venit quis ad locum, ubi *amatur; dabit* ideo *Pater* caelestis *spiritum bonum petentibus se,* quod figuratum est Actuum primo, ubi venit Spiritus sanctus in discipulos congregatos in loco, ubi *erant perseverantes unanimiter in oratione.* Movet enim eum in loco sanctae devotionis et orationis odor sanctae devotionis." *Dom infra octavam Ascen,* 2 (IX, 329b). That the Holy Spirit descended on the apostles at Pentecost does not mean, however, that the Spirit was not present and at work in the world before Pentecost. On this question, see: *I Sent,* d. 15, p. 2, dub. 3 (I, 274b-275a).

[119] *Brev,* p. 4, c. 10 (V, 251b); *Comm Lc,* c. 11, n. 35 (VII, 288a); *Comm Lc,* c. 24, n. 62 (VII, 603a); *Dom 4 post Pascha,* 1 (IX, 309b-310a); and *Dom infra octavam Ascen,* 2 (IX, 329b).

[120] "Iste Spiritus datur *petentibus* et desiderantibus, secundum illud Psalmi: 'Os meum aperui et attraxi spritum.' " *Comm Lc,* c. 11, n. 35, (VII, 288a). The psalm text is Ps 119: 131.

[121] *Comm Lc,* c. 11, n. 35 (VII, 288a).

Finally, so he might inflame to charity, he sent the fire of
the Holy Spirit on the day of Pentecost. And because no
one is filled with this fire except the one who petitions,
seeks and knocks with the insistent and importune desire
of hope, therefore, he did not send [the fire of the Holy
Spirit] immediately after the Ascension, but after an
intervening period of ten days in which the disciples
prepared themselves [by] fasting, praying and groaning
for the reception of the Holy Spirit.[122]

Humility, in addition to devotion and desire, is also an important
disposition encouraging the advent of the grace of the Holy Spirit.
Bonaventure maintains in the work, *Evangelical Perfection,* that only those
who are humble will receive the grace of the Holy Spirit.[123] In a homily on
humility and Francis of Assisi, he speaks of the bond between humility, the
grace of the Holy Spirit, and prayer.[124] After singling out the discovery or
reception of grace as one of the fruits of humility, he likens the discovery of
grace to the discovery of water: just as it is impossible to find water without
digging a well, so, too, the living water of grace is found only by digging an

---

[122] "Postremo, ut *inflammaret ad caritatem, misit ignem Spiritus sancti in die Pentecostes.*
Et quia nullus hoc igne impletur, nisi qui petit, quaerit et pulsat cum instanti et importuno
spei desiderio; ideo non statim post ascensionem misit, sed decem dierum spatio interiecto,
in quo discipuli ieiunantes, orantes et gementes disposuerunt se ad Spiritus sancti
susceptionem." *Brev,* p. 4, c. 10 (V, 251b). See also: *Comm Lc,* c. 24, n. 62 (VII, 603a).

[123] *Perf ev,* q. 1, concl. (V, 121b). On humility and the reception of the Holy Spirit, see
also: *Dom 3 Adventus,* 2 (IX, 64a); *In Pent,* 7 (IX, 338b-339a); and *De S. P. Franc,* 5
(IX, 595a-b). Given Bonaventure's insistence on the need for humility on the part of those
seeking the gift of the Holy Spirit, it is not suprising to read in the *Commentary on the
Sentences* that humility is a disposition for spiritual adoption; see: *III Sent,* d. 10, a. 2, q.
2, concl. ad 4 (III, 237b).

[124] *De S. P. Franc,* 5 (IX, 595b).

111

interior well by means of humility. Such humility removes pride and prepares an appropriate place for the grace of the Holy Spirit. Furthermore, it assures the reception of grace in prayer for God looks with favor on the humble heart. Relying once again in the same homily on an analogy to water, Bonaventure compares the divine response to humble prayer, evidenced in the advent of the Holy Spirit, to that of water flowing down into a valley:

> And just as water flows to the valleys, so, too, does the grace of the Holy Spirit flow down to the humble. And just as water ascends higher, the greater it descends, so, too, prayer which proceeds from a humble heart draws nearer and resounds in the ears of God so that it may obtain grace . . . .[125]

The advent of the Holy Spirit, described above in terms of the flowing water of grace received in prayer, is also spoken of as a river of grace flowing from the Father and the Son into the Church.[126] Those partaking of the river of living water are carried by its current back to the divine source.[127] Although this gift of grace is given by the entire Trinity,[128] it flows

---

[125] "Et sicut aqua confluit ad valles, sic gratia Spiritus sancti defluit ad humiles; et sicut aqua tanto altius ascendit, quanto magis descendit, sic oratio, quae de corde humiliatio procedit, magis propinquat et resonat auribus Dei, ut impetret gratiam." *De S. P. Franc,* 5 (IX, 595b).

[126] *In Pent,* 3 (IX, 335a-b) and *In Pent,* 8 (IX, 339b-341a). Both these homilies speak of the Church as a type of garden irrigated by the Holy Spirit. Along the same line, see: *Plant par,* n. 8 (V, 577a). On the imagery of water, grace and the Holy Spirit, see also: *Comm Jn,* c. 4, n. 18-22 (VI, 292a-293a); *Comm Jn,* c. 7, n. 56 (VI, 350a); *In Pent,* 4 (IX, 335b); and *De assum B.V.M.,* 4 (IX, 696a). On the symbolic interpretation of water, see: Dorothea Forstner, *Die Welt der Symbole* (Innsbruck: Tyrolia Verlag, 1961) 89-96 and Gérard de Champeaux and Sébastien Sterckx, *I simboli del medio evo,* trans. Monica Girardi (Milano: Jaca Book, 1981) 228-229.

[127] "Respondet Chrysostomus, quod *flumina Spiritus sancti* dicuntur eius dona et gratiae. Gratia autem recte dicitur *flumen fluens*, non quia ab uno fluat in alterum, sed quia, cum mentem intraverit, omni fonte magis manat nec deficit nec stat, sed *fluit* et *refluit. Fluit* a

112

from the Father, who is the original principle[129] and font of grace[130] from whom all things go forth and return.[131] The Father communicates the gift of grace through the Son,[132] who becomes a font of living water for those thirsting for the goodness of God. The Son is the font from whom the waters of life descend to earth and ascend to heaven; it is he who comes to offer to the thirsty the waters of grace springing up to eternal life.[133] This water of grace refreshes and quenches the thirst of those longing for the living God;[134] hence

Deo et facit hominem *refluere* in Deum, iuxta proprietatem aquae, quae tantum ascendit in fluxu, quantum descendit. Propterea scribitur supra quarto: *Fiet in eo fons aquae salientis in vitam aeternam*; ideo Ecclesiastae primo: *Ad locum, unde exeunt flumina, revertuntur, ut iterum fluant.*" *Comm Jn*, c. 7, n. 58, resp. (VI, 350a). For the reference to John Chrysostom, see: *In Joannem*, Homilia 51, n. 1, *PG* 59, 284. The Scriptures quoted are Jn. 4: 14 and Ec. 1: 7, respectively. De Champeaux and Sterckx in *I simboli*, (228) identify the flowing of water in and out of the garden of Paradise with the "exitus-reditus," or emanation theme of theology: "La Bibbia indica che 'un fiume usciva dall'Eden per innaffiare il giardino, e di là si divideva per formare quattro bracci'. . . Questi fiumi, mentre partono dalla montagna per simboleggiare il movimento di emanazione e vivificazione, vi ritornono per simboleggiare il ritorno al Paradiso el il compimento di ogni cosa da parte del creatore. Su questo tema dell'*exitus-reditus*, emanazione-ritorno, si elaborerà una reflessione teologica. L'opera della creazione materiale, avendo la sua origine nel Paradiso terrestre, è l'immagine perfetta dell'opera della creazione spirituale e di quella della ricreazione universale richiesta dalle distruzioni del peccato e più ancora dalla vocazione trascendente di tutto il cosmo purificato per essere assunto nel mistero totale di Cristo. " The "exitus-reditus" theme lies at the core of Bonaventure's theology; see: Hayes, *The Hidden Center*, 12-13.

[128] *III Sent*, d. 10, a. 2, q. 3, concl. ad 1 (III, 238a) and *In Pent*, 7 (IX, 337b).

[129] *De donis*, coll. 1, n. 4 (V, 457b).

[130] *De assum B.V.M.*, 4 (IX, 696a).

[131] *I Sent*, d. 31, p. 2, dub. 7 (I, 552a). In this text the Father is spoken of as "fontale principium." He is spoken of elsewhere as the "fontalis plenitudo." On the Father as the "fontalis plenitudo," see: Alejandro de Villalmonte, "El Padre Plenitud fontal de la Deidad," in vol. 4 of *SB*, 221-242. See also: Ewert Cousins, *Bonaventure and the Coincidence of Opposites* (Chicago: Franciscan Herald Press, 1978) 52-54 and Franz Courth, *Trinität in der Scholastik*, vol. 2 (Faszikel 1b) of *HDG*, 132-133.

[132] *I Sent*, d. 18, au., q. 1, concl. (I, 324a) and *De assum B.V.M.*, 4 (IX, 695b-696a).

[133] *Coll Jn*, coll. 14, n. 1-3 (VI, 554a-555b) and *De assum B.V.M.*, 4 (IX, 696a). On Christ as the font of grace, see also: *Comm Jn*, c. 4, n. 9 (VI, 290a) and *In Pent*, 8 (IX, 340a-341a).

the admonition in the *Tree of Life*:

> . . . apply your mouth *so you may draw water from the*
> *Saviour's fountains*. This is certainly the *fountain rising*
> *from the middle of paradise*, which *divided into four*
> *sources*, and poured into devout hearts, makes fertile and
> irrigates the whole earth.[135]

Prayer provides the means to draw the water of grace flowing from the Father through the Son: "For prayer is the vessel by which the grace of the Holy Spirit is drawn from the font of overflowing delight of that most blessed Trinity."[136] Those thirsting for the grace of the Holy Spirit should direct their prayer to the Son since it is through him that grace reaches those in need.[137] The exegesis of Christ's encounter with the Samaritan women (Jn. 4:

---

[134] *Coll Jn,* coll. 14, n. 2-3 (VI, 555a-b); *Comm Jn,* c. 4, n. 22, (VI, 292b-293a) and *In Pent,* 8 (IX, 341a).

[135] ". . . os appone, *ut haurias aquas de fontibus Salvatoris.* Hic enim est *fons egrediens de medio paradisi,* qui, *in quatuor divisus capita* et in corda devota diffusus, fecundat et irrigat universam terram." *Lig vit,* fr. 8, n. 30 (VIII, 79b-80a).

[136] "Oratio enim hausorium est, quo Spiritus sancti gratia hauritur de fonte supereffluentis dulcedinis illius beatissimae Trinitatis." *Perf vit,* c. 5, n. 5 (VIII, 119a).

[137] *Dom 13 post Pent,* 1 (IX, 404b). On the question of prayer to Jesus, see: A. Klawek, *Das Gebet zu Jesus. Seine Berechtigung und Übung nach den Schriften des Neuen Testaments* (Münster: Verlag der Aschendorffschen Verlagsbuchhandlung, 1921); Irénée Hausherr, *The Name of Jesus,* trans. Charles Cummings (Kalamazoo, Michigan: Cistercian Publications, 1978); and Salvatore di Cristina, *Preghiera e devozione a Cristo nei Padri* (Milano: Edizioni O.R., 1987). See also: Josef Andreas Jungmann, *Die Stellung Christi im liturgischen Gebet* (Münster: Verlag der Aschendorffschen Verlagsbuchhandlung, 1925) and Oktavian Schmucki, "Die Stellung Christi," 188-212, esp. 188-202 and 210-212. In this context it should be noted that, while Bonaventure on many occasions speaks of praying to the Son as well as to the Father for the gifts of grace, he is most reluctant to speak of praying to the Holy Spirit for the same gifts. This is not surprising since he writes in the *Commentary on the Sentences:* "Ad illud quod obiicitur, quod postulatio orationis respicit totam Trinitatem; dicendum, quod verum est *ex consequenti,* licet quaedam orationes dirigantur ad Patrem, quaedam ad Filium." *III Sent,* d. 17, a. 2, q. 1, concl. ad 4 (III, 372b). In another book of the *Commentary on the Sentences,* he points out that prayers of petition are not directed to the Holy Spirit because of the very nature of the Holy Spirit as gift: "Quod vero quaeritur de Spiritu sancto, dicendum est, quod quia est donum, in quo omnia dona donantur, ideo petendus est ipse,

1-30), found in the *Commentary on John*, bears out this point.[138] Here Bonaventure depicts Christ as the font of living water from whom the gift of the Holy Spirit is to be drawn in prayer. This prayer requires a recognition of the nature of the living water offered by Christ along with his ability to offer such water. The water he offers is the grace of the Holy Spirit,[139] which perfectly refreshes the thirst for God.[140] Had the Samaritan appreciated the nature of the gift Christ had to offer, as well as his power to do so, then she might have chosen to ask him for it. Had she decided to pray, her request would have been granted for Christ satisfies the petitions of those praying for the grace of the Holy Spirit.[141]

---

non porrigenda est ei petitio." *IV Sent*, d. 45, a. 3, q. 1, concl. ad 3 (IV, 949b). Bonaventure's teaching on prayer to the Holy Spirit reflects the liturgical practice of the Western Church of his day. Josef Jungmann in *Missarum Sollemnia* (Freiburg: Herder, 1958) 486-487, note 25, writes: "In weiterem Verfolg des trinitarischen Gedankens und angesichts der inzwischen durchgedrungenen Christusorationen werfen schon mittelalterliche Erklärer die Frage auf, warum keine Oration an den Heiligen Geist gerichtet sei. Darauf antwortet Hugo von St. Cher, Tract. de missa (Sölch 15): *Quia Spiritus Sanctus est donum et a dono non petitur sed a largitore doni.* . . . Obwohl die Antwort spekulativ nicht zwingend ist, ist sie kerygmatisch richtig, d. h. es soll die theoretische Möglichkeit von Orationen an den Hl. Geist nicht ausgenützt werden, damit die Grundlinien der Heilsordnung, die durch Christus zu Gott führt, sich im Bewußtsein der Beter nicht verwischen." For a discussion of this same question of prayer to the Holy Spirit, see also: Otto Hermann Pesch, *Das Gebet* (Verlag Winfried Werk) 115-118. Pesch (115) says: "Zum Heiligen Geist betet man im Neuen Testament nicht. Er selber ist der Erbetene, die Gabe, um die man bittet. Man betet nicht *zum* Geist, man betet *um den* Geist. So ganz deutlich etwa Lk 11, 13 und Jo 14, 16f." A reading of Bonaventure's sermons indicates that he deviated from his own teaching on petitionary prayer to the Holy Spirit on at least one occasion. This exception is found in a homily on the Ascension which reads: "Oportet igitur, quod petamus a Spiritu sancto scientiam, quia *omnis, qui petit, accipit* . . . ." *In Ascen*, 1 (IX, 314b).

[138] *Comm Jn*, c. 4, n. 1- 62 (VI, 289a-299a).

[139] *Comm Jn*, c. 4, n. 18 (VI, 292a-b).

[140] *Comm Jn*, c. 4, n. 21-22 (VI, 292b-293a).

[141] "*Respondit Iesus et dixit ei: Si scires donum Dei. Donum Dei* est Spiritus sanctus, de quo Actuum secundo: 'Poenitemini, et baptizetur unusquisque vestrum, et accipietis donum sancti Spiritus.' Spiritus sanctus dicitur *donum*, quia non debet vendi; Actuum octavo: 'Pecunia tua tecum sit in perditionem, quoniam donum Dei existimasti pecunia possideri.' Si hoc, inquam, cognosceres, *et quis est, qui dicit tibi: Da mihi bibere*, quoniam scilicet

The grace of the Holy Spirit, which Christ gives as living water to those petitioning him, is also symbolically described in terms of light.[142] In fact, among all natural materials, Bonaventure considers the light of the sun the most representative of the nature and effect of grace.[143] As light flows from the sun and illuminates the air, so, too, does the spiritual light of grace flow from God, as from a spiritual sun, to illuminate, reform, gratify, and enliven the soul. The light of grace issues from the font of the Father of lights,[144] conforms the soul to the divine source,[145] and leads it through the Son back to the Father.[146] This grace descends from the Father of Lights

---

ipse dator sancti Spiritus; non fecisses quaestionem, sed doni postulationem. Ideo dicit: *Tu forsitan petisses ab eo; forsitan* non est nota dubitationis, sed libertatis arbitrii; et ille petitioni tuae satisfecisset. Ideo dicit: *Et ille dedisset tibi aquam vivam; tibi,* petenti; *dedisset;* Matthaei septimo: 'Omnis, qui petit, accipit, et qui quaerit invenit, et pulsanti aperietur.'" *Comm Jn* c. 4, n. 18 (VI, 292a-b).

[142] *De donis*, coll. 1, n. 9 (V, 459a). See also: *Brev*, p. 5, n. 4 (V, 257a).

[143] *II Sent*, d. 26, au., q. 2, concl. (II, 636a). On grace and light, see also: *IV Sent*, d. 18, p. 2, dub. 3 (IV, 496a). On the theme of light in Bonaventure's writings, see: Emma Thérèse Healy, comm., *Saint Bonaventure's De reductione artium ad theologiam*, trans. intro, and comm., Emma Thérèse Healy (Saint Bonaventure, N.Y.: The Franciscan Institute, 1955) 45-110; Gilson, *The Philosophy of St. Bonaventure*, 250-259 and with reference to the Gothic architecture: Remigius Boving, *Bonaventura und die französische Hochgotik* (Werl/Westfalen: Franziskus Druckerei, 1930) 85-96. On the symbolism of light (and of the sun) in the Christian tradition, see: Forstner, *Die Welt der Symbole*, 117-123.

[144] *Red art*, n. 1 (V, 319a). The reference to the Father as the "Father of Lights" is based on Jas 1: 17. This text reads in *The New Catholic* (300) translation of the Vulgate as follows: " Every good gift and every perfect gift is from above, coming down from the Father of Lights, with whom there is no change nor shadow of alteration." Bonaventure frequently interprets the "good" and "perfect" gift as the gift of the Holy Spirit; see among many texts: *I Sent*, d. 14, a. 2, q. 1, concl. (I, 250a) and *Brev*, p. 5, c. 1 (V, 252a).

[145] *II Sent*, d. 26, au., q. 2, concl. (II, 636a).

[146] *Hex*, coll. 1, n. 17 (V, 332a-b); *De donis*, coll. 1, n. 9 (V, 459a) and *Comm Ec*, c. 1, p. 1 (VI, 13b). The imagery of light, like that of water, was used by medieval writers to convey their teaching on emanation. On the theme of light and emanation in medieval thought, see: M. D. Chenu, *Nature, Man and Society in the Twelfth Century. Essays on New Theological Perspectives in the Latin West*, pref. Etienne Gilson, ed. and trans. Jerome Taylor and Lester K. Little (Chicago: The University of Chicago Press, 1979) 52, note 2.

through the Son,[147] who is also a font of eternal light,[148] an allegorical "sun," so to speak, illuminating the inhabitants of the earth. He is, as the *Commentary on Ecclesiastics* says, the "Sun of justice" which rose at the time of the nativity to illuminate all the world with the light of the Holy Spirit. At the time of the passion, this same "Sun of justice" set to redeem the world only to return to its place in the heavens with the Ascension.[149] After the Ascension, the world continues to be illuminated by the Holy Spirit, who, descending from the Son like fire upon the members of the Church, illuminates the way leading back to heaven.[150]

The return of the "Sun of justice" to the heavens set the stage for the illuminating advent of the Holy Spirit, which is to be sought in prayer. In the *Collations on the Six Days* Bonaventure writes: "For certainly just as a cloud ascends on high so that it may rain later, so Christ ascended that he might give his gifts; when *the sun was raised and the moon stood in its place.*"[151] These gifts of grace from Christ[152] are crucial to the life of the soul, for: ". . . just as the sun illuminates continually, so should the soul receive illuminations

---

[147] *De donis*, coll. 1, n. 4-5 (V, 457b-458a).

[148] *Lig vit,* fr. 12, n. 47 (VIII, 85a-b). See also: *In Ascen*, 1 (IX, 315b).

[149] *Comm Ec*, c. 1, p. 1 (VI, 13a-b). See also: *Hex*, coll. 13, n. 26 (V, 391b). On Christ as the "Sun of justice," see also: *II Sent*, d. 26, au., q. 2, concl. (II, 636a) and *De sancto Marco,* 1 (IX, 519a). On Christ, sun symbolism, and prayer in the early Church, see: Franz Joseph Dölger, *Sol Salutis. Gebet und Gesang im christlichen Altertum* (Münster: Verlag der Aschendorffschen Verlagsbuchhandlung, 1920).

[150] *In Pent*, 9 (IX, 341b-342a). This homily goes on to describe how the fire of the Holy Spirit inflames the heart. This inflamation of the affections, which is attributed to grace as fire, is also a property of grace as light. In fact, it is a consequence of the illumination brought about through the light of grace. See: *IV Sent*, d. 18, p. 2, dub. 3 (IV, 496a).

[151] "Sicut enim nubes ascendit in altum, ut postmodum pluat; sic ascendit Christus, ut dona sua daret; cum *elevatus est sol, et luna stetit in ordine suo.*" *Hex*, coll. 3, n. 19 (V, 346b).

[152] *Hex*, coll. 3, n. 19 (V, 346b).

continually from the grace of the Holy Spirit."[153] Prayer is one way to receive this illumination according to the exegesis of the healing of the blind beggar (Lk. 18: 35-43) found in the *Commentary on Luke*.[154] Here, Bonaventure interprets the mendicant's request to see, which is directed to Christ, as a plea for the light of divine wisdom. In response to his prayer, Christ healed the mendicant both physically and spiritually.[155] The desire of the blind mendicant to see serves as an example of prayer for others who wish to be illuminated by grace. Bonaventure includes himself among this group as his remarks reveal in a homily on Saint Mary Magdalene:

> *Standing still, however, Jesus ordered the blind man to be brought to him.* It is read in the Gospel that as the Lord was passing by along the road, a blind man was standing along the way. That blind man designates the human race or everyone who needs to be illuminated by the knowledge of divine matters; the one, however, who reckons that he is not in need of the illumination of the knowledge of divine matters, is blind and more than blind. Hence in Proverbs: *Have you seen a person appearing to himself to be wise? The foolish person will have more hope than that one.* And in the Apocalypse it is said: *You say that I am rich, wealthy and in need of nothing. You do not know that you are wretched,*

---

[153] ". . . sicut sol continue illuminat, sic anima continue debet recipere illuminationes a gratia Spiritus sancti." *Hex*, coll. 13, n. 30 (V, 392b).

[154] *Comm Lc*, c. 18, n. 58-66 (VII, 470a-472b).

[155] *Comm Lc* c. 18, n. 64 (VII, 471b-472a). Wisdom is a gift of the Holy Spirit which is discussed in the last section of this chapter (2.2.2.7.) and in Chapter Four.

miserable, poor, blind and naked. Therefore I, and every person, should be an imitator of the blind man and call out, that is, pray to the Lord, so he will illuminate him. The blind man did not ask for clothes or money, but instead, when the Lord said: *What do you wish that I do for you,* he responded, *Lord, that I may see.* And in a way similar to his example, we should ask for the light of grace and doctrine. [156]

2. 2. 2.   The "Our Father" and the Seven Gifts of the Holy Spirit

One way to pray for the advent of the Holy Spirit is to address the Father with the words of the Our Father. As Bonaventure says in the *Collations on the Gifts,* Jesus taught his disciples the petitions of the Our Father so they might pray accordingly and receive the seven gifts of the Holy Spirit from the Father of lights.[157] These seven gifts are: fear, piety,

---

[156] *"Stans autem Iesus iussit, caecum adduci ad se.* In Evangelio legitur, quod transeunte Domino per viam, stabat caecus secus viam. Caecus iste designat genus humanum sive omnem, qui indiget illuminari cognitione divinorum; qui autem reputat, se non indigere illuminatione cognitionis divinorum, caecus est et plus quam caecus. Unde in Proverbiis: *Vidisti, hominem sapientem sibi videri? Magis illo spem habebit insipiens;* et in Apocalypsi dicitur: *Dicis, quod dives sum et locupletatus et nullius egeo; et nescis, quia tu es miser et miserabilis et pauper et caecus et nudus.* Igitur ego et quilibet homo debet esse imitator caeci et clamare, id est orare, ad Dominum, ut ipsum illuminet. Caecus non petiit vestem vel pecuniam, sed dicente Domino: *Quid tibi vis, faciam;* respondit: *Domine, ut videam.* Similiter et nos exemplo eius debemus petere lumen gratiae et doctrinae." *De S. Maria Magdalena,* 1 (IX, 554b-555a). The Scripture texts referred to are: Lk. 18: 40; Pr. 26: 12; Rev. 3: 17 and Lk. 18: 41.

[157] "Ista septem dona Spiritus sancti tanguntur in oratione dominica. Ista dona non habentur nisi a Patre luminum; ideo Christus volens nos docere, quomodo possumus ea obtinere, docet nos ista petere in oratione dominica." *De donis,* coll. 2, n. 4 (V, 463a). On the Our Father as a prayer for the seven gifts of the Holy Spirit, see also: *III Sent,* d. 34, p. 1, a. 1, q. 2, concl. ad 1 (III, 740b-741a); *Brev,* p. 5, c. 10 (V, 264b); *Comm Lc,* c. 11, n. 9 (VII,

knowledge, fortitude, counsel, understanding, and wisdom. In this interpretation of the Our Father, Bonaventure follows an exegetical tradition
going back at least as far as Augustine, which considers each of the seven
petitions of the Matthean version of the Our Father (Mt. 6: 9-13) as a request
for one of the seven gifts of the Holy Spirit.[158] The seven gifts of the Holy
Spirit, originally identified by the prophet Isaiah with the Spirit of the Lord
(Is. 11: 2), are to be distinguished from other gifts of grace. While every
infused grace is a gift, only the seven gifts of the Holy Spirit are gifts in the
strict sense of the word.[159]

The seven gifts of the Holy Spirit assist the poor to progress in the life
of grace,[160] dispose them toward spiritual perfection,[161] and conform them to
Christ.[162] Their reception of these seven gifts, when praying the Our Father,

---

279b); and *Lig vit,* fr. 12, n. 49 (VIII, 86a-b).

[158] For Augustine's exegesis, see: Augustine, *De sermone Domini 2,* II, 38 in *De sermone
Domini in monte. Libros Duos, CChr,* 35, 128-130. For a medieval example of this
tradition, see: Hugh of St. Victor, *De quinque septenis, PL* 175, 407-410. On the seven
gifts of the Holy Spirit in Bonaventure's theology, see: Bonnefoy, *Le Saint-Esprit et ses
dons,* esp. 106-108 in regard to prayer for the gifts; Bernardo Aperribay, intro., vol. 5 of
Obras de San Buenaventura, 51-84; Eliodoro Mariani, intro. and comm., *I sette doni dello
spirito santo* (Vicenza: L.I.E.F., 1985) and Jörg Splett, "Der Geist der Gaben," *WW* 45
(1982): 72-79. On the seven gifts of the Spirit in general, see: Karl Boeckl, *Die sieben
Gaben des heiligen Geistes in ihrer Bedeutung für die Mystik nach der Theologie des 13.
und 14. Jahrhunderts* (Freiburg: Herder, 1931); esp. 76-89 in regard to Bonaventure; A.
Gardeil, "Dons du Saint-Esprit" in vol. 4/2 of *DThC,* 1728-1781, esp. 1768 and 1777 in
reference to the Our Father; Gustave Bardy, "Dons du Saint-Esprit I. Chez le Pères" in vol.
3 of *DS,* 1579-1587 and François Vandenbrouck, "Dons du Saint-Esprit IV. Le moyen
âge" in vol. 3 of *DS,* 1587-1603.

[159] *Brev* p. 5, c. 5 (V, 257a). See also: *III Sent,* d. 34, p. 1, a. 1, q. 2, concl. and ad 1
(III, 740b).

[160] *III Sent,* d. 34, p. 1, a. 1, q. 3, concl. (III, 742b).

[161] *Brev,* p. 5, c. 6 (V, 259a-b). See also: *De donis,* coll. 2, n. 3 (V, 463a).

[162] " . . . alii habitus dati nobis, ut conformemur ei (Christ) in *patiendo*; et huiusmodi
habitus sunt *dona,* per quae Christus erat dispositus ad sustinendam rectissime passionem
ad gloriam Dei et nostram utilitatem; et per habitus huiusmodi donorum debemus sibi
conformari in *patiendo.*" *III Sent,* d. 34, p. 1, a. 1, q. 1, concl. (III, 737a). On the

presupposes the rectification of the virtues of temperance, justice, prudence, patience, hope, faith, and love.[163] The seven gifts of the Holy Spirit further the spiritual growth begun in the rectification of the virtues by repelling the deviations of vice; aiding the natural powers of the soul; assisting the seven virtues; helping the soul to suffer with the spirit with Christ; encouraging resistance against evil and progress in good; fostering contemplation; and facilitating action and contemplation.[164] The seven gifts of the Holy Spirit also prepare the way for the perfection of the spiritual life. The *Breviloquium* describes this perfection in terms of beatitude because it resembles the ultimate end of grace. It is designated by the seven beatitudes of the Sermon on the Mount (Mt. 5: 3-9): poverty of spirit, meekness, mourning, the thirst for justice, mercy, purity of heart, and peace.[165]

The seven gifts of the Holy Spirit, which lead to spiritual perfection, are requested in a prayer found at the conclusion of the *Tree of Life*. In this prayer, Bonaventure recalls that the Our Father is itself a prayer for the gifts of the Holy Spirit:

> We pray, therefore, to the most clement Father through

---

meaning of the term "habitus," see: Jacques Guy Bougerol, "Habitus," *LSB*, 79-80.

[163] According to the *Commentary on the Sentences*, no one receives the gifts of the Holy Spirit by praying the Our Father unless they are already rooted in the virtues and, thus, able to merit the gifts; see: *III Sent*, d. 34, p. 1, a. 1, q. 2, concl. ad 1 (III, 740b-741a). The rectification of the seven virtues is the work of sanctifying grace which orders the soul toward God, neighbor, and self and renders the soul capable of meriting further grace; see: *Brev*, p. 5, c. 4 (V, 256b). These seven virtues, when rectified by grace, conform those who possess them to Christ by helping them to act as Christ acted; see: *III Sent*, d. 34, p. 1, a. 1, q. 1, concl. (III, 737a).

[164] *Brev*, p. 5, c. 5 (V, 257a-258a).

[165] *Brev*, p. 5, c. 6 (V, 258b). These seven beatitudes are also listed in the *Collations on the Gifts* but are spoken of as virtues, see: *De donis*, coll. 2, n. 3 (V, 463a). When speaking of the beatitudes, it should be noted that they, like the seven virutes and seven gifts of the Holy Spirit, foster conformity to Christ; see: *III Sent*, d. 34, p. 1, a. 1, q. 1, concl. (III, 737a) and *Comm Lc* c. 6, n. 62 (VII, 152b).

you, his Only-begotten Son, who became man for us, was crucified and glorified, so that from his treasures he may send into us the Spirit of seven-fold grace, who *rested* upon you in all fullness: the spirit, I say, of *wisdom* so we may taste the life-giving flavors of the fruit of the tree of life, which truly you are; also the gift of *understanding* whereby the contuitions of our mind may be illuminated; the gift of *counsel* whereby we may follow your footsteps along the correct paths; the gift of *fortitude*, whereby we may be able to weaken the violence of the attacking enemies; the gift of *knowledge* whereby we may be filled with the lights of your sacred doctrine to distinguish good and evil; the gift of *piety* whereby we may receive a merciful heart; the gift of *fear*, whereby, drawing back from every evil, we may be calmed by reverential consideration of your eternal Majesty. - You wished that we ask for these things in that sacred prayer which you taught us; and now we ask to obtain these things to the praise of your most holy name, to which with the Father and the Holy Spirit, be all honor and glory, thanksgiving, splendor, and authority for ever and ever. Amen.[166]

---

[166] "Oramus igitur clementissimum Patrem per te, Unigenitum eius pro nobis hominem factum, crucifixum et glorificatum, ut de thesauris suis emittat in nos Spiritum gratiae septiformis, qui super te in omni plenitudine *requievit*: spiritum, inquam, *sapientiae*, quo fructum *ligni vitae,* quod vere tu es, videlicet sapores vivificos degustemus; donum etiam *intellectus*, quo mentis nostrae contuitus illustrentur; donum *consilii*, quo post tuorum vestigia gressuum rectarum semitarum itineribus incedamus; donum *fortitudinis*, quo impugnantium hostium violentias enervare possimus; donum *scientiae*, quo sacrae doctrinae tuae repleamur fulgoribus ad discretionem boni et mali; donum *pietatis*, quo induamus misericordiae viscera; donum *timoris*, quo, recedentes ab omni malo, aeternae

2. 2. 2. 1. Fear of the Lord

In his exegesis of Our Father, Bonaventure teaches that the first petition: "Our Father, who is in heaven, hallowed be your name," is a request for
the fear of the Lord.[167] This gift drives the vice of pride from the soul and
prepares those growing in the spiritual life for the beatitude of poverty of
spirit.[168] Its acquisition is furthered by reflection on its origin, usefulness,
and perfection.[169] The fear of the Lord originates in the consideration of the
sublimity of divine power, the discernment of divine wisdom, and the
severity of divine vindication. It is a useful gift because it assures the poor of
receiving the continual blessings of grace: it, and not wealth, intelligence or
power, draws down the mercy of God. In addition, its utility is attested to by
the fact that it restores the rectitude of divine justice lost through sin and ob-
tains the illumination of divine wisdom. The perfection[170] of the gift of fear is

---

Maiestatis tuae reverentiali pondere tranquillemur. - Haec enim nos in illa sacra tua quam
nos docuisti oratione petere voluisti; haec et nunc per crucem tuam petimus obtinere ad laudem sanctissimi nominis tui, cui cum Patre et Spiritu sancto omnis sit honor et gloria,
gratiarum actio, decus et imperium per infinita saecula saeculorum. Amen." *Lig vit*, fr. 12,
n. 49 (VIII, 86a-b). On Eckbert of Schönau's influence on this prayer, see: O'Connell,
The "Lignum Vitae" of St. Bonaventure, 157-159.

[167] *De donis,* coll. 2, n. 4-5 (V, 463a-b).

[168] *Brev* p. 5, c. 6 (V, 259a) and *De donis,* coll. 2, n. 3 (V, 463a). On the gift of fear, see
also: *III Sent,* d. 34, p. 2 (III, 753a-770b).

[169] *De donis,* coll. 2, n. 6-21 (V, 463b-467b). To reflect in this way is to take to heart the
invitation of Ps. 33: 12: "Come, children, listen to me, and I will teach you the fear of the
Lord." The invitation is directed to the adopted sons and daughters of God: "*Venite, filii,*
etc. Verba ista sunt Prophetae David, in quibus invitat filios gratiae Dei et filios adoptionis
ad addiscendam istam lectionem . . . ." *De donis,* coll. 2, n. 6 (V, 463b).

[170] Perfection here should not be confused with the previously mentioned perfection of the
beatitudes. The perfection of the beatitudes is proper to the state of the perfect, while the

manifested in the perfect sanctification or purification of conscience, in the perfect readiness of obedience, and in the perfect steadfastness of trust.

2. 2. 2. 2. Piety

The second petition of the Our Father: "Your kingdom come," asks for the consummation of human salvation brought about by the gift of piety.[171] Piety roots out the vice of envy and disposes the poor to receive the beatitude of meekness.[172] When speaking of piety in the *Collations on the Gifts,* Bonaventure focuses on how it is to be practiced and then goes on to describe its origin and utility.[173] The practice of piety is three-fold: it entails the affective worship of God symbolized by King David, the custody of interior sanctity leading to a peaceful conscience, and the merciful actions marked by patience and charity. Piety originates in the Trinity, Christ, and the Church. The piety of the Trinity is revealed progressively in deeper ways in the works of nature, grace, and glory.[174] The Son of God, who was moved by

---

perfection of fear, as with the perfection of all the seven gifts of the Holy Spirit, is proper to the state of those progressing in the spiritual life. The perfection of the *virtutes* is proper to the state of beginners in the spiritual life. On this point, see: Bonnefoy, *Le Saint-Esprit et ses dons,* 94 and 216-217.

[171] *De donis,* coll. 2, n. 5 (V, 463b). On piety in Bonaventure's thought, see: Zelina Zafarana, "Pietà e devozione in san Bonaventura," in *Da Gregorio VII a Bernardino da Sienna: saggi di storia medievale,* ed. O Capitani, C. Leonardi, E. Menestò, and R. Rusconi (Firenze: "La Nuova Italia" Editrice, 1987) 118-122.

[172] *De donis,* coll. 2, n. 3 (V, 463a). See also: *Brev,* p. 5, c. 6 (V, 259a-b).

[173] *De donis,* coll. 3, n. 1-19 (V, 468a-473b). An earlier, more restrictive, treatment of piety is found in *III Sent,* d. 35, au., q. 6 (III, 784a-786b). The importance of the teaching on piety, which is found in the third collation of the *Collations on the Gifts,* is underlined by Aimé Solignac: "Ce sermon universitaire, prononcé devant le clergé parisien au cour du Carême, 1268, est sans doubt l'exposé le plus riche de l'époque médiéval sur notre sujet." See: Aimé Solignac, "Piété II. moyen âge" in vol. 12 of *DS,* 1719. On the historical background and teaching of the *Collations,* see: Bougerol, *Introduction,* 125-130.

124

piety to take on human poverty, is also a source of piety. In fact, all of his life, from the Incarnation to the liberation of those in misery, is the sacrament of piety. The Church is a source of piety by means of the sanctifying presence of the Holy Spirit. Finally, the gift of piety is useful because it assists in the discovery of salvific truth, the struggle against evil, and the effort to partake in the goodness of God.

2. 2. 2. 3. Knowledge

The fulfillment of divine law by means of the gift of knowledge is sought in the third petition: "Your will be done."[175] This gift of the Holy Spirit eradicates anger and prepares the poor for the beatitude of mourning.[176] As a gift of the Holy Spirit in the proper sense of the word, it is a gratuitous mode of knowledge to be differentiated from philosophical, theological, and glorious, or eternal, knowledge[177] The gift of gratuitous knowledge is eminently practical: it directs those who receive it to act in accord with the teachings of faith and to show mercy without discrimination to both the good and evil. These works, as a consequence, extend beyond the dictates of the natural law of mutual benevolence to include those in accord with the divine law of grace revealed in the exemplary life of Christ.[178] The gift of gratuitous knowledge, or "the knowledge of the saints," as

---

[174] *De donis*, coll. 3, n. 11 (V, 470b-471a). By identifying piety with God, Bonaventure follows the unique teaching of Gregory the Great; see: Solignac, "Piété, 1715.

[175] *De donis*, coll. 2, n. 5 (V, 463b).

[176] *De donis*, coll. 2, n. 3 (V, 463a). See also: *Brev*, p. 5, c. 6 (V, 259b).

[177] *De donis*, coll. 4, n. 4 (V, 474a-b).

[178] *III Sent*, d. 35, au., q. 2, concl. (III, 776b).

Bonaventure also terms it,[179] likewise, provokes spiritual grief by unmasking human shortcomings and sins.[180] The grief flowing from this knowledge is expressed in personal compunction, compassion for others, and the assiduous striving for the honor of God.

2. 2. 2. 4. Fortitude

The subject of the fourth petition: "Give us today our daily bread," is the gift of fortitude which is likened to bread because it, too, in analogous fashion, restores strength and instills courage into human hearts.[181] This gift of the Holy Spirit destroys the vice of sloth and introduces in its place a hunger for the beatitude of justice;[182] a hunger so strong it leads to willful acceptance of physical death rather than the loss of justice.[183] Like the gift of piety, fortitude has a three-fold source.[184] It comes first of all from God, who, as the First Principle, is the principle of all solidity and strength. Secondly, it comes from God through the divine Word, who revealed the strength of God in the midst of the human weakness. Thirdly, it comes from God in the indwelling of the Spirit of the Lord, who proffers strength to an otherwise infirm soul. The poor are disposed for the gift of fortitude by

---

[179] *De donis*, coll. 4, n. 19 (V, 477b).

[180] *De donis*, coll. 4, n. 22 (V, 478a-b).

[181] *De donis*, coll. 2, n. 5 (V, 463b). On the gift of fortitude, see also: *III Sent*, d. 35, au., q. 5 (III, 782a-784b).

[182] *De donis*, coll. 2, n. 3 (V, 463a).

[183] *Brev*, p. 5, n. 6 (V, 259b).

[184] *De donis*, coll. 5, n. 5-8 (V, 480a-481a).

practicing the virtues of faith, hope, and love.[185] The subsequent reception of fortitude facilitates bold actions of evangelization, the overpowering of evil, and the endurance of tribulation.[186] The practice of fortitude is evident in the Mother of God. Instead of fleeing from tribulation like those afraid to lose something that is of importance to them,[187] Mary willingly offered the fruit of her womb for the salvation of humanity.[188]

2. 2. 2. 5. Counsel

The fifth petition: "Forgive us our debts as we forgive are debtors," asks the Father for the remission of sin through the gift of counsel.[189] This gift removes the vice of avarice[190] and disposes the poor for the beatitude of mercy by counseling the practice of mercy. The practice of mercy, which God counsels by means of the Scriptures, is a most pleasing sacrifice[191] assuring the forgiveness of the debts incurred by sin.[192] The gift of counsel works in tandem with the gift of fortitude: it directs the choice of the best

---

[185] *De donis*, coll. 5, n. 9-12 (V, 481a-482a).

[186] *De donis*, coll. 5, n. 13-15 (V, 482a-483b).

[187] *De donis*, coll. 5, n. 15 (V, 482b-483a).

[188] *De donis*, coll. 6, n. 15 (V, 486b).

[189] *De donis*, coll. 2, n. 5 (V, 463b).

[190] *De donis*, coll. 2, n. 3 (V, 463a).

[191] *Brev*, p. 5, c. 6 (V, 259b).

[192] *Comm Lc*, c. 11, n. 15 (VII, 281b). See also the section of this chapter (2.1.3.4.) dealing with the Lucan Our Father.

way to follow in the footsteps of Christ,[193] and fortitude provides the strength to put the choice into practice.[194] Bonaventure teaches that the gift of counsel includes a distrust of self and a willingness to seek counsel from another.[195] Yet before seeking counsel, it is important to discern the difference between good and evil counselors, or directors. For Bonaventure, Christ is the foremost good director whose teaching and example of life provide an eternal source of truth to those seeking counsel. Others, like Francis of Assisi, who followed the counsels of Christ by giving alms, living humbly, poorly, and obediently are also good counselors. On the other hand, those who discourage this following of Christ should be shunned as evil counselors.

2. 2. 2. 6. Understanding

The gift of understanding, which wards off the deceits of the evil, is requested in the sixth petition: "And lead us not into temptation."[196] It eradicates the vice of gluttony[197] and leads to purity of heart through the consideration of truth.[198] The gift of understanding is the subject of the eighth collation in the *Collations on the Gifts*. Here Bonaventure outlines the three-

---

[193] *Lig vit,* fr. 12, n. 49 (VIII, 86a) and *III Sent,* d. 35, au., q. 5, concl. ad 4 (III, 784a).

[194] *III Sent,* d. 35, au., q. 4, concl. ad 1 (III, 781b) and *III Sent,* d. 35, au., q. 5, concl. ad 4 (III, 784a).

[195] *De donis,* coll. 7, n. 13-19 (V, 491b-493b).

[196] *De donis,* coll. 2, n. 5 (V, 463b).

[197] *De donis,* coll. 2, n. 3 (V, 463a).

[198] *Brev,* p. 5, c. 6 (V, 259b). On the gift of understanding and the consideration of truth, see: *III Sent,* 35, au., q. 3, concl. (III, 778a-b). This theme is discussed further in Chapter Four.

fold disposition necessary for receiving the gift of understanding: sanctity of life, meekness, and the surrender of the intellect to the truth of faith.[199] While he also singles out the moral, scientific and contemplative aspects of understanding,[200] he only develops the first two aspects. Moral understanding concerns the avoidance of evil, the accomplishment of good, and the expectation of eternal life.[201] Scientific understanding is concerned with the knowledge of first causes, conclusions, and principles.[202] The contemplative aspect of understanding, which is treated in the third collation of the *Collations on the Six Days,*[203] concerns the understanding of the Uncreated Word through whom all things are made, the Incarnate Word through whom all things are redeemed, and the Inspired Word through whom all things are revealed.

2. 2. 2. 7. Wisdom

The seventh petition: "But deliver us from evil. Amen," seeks the subjection of the flesh by means of the gift of wisdom.[204] The reception of this gift of the Holy Spirit uproots the vice of luxury and leads to the beatitude of peace,[205] which is characteristic of the adopted sons and daughters of God.[206]

---

[199] *De donis*, coll. 8, n. 2-5 (V, 494a-496a).

[200] *De donis*, coll. 8, n. 6 (V, 495a).

[201] *De donis*, coll. 8, n. 7-11 (V, 495a-496a).

[202] *De donis*, coll. 8, n. 12-20 (V, 496a-498b).

[203] *Hex*, coll. 3, n. 1-32 (V, 343a-348b). Concerning the Uncreated, Incarnate and Inspired Word in Bonaventure's theology, see: Winfried Schachten, *Intellectus Verbi.*

[204] *De donis*, coll. 2, n. 5 (V, 463b).

Wisdom brings about peace through union with God, who, as the most high Truth and Good, is the end and repose of all rational appetites.[207] In the *Commentary on the Sentences*, Bonaventure takes care to distinguish the gift of wisdom from other modes of wisdom such as philosophical, metaphysical and pious wisdom.[208] As a gift of the Holy Spirit, it is an experiential knowledge of God. Even though wisdom is a gift which descends as light from the Father of lights,[209] its donation presupposes several dispositions found in the *Collations on the Gifts*. In addition to the dispositions of desire and justice mentioned at the beginning of the ninth collation,[210] seven others are developed further on in the same collation:[211] modesty of the flesh, innocence of thought, moderation in speaking, docility of the affections, generosity in works of mercy, maturity in judgment, and simplicity of intention.

---

[205] *De donis*, coll. 2, n. 3 (V, 463a).

[206] " . . . donum sapientiae et pacis, per quam vocamur filii Dei." *Comm Lc*, c. 11, n. 11 (VII, 280a). The theme of wisdom and peace is taken up at length in Chapter Four.

[207] *Brev*, p. 5, c. 6 (V, 259b).

[208] *III Sent*, d. 35, au., q. 1, concl. (III, 774a). On the philosophical, metaphysical, pious and experiential modes of wisdom, see also: Boehner, comm., *St Bonaventure's Itinerarium*, 129-131, n. 1, esp. 130 in reference to wisdom and peace.

[209] *De donis*, coll. 9, n. 5 (V, 500a).

[210] *De donis*, coll. 9, n. 1 (V, 499a).

[211] *De donis*, coll. 9, n. 8-17 (V, 500b-503b).

2. 3. Summary

This present chapter began by examining prayer as a concrete way in which the poor imitate the example of Christ and are, thereby, conformed to him as adopted sons and daughters of God. Their prayerful imitation of Christ, which is fostered by the grace they have received as members of the Church, is a reflection of their share in the perfection of Christ. Following the example of Christ, who Bonaventure notes prayed throughout his life, the poor should strive to make prayer a permanent characteristic of their own lives. In their attempt to integrate their lives with prayer, they should pay particular attention to Christ's prayer in the Garden of Gethsemane.

In the prayer in Gethsemane, Christ showed himself to be obedient to the Father's will. Such obedience, which marks the relationship between a father and son on the anthropological level, also reveals the inner dynamic of the ontological relationship between Christ and the Father. According to Bonaventure, Christ handed himself over to the Father in an act of obedient love, which itself is in response to the love he had received from the Father as the only begotten Son. In the light of Christ's obedience, the obedient prayer of the poor becomes an act of conformity with Christ, which goes beyond the exterior imitation of an exemplary action of Christ, to include an analogous sharing of, and entrance into, the mystery of his sonship.

Obedience in imitation of Christ assures the poor that the Father will answer their prayer. One way they can turn with confidence to the Father in prayer is with the words of the "Our Father." This prayer, which Jesus taught his disciples in response to their desire to follow his example of prayer, is the most noble of prayers since it is a concise summary of all prayer and of everything needing to be requested in prayer. As Bonaventure points out in his exegesis of the five petitions found in the Lucan version of the Our Father, the nobility of this prayer is also manifested in the descending order of dignity expressed by the petitions: the first two petitions concern the consummation of divine glory through the sanctification of the divine name and reverential obedience to God; the third petition turns its attention to the physical and spiritual needs of the poor; and the fourth and fifth petitions treat the cancelation of the debts incurred by sin and the avoidance of the punishment which accompanies sin.

The prayer of the poor to the Father, be it with the words of the Our Father or with some other prayer, is grounded in the belief that God is the source of all goodness and most generous in sharing that goodness with those who call out in prayer. The Father, together with the Son, expresses this generosity toward the poor in the donation of the Holy Spirit. The gift of the Holy Spirit, which is sought in prayer sealed by devotion, desire and humility, descends from the Father through the Son and enriches the poor with sanctifying grace. This gift of sanctifying grace descends in analogical fashion like water from the mountains or light from the sun to conform the poor into the image of the Son of God. As they are conformed to the only begotten Son, the poor are made acceptable to God as adopted sons and daughters and prepared to receive the inheritance of the Kingdom of God.

The advent of the Holy Spirit, who dwells within the soul by means of sanctifying grace and transforms the poor into sons and daughters of God, is encouraged by those who pray the Our Father. In his exegesis of Matthew's version of the Our Father, Bonaventure teaches that each of Matthew's seven petitions is a request for one of the seven gifts of the Holy Spirit. The seven

132

gifts, which Bonaventure maintains are gifts in the proper sense of the word, are the gifts mentioned in Is. 11: 2: fear of the Lord, piety, knowledge, fortitude, counsel, understanding and wisdom. These seven gifts of the Holy Spirit enable the poor to make progress in the spiritual life by assisting them in the struggle to eradicate vice from the soul and by preparing them for the introduction of the beatitudes of spiritual perfection.

Chapter Three: Unceasing Prayer

The prayer of the poor, which is an essential element in the dynamics of spiritual adoption, is not an isolated expression of indigence restricted to a specific time or place. Christ's example of praying throughout his life suggests that the entire sphere of human activity should be permeated by unceasing prayer.[1] In addition, as Bonaventure writes in the *Perfection of Life*, such continuous prayer is of great benefit to those who practice it: "Devout prayer is of so great a worth, however, that it is effective in all circumstances and a person is able to profit through it at all times . . . ."[2] In the *Commentary on Luke*, he delineates ten specific ways the poor profit from continuous prayer: these benefits range from the easing of divine punishment to the reception of eternal life.[3]

The present chapter examines Bonaventure's concept of unceasing prayer in two sections. The first develops the three principle ways unceasing prayer is practiced: vocal prayer, the desire for the good, and the choice to

---

[1] *Comm Lc*, c. 3 n. 50-51 (VIII, 82b) and *Comm Lc*, c. 11, n. 2 (VII, 277b). For an insight into the medieval approach to unceasing prayer and specific times of prayer within the wide sphere of human activity, see: Gunther of Paris, *De oratione, jejunio et eleemosyna,*" Liber 8, c.1 *PL* 212, 163-168.

[2] "Est autem tantae virtutis devota oratio, ut ad omnia valeat et in omni tempore homo possit per eam lucrari . . . ." *Perf vitae*, c. 5, n. 1 (VIII,117a).

[3] *Comm Lc*, c. 18, n. 3 (VIII, 449a-b). Bonaventure lists 10 specific benefits derived from unceasing prayer: the easing of divine judgment, the remission of sins already committed, the repelling of spiritual attacks, the restoration of natural virtue, the conservation of temporal peace, the custody of a tranquil conscience, the inflamation of divine grace, the illumination of divine wisdom, the opening of the heavenly door and the acquisition of eternal reward.

live justly. The second section focuses on unceasing prayer as a form of spiritual warfare against concupiscence necessitated by the choice of the poor to seek after eternal goods instead of temporal goods. Both sections take into account the biblical, patristic and medieval traditions out of which Bonaventure develops his teaching. The biblical admonition to pray without ceasing, seen most clearly in the Gospel of Luke and in the Pauline literature, is deeply etched into the foundations of his teaching on prayer.[4] He also draws from the teaching on unceasing prayer which was developed in the early church, furthered by the medieval church,[5] and strikingly incarnated in the spirituality of Francis of Assisi.[6]

---

[4] For a study on the New Testament understanding of unceasing prayer, see: Radbert Kerkhoff, *Das unablässige Gebet. Beiträge zur Lehre vom immerwährenden Beten im Neuen Testament* (München: Karl Zink Verlag, 1954); and with special reference to the Pauline literature: Stanley, *Boasting in the Lord*, 100-107. On the general biblical doctrine of unceasing prayer and its expression in a systematic theology of prayer, see: John Wright, *A Theology of Christian Prayer* (New York: Pueblo Publishing Company, 1979) 161-171.

[5] For studies with appropriate bibliography on unceasing prayer in early Christian monasticism, see: Irénée Hausherr, *The Name of Jesus*, 119-189 and Antoine Guillaumont, "Le problème de la prière continuelle dans le monachisme ancien," in *L'experience de la prière dans les grandes religions*, ed. Henri Limet and Julien Ries (Louvain-la-Neuve: Centre d'Histoire des Religions, 1980) 285-294. A description of the medieval monastic understanding and practice of unceasing prayer is found in Jean Leclercq, François Vandenbroucke and Louis Bouyer, *The Spirituality of the Middle Ages*, vol. 2 of *A History of Christian Spirituality*, trans. The Benedictines of Holme Eden Abbey, Carlisle (New York: The Seabury Press, 1968) 106-110.

[6] *Leg maj*, c. 1, n. 4-5 (VIII, 506b-507a). Francis himself speaks of unceasing prayer in both the *Earlier Rule*, c. 22, n. 29 and the *Later Rule*, c. 10, n. 9. See: Eßer, *Die Opuscula*, 397 and 370, respectively. The text from the *Later Rule* concerning unceasing prayer is quoted in *Const Narb*, rub. 4 (VIII, 453b).

3. 1.   Three Ways of Unceasing Prayer

Bonaventure does not outline extensively in any one work the nature and practice of unceasing prayer. The *Commentary on the Gospel of Luke* does, however, offer a point of departure for the development of his thought on the subject. In his exegesis of the parable of the judge and the widow (Lk. 18: 1-8),[7] he reminds his readers that the Lord taught this parable in order to encourage the practice of unceasing prayer. He then proceeds to clear up any possible misconceptions as to the meaning of the Lord's injunction to pray always (Lk. 18: 1). To pray always means certain times of the day are to be set aside for prayer; therefore, he considers the Liturgy of the Hours to be a valid response to the Lord's command to pray without ceasing. Bonaventure also readily admits the command to prayer without ceasing denotes an understanding and praxis of prayer which goes beyond the Liturgical Hours, for: ...   *"to pray always* here is understood such that prayer is always either in the *mouth* by means of asking, or in the *heart* by means of desire, or in *work* by means of preparation."[8]

The various categories that Bonaventure uses to define unceasing prayer illustrate the extensive nature of this manner of prayer. These categories indicate a mode of prayer which touches many levels of human

---

[7] *Comm Lc,* c. 18, n. 1-9 (VII, 448a-451a). On this same parable and unceasing prayer, see: *Dom 9 post Pent,* 1 (IX, 389b).

[8] "... *semper orare* hic intelligitur, ut oratio semper vel sit in *ore* per postulationem, vel sit in *corde* per desiderium, vel sit in *opere* per praeparationem." *Comm Lc,* c. 18 n. 2 (VII, 448b).

activity and is inclusive of private and liturgical prayer. The broad definition of unceasing prayer found in the exegesis of Lk. 18: 1-8 is reflected in Bonaventure's interpretation of Lk. 11: 9: ". . . ask, and it will be given you; seek, and you will find; knock, and it will be opened to you."[9] Jesus's threefold admonition is an invitation to prayer including some of the same elements mentioned in the exegesis of Lk. 18: 1-8: ". . . to ask regards an act of the mouth, to seek an act of the heart, and to knock [an act of] work."[10] Each of these spiritual movements is a particular dimension of the one reality of unceasing prayer and should be considered a type of petition. Together they constitute, according to Bonaventure, a continuous, all encompassing petition directed toward God.[11]

3. 1. 1. Vocal Prayer

Bonaventure's exegesis of Lk. 18: 1-8 and Lk. 11: 9 points to vocal prayer as one manner of fulfilling the scriptural admonition to pray always. He describes unceasing prayer as: "an act of the mouth," and: "in the mouth by means of asking." The word "mouth" suggests an audible form of prayer. Such prayer, which is characterized by the pronunciation of words, is called vocal prayer.[12] The use of the phrase "by means of asking" indicates that

---

[9] *Comm Lc*, c. 11 n. 25-27 (VII, 284b-285b).

[10] ". . . *petere* respiciat actum oris; *quaerere*, actum cordis; *pulsare*, operis." *Comm Lc*, c.11, n. 26 (VII, 285a).

[11] *Comm Lc*, c. 11, n. 25 (VII, 284b-285a).

[12] *IV Sent,* d. 15, p. 2, a. 2, q. 3, concl. (IV, 374a). For an insight into the Franciscan understanding and practice of vocal prayer in Bonaventure's day, see: David of Augsburg, *De exterioris et interioris hominis compositione,* ed. PP. Collegii S. Bonaventurae (Quaracchi: Collegium S. Bonaventurae, 1899) 296-300. See also: *De orat,* membrum 3, a.

138

vocal prayer has a petitionary character. This view is confirmed by the explanation of vocal prayer offered in the *Breviloquium*: "[God] does not wish to be prayed to with *mental* prayer alone, which is 'the ascent of the intellect into God,' but also with *vocal* prayer, which is 'the petition of fitting things from God . . . .'"[13]

One of the most obvious forms of unceasing vocal prayer is the Liturgy of the Hours. In his exegesis of the parable of the widow and the judge, Bonaventure expresses the same idea which had previously been developed among the Christian communities of the patristic era: the Liturgy of the Hours, offered seven times a day, constitutes a legitimate form of unceasing prayer.[14] Praying always in this sense does not mean that every moment of the day must be filled with prayer, but, rather, that fixed times of prayer be observed throughout the day. The Liturgy of the Hours qualifies as unceasing prayer because it is in harmony with the prophetic practice of praying seven times a day mentioned in Psalm 119: 164:

> . . . *Because it is necessary to pray always and never cease;*
> which should be understood in such a way that the *always*
> is not spread throughout every moment, but throughout
> fixed times like that which is said according to the

2, resp. 690a-691a.

[13] "Vult autem orari non solum oratione *mentali*, quae est, 'ascensus intellectus in Deum,' verum etiam *vocali*, quae est 'petitio decentium a Deo . . . .'" *Brev*, p. 5, c. 10 (V, 263b). These two definitions of prayer, which come from John of Damascus (*De fide orthodoxa*, Liber 3, c. 24, *PG* 94, 1090), are the first definitions listed in *De orat*, membrum 1, a. 1, 667b. Prayer as the "ascent of the intellect" into God is discussed in Chapter Four.

[14] On the practice of the seven-fold recitation of the Liturgy of the Hours in the patristic period, see: Josef Jungmann, *Christliches Beten in Wandel und Bestand* (München: Verlag Ars Sacra, 1969) 44 and 172, note 10. See also: Robert Taft, *The Liturgy of the Hours in East and West. The Origins of the Divine Office and Its Meaning for Today* (Collegeville, Mn.: The Liturgical Press, 1986) 84-87.

prophetic instruction in the Psalm: 'Seven times a day I have given praise.' And the Church observes this practice; thus the Gloss: '*Always,* [is to be understood as] daily in the canonical hours according to the custom of the Church.'[15]

The Liturgy of the Hours, understood as continuous prayer, is more than a fulfillment of the scriptural call to pray seven times a day. It is more than a commemoration of various moments in the Paschal Mystery.[16] The Liturgy of the Hours is also bound to the reception of the Holy Spirit. Thus, Bonaventure goes beyond traditional prophetic and christological interpretations of the liturgical hours to give them a pneumatological underpinning. This interpretation links the seven hours with the seven gifts of the Holy Spirit. From this perspective, the unceasing prayer of the Church becomes a continuous manifestation of praise assuring the reception of the Holy Spirit. This prayer, which elicits the advent of the Holy Spirit, is a vocal prayer re-

---

15 " . . . *Quoniam oportet orare semper et non deficere;* quod debet intelligi, ut *semper* non distribuat pro omni parte temporis, sed pro horis statutis, iuxta quod secundum institutionem propheticam dicitur in Psalmo: 'Septies in die laudem dixi.' Et hunc modum observat Ecclesia; unde Glossa: '*Semper,* canonicis horis quotidie secundum morem Ecclesiae.'" *Comm Lc,* c. 18 n. 2 (VII, 448b). See also: *Dom 9 post Pent,* 1 (IX, 389b) and *De modo vivendi* (IX, 723b). The psalm text referred to in the above quote is Ps. 118: 164. The Quaracchi editors note (VII, 448b, note 8) that the *Gloss* mentioned above, which they attribute to Bede, is from the *Glossa Ordinaria* on Lk. 18: 1 found in *Biblia Sacra cum Glossa interlineari, ordinaria et Nicolai Lyrani Postilla.* Venice: 1588. This source was not available to this author. Another text on Lk. 18: 1 from Bede linking constant prayer and the Liturgy of the Hours is found in Bede, *In Lucae Evangelium Expositio, CChr* 120, 322.

16 On the identification of the Paschal Mystery with the various hours of prayer in the early church, see: Emmanuel von Severus, "Gebet I," in vol. 8 of *RAC,* 1219-1222. This development is reflected later in a work printed among the works of Hugh of St. Victor; see: *Miscellanea,* Liber 7, *PL* 177, 873-874. It is also found in the work of the Franciscan William of Middleton, who was a contemporary of Bonaventure and, likewise, master at the University of Paris; see: William of Middleton, *Opusculam super Missam,* ed. Willibrord Lampen (Quaracchi: Collegium S. Bonaventurae, 1931) 17-19.

quiring clear, distinct, and devout recitation.[17]

The Liturgy of the Hours, and in fact all vocal prayer, needs to be properly understood if it is to be beneficially practiced.[18] The repetition of words alone, even if they are the psalms, does not assure authentic, efficacious prayer. The mindless recitation of prayers resembles the useless babbling of the pagans which Jesus condemned.[19] Bonaventure classifies such prayer as pure vocal prayer. It is evident in the case of the person who vocalizes a prayer, yet has no comprehension of what the words of the prayer mean or the end for which the prayer is being offered. When both the sense and purpose of the words are lost, prayer is to be considered a waste of time.[20]

---

[17] *De modo vivendi* (IX, 723b). The liturgical hours are also linked with the gifts of the Holy Spirit by Gunther of Paris in *De orat., jej. et eleem.* Liber. 8, c. 4, *PL* 212, 166. Bonaventure says that praise is one of the reasons why the Church offers the Liturgy of the Hours. He also sees the celebration of the Hours as a way of encouraging devotion; see: *IV Sent*, d. 12, p. 1, dub. 5 (IV, 288b).

[18] While vocal prayer is not restricted to the Liturgy of the Hours, both forms of prayer are certainly connected closely with each other as the *Leg maj* indicates when describing the prayer life of the early Franciscan friars at Rivotorto; see: *Leg maj*, c. 4, n. 3 (VIII, 513a-b). On the identification of vocal prayer by the Franciscans with the Liturgy of the Hours, see: Dupuy, "Oraison," 837. Bonaventure considers vocal prayer to be an important element of the sacramental praxis because of the relationship between the effective power of the word and the regeneration brought about by Christ, the Word made flesh. See: *IV Sent*, d. 23, a. 1, q. 4, concl. (IV, 595a); *IV Sent*, d. 3, p. 1, a. 1, q. 2, concl. (IV, 67b); *III Sent*, d. 1, a. 2, q. 3, concl. (III, 29b) and *I Sent*, d. 27, a. 1, p. 2, q. 4 (I, 488a-490b). On vocal prayer and liturgical prayer, see also: *De orat*, membrum 3, a. 2, resp., 690b. This text identifies the Liturgy of the Hours as a sacramental form of prayer which encourages devotion.

[19] On this point, see: Ludger Meier, "Evangelische Lebensform und mündliches Beten," *FS* 32 (1950): 266.

[20] *IV Sent*, d. 15, p. 2, a. 2, q. 3, concl. (IV, 374a). Almost the exact same text can be found in the discussion on vocal and mental prayer in *De orat*, membrum 3, a. 2, 690a. Similar texts which give a three-fold definition of prayer are found in *IV Sent*, d. 15, p. 2, a. 1, q. 4, concl. (IV, 368a) and *De orat*, membrum 1, a. 2, 676b. These similarities between *IV Sent* and *De orat* raise the question of the relation between Bonaventure's writings on prayer and the *De orat*. According to Doucet, Bonaventure's *IV Sent* predates Book IV of Alexander of Hales' *Summa* which was most likely composed by William of

Bonaventure's desire to avoid the dangers of vocal prayer surfaces in the *Rule of Novices* where he urges the novices to make the necessary effort to understand what they are saying during the celebration of the Hours. He tells them if they do not understand what is being said, they should, nevertheless, remain reverent since the reception of grace is dictated by reverence in prayer and not the complete understanding of the words composing the prayer: "Be eager to understand the things which you are saying, if you are able; if however you are unable to understand, be reverent, because as Wisdom says, *good grace will come to you in proportion to [your] reverence.*"[21] An atmosphere favorable to reverence is encouraged by insisting on a proper body posture mirroring the dignity of prayer; the novices are, after all, not only in the presence of fellow friars, but of the entire celestial court.[22]

Given the seriousness of prayer, it is not surprising that Bonaventure cautions the novices not to abuse the time set aside for the Liturgy of the Hours by letting their hearts wander far from the Lord.[23] Reverence, accompanied by humility and fear of the Lord, enables the novice to avoid the danger of useless vocal prayer since these dispositions keep the heart

---

Middleton; see Victorin Doucet, "The History of the Problem of the Authenticity of the Summa," *FSt* 7 (1947): 311. Since *De orat* is found in Book IV of Alexander's *Summa,* it appears that Bonaventure's teaching on prayer may have been a source for William of Middleton as he composed the *De orat.*

[21] "Et stude intelligere ea quae dicis, si potes, si vero non potes intelligere, reverere, quia, sicut dicit Sapiens, *pro reverentia accedet tibi bona gratia.*" *Reg nov,* c. 1, n. 1 (VIII, 476a). The text from *Ecclesiasticus* is Sir. 32: 9. Cfr.: the translation of Sir. 32: 9 in the *New Catholic Edition* and *The New Oxford.*

[22] *Reg nov,* c. 1, n. 2 (VIII, 476a). On posture and prayer in medieval times, see: Richard Trexler, *The Christian at Prayer. An Illustrated Prayer Manual Attributed to Peter the Chanter (d.1197)* (Binghamton, New York: The Center for Medieval and Early Renaissance Studies, 1987).

[23] *Reg nov,* c. 1, n. 1 (VIII, 475a-476a).

oriented toward God and, consequently, on the texts being recited. Attention must be given so that the Hours can be said without mistakes. Yet, despite the importance of proper and attentive reading, the perfect recitation of the liturgical texts is not the end of prayer. Those who pray vocally, without the participation of the heart, are merely praying externally and can be compared to the hypocrites whom Christ condemned:

> And pay attention to the book, lest at some time, having been led by negligence or shame, you may omit some word of the office; and do not say your hours with only the pronunciation of the exterior voice, like cunning hypocrites about whom the Lord complains through the Prophet, saying: *This people honors me with [their] lips, but their heart is far from me.*"[24]

Bonaventure's concern that the novices conscientiously celebrate the Liturgy of the Hours is understandable given the therapeutic value he assigns to vocal prayer. The primary aim of therapeutic prayer is to affect those praying and not the God to whom it is addressed.[25] Vocal prayer, as a type of petition, is addressed to God and at the same time looks to change those en-

---

[24] "Et sis semper sollicitus ad librum, ne aliquando negligentia vel verecundia ductus, aliquod verbum officii praetermittas; et non dicas horas tuas solummodo prolatione vocis exterioris, sicut hypocritae versipelles, de quibus conqueritur Dominus per Prophetam, dicens: *Populus hic labiis me honorat, cor autem eorum longe est a me.*" *Reg nov,* c. 1, n. 3 (VIII, 476b). The Scripture references are Is. 29: 13 and Mt. 15: 8. On the proper role of vocal prayer with reference to the Franciscan tradition, see: Anton Rotzetter, *Selbstverwirklichung des Christen* (Zürich: Benziger, 1983) 139-148. On the Liturgy of the Hours and the early friars, see: Oktavian Schmucki, *Gotteslob und Meditation nach Beispiel und Anweisung des hl. Franziskus von Assisi* (Luzern: St. Fidelis Druckerei, 1980) 11-31.

[25] The therapeutic aspect of Christian prayer is discussed in Vincent Brümmer, *What are we doing when we pray? A Philosophical Inquiry* (London: SCM Press, 1984) 16-28 and Hans Martin-Barth, *Wohin - woher mein Ruf,* 49-61.

gaged in prayer. As Bonaventure points out in the *Commentary on the Sentences,* vocal prayer is especially helpful for those who are not sensitive to spiritual matters: ". . . and there are many such people, and most of all those who are not spiritual men, for the awakening of whose affections vocal prayers were instituted."[26] Thus, vocal prayer is helpful for those learning how to pray;[27] its affective action would be of particular assistance for the novices who are at the beginning of a systematic introduction into the spiritual life in general and the art of prayer in particular.

The therapeutic aspect of vocal prayer arises from the poverty of the human condition evident during periods of prayer. Many difficulties can hinder, and eventually suffocate, the attempts of those who pray. In the *Breviloquim,* Bonaventure states that vocal prayer is an effective tool against some of these obstacles. It overcomes the lack of affections, the inability to be recollected, and the inordinate fear of God. Vocal prayer allows the desire for divine gifts, which is a source of petition, to be channeled into a request which is fervent, recollected and confident:

> . . . so that our desire may efficaciously reach upward to
> receive divine gifts, it is necessary that our *affection* be
> fervent, our *thought* collected together, and our *ex-*

---

[26] ". . . et multi sunt tales, et maxime illi qui non sunt viri spirituales, ad quorum affectus provocandos institutae sunt vocales orationes." *IV Sent,* d. 15, p. 2, a. 2, q. 3, concl. (IV, 374b).

[27] It is worthwhile noting the difference between the teaching on prayer in works such as the *Reg nov* and *Perf vitae.* In the *Reg nov,* Bonaventure is speaking to those who are being introduced to liturgical prayer, in particular, and to the art of prayer, in general. In the *Perf vitae,* he is speaking to those whom he admits know more about prayer than him. There is no development of vocal prayer in *Perf vitae,* yet, it plays an important role in the *Reg nov.* The difference between the two works reflects the notion that vocal prayer is of special significance for those who are beginning to learn how to pray. The different level of teaching on prayer (without specific reference to vocal prayer) in the two works is mentioned briefly by Grünewald, *Franziskanische Mystik,* 66-67.

pectation certain and firm; and because our heart is frequently tepid, frequently distracted, and even frequently terribly frightened because of the remorse of sin, and not daring to appear on its own before the divine presence: hence it is that God intended that we pray not only *mentally* but also *vocally* to awaken our affection by the words and to recollect our thoughts by the sense of the words.[28]

The vocalized cry for divine assistance does not inform God of what people need or desire since God already knows all things.[29] Instead, it functions as a therapeutic stimulus and support for a deeper, interior mode of prayer which Bonaventure calls "mental prayer." Vocal prayer should lead to mental prayer, for: ". . . *vocal* prayer is ordered to *mental* [prayer] and not the other way around."[30] As a specific form of prayer, vocal prayer is useful

---

[28] ". . . ut desiderium efficaciter sursum tendat ad impetrandum dona divina, necesse est, quod *affectio* nostra sit fervida, et *cogitatio* in unum collecta, et *exspectatio* nostra sit certa et firma; et quia cor nostrum frequenter est tepidum, frequenter dispersum, frequenter pavidum propter peccati remorsum nec audens per se ipsum comparere ante divinum conspectum: hinc est, quod Dominus voluit, nos non tantum orare *mentaliter*, verum etiam *vocaliter* ad nostri affectus excitationem per verba et ad recollectionem cogitationum per sensum verborum." *Brev,* p. 5, c. 10 (V, 264a). See also: *IV Sent,* d. 15, p. 2, a. 2, q. 3, concl. ad 3 (IV, 374b-375a) and *IV Sent,* d. 27, p. 2, a. 1, q. 2, concl. ad 3 (IV, 440a).

[29] *IV Sent,* d. 15, p. 2, a. 2, q. 3, concl. ad 3 (IV, 375a) and *IV Sent,* d. 27, p. 2, a. 1, q. 2, concl. ad 3 (IV, 440a).

[30] ". . . *vocalis* oratio ordinatur ad *mentalem*, et non e converso." *IV Sent,* d. 15, p. 2, a. 2, q. 3, concl. (IV, 374a). See also: *IV Sent,* d. 15, p. 2, a. 2, q. 3, concl. ad 3 (IV, 375b). Mental prayer is described by Bonaventure as the "ascensus intellectus in Deum" in p. 5, c. 10 of the *Brev* (V, 263b). The ascent of the intellect is not limited to an intellectual, speculative, activity. "Intellectus," as Jean Châtillon writes, was used, along with "anima," "cor," and "mens," from the time of Augustine and Gregory to the Middle Ages, to describe the spiritual center of the human being; see: Jean Châtillon, "Cor et cordis affectus 3. Cordis affectus au moyen âge" in vol. 2 of *DS*, 2289. The ascent of the intellect into God also includes the cry for mercy raised by those, who, conscious of their poverty and God's goodness, turn to him for help. On Bonaventure's various interpretations of the ascent of the intellect into God, see: *III Sent,* d. 17, a. 2, q. 1, concl. ad 3 (III, 372a-b) and

to the degree that it fosters mental prayer.[31] The words proper to vocal prayer are said to have a positive impact when they inflame the heart and direct it into God. They are, however, to be abandoned when they keep the affections from passing over into God. This type of prayer, combining words and affections, stands between pure vocal prayer and pure mental prayer. As such, it is a "mixed" form of prayer.[32] In juxtaposition to pure vocal prayer and mixed prayer, Bonaventure describes pure mental prayer as a type of prayer taking place when the heart speaks to God without moving the lips.[33]

Vocal prayer also has a pedagogical dimension that builds upon and complements its therapeutic dimension. While vocal prayer moves and

---

IV Sent, d. 45, a. 3, q. 1, concl. ad 2 (IV, 948b). See also: *De orat,* membrum 1, a. 1, resp. 669a.

[31] *IV Sent,* d. 15, p. 2, a. 2, q. 3, concl. (IV, 374a-b). The first use of the term "oratio mentalis" is attributed to David of Augsburg by Friedrich Wulf in "Das innere Gebet (oratio mentalis) und die Betrachtung (meditatio)," *GL* 25 (1952): 385. It should be noted, however, that the term also appears in *De oratione* from MS Codex Vatic. Palat. lat. 612; see: Doucet, *De quaestionibus S. Bonaventurae,* 486. If *De oratione* can be attributed to John of La Rochelle as Brady suggests (see note 6 in the Introduction), there is reason to suspect that the first use of the term could be traced back to the Franciscan theologians at the University of Paris and not to David of Augsburg. For David of Augsburg's description of mental prayer, see: David of Augsburg, *De hominis compositione,* 319-324. On mental prayer in the Christian tradition, see (in addition to Wulf's article): Dupuy, "Oraison," 836-837.

[32] *IV Sent,* d. 15, p. 2, a. 2, q. 3, concl. (IV, 374b). Bonaventure says of "mixed" prayer: "Alia est *mixta,* in qua scilicet orat mentaliter et vocaliter." For a description of "mixed" prayer, see also David of Augsburg's *De hominis compositione,* 300-307. Bonaventure discusses the role of vocal prayer in the inflammation of the heart in regard to the question of making satisfaction for sins; see: *IV Sent,* d. 15, p. 2, a. 2, q. 3, concl. (IV, 374b). Here he notes that a prayer from the heart, marked by tears, is most satisfactory; yet, no priest can require such a prayer from a penitent since it depends on grace. Vocal prayer, imposed as a penance by the priest and recited by the penitent, can draw the penitent to this most pleasing form of prayer. Regardless of the state of the penitent, vocal prayer remains satisfactory, as does mental prayer, as long it is rooted in charity. On this last point, see: *IV Sent,* d. 15, p. 2, a. 2, q. 3, concl. ad 3 (IV, 374b). Prayer, along with almsgiving and fasting, brings satisfaction for sins; see: *IV Sent,* d. 15, p. 2, a.1, q. 4, a. 2, q. 1, 2, and 3 (IV, 367a-375b). On prayer and satisfaction for sins, see also: *De orat,* membrum 5, a. 4, 733b-734b.

[33] *IV Sent,* d. 15, p. 2, a. 2, q. 3, concl. (IV, 374a).

focuses the affections of those who may find it difficult to pray, it also teaches them how to pray by giving them a concrete, audible model which they can imitate. This is why Christ prayed out loud in the presence of his apostles on the night before he died. These audible words of prayer, in addition to consoling and acquiring salvation for the apostles, taught them how to pray.[34] Bonaventure also sees the pedagogical dimension of vocal prayer exemplified in Francis of Assisi's attempt to teach his followers to pray. In the *Major Life of St. Francis,* he writes that the friars approached Francis and asked him to instruct them as to how they should pray. Francis responded to their wish by reciting for them such formulary prayers as the "Our Father" and the "We adore you, O Christ."[35]

Given the therapeutic and pedagogical importance of vocal prayer, it is clear that this form of prayer plays a significant role in Bonaventure's teaching on prayer. Nevertheless, it is a role which is subordinated to mental prayer. As a form of unceasing prayer, vocal prayer is of great assistance to those who are learning the art of prayer. Furthermore, it helps those plagued in prayer by difficulties such as distractions, emptiness, and fear. Vocal prayer can also lead penitents to a deeper, more satisfactory, form of prayer. Yet, despite all these positive aspects, vocal prayer is subordinate to mental prayer because God is above all concerned with the desires of the heart and not with the words expressed by those praying. This point is brought home by Bonaventure when, quoting both Gregory the Great and Scripture, he urges novices to prepare themselves well for prayer lest they fail to taste the divine goodness. Those who pray with the voice to the neglect of the heart

---

[34] *Comm Jn,* c. 17, n. 21, resp. (VI, 471b).

[35] *Leg maj,* c. 4, n. 3 (VIII, 513a-b).

only shout out words which are rarely efficacious. They cannot be considered as people of prayer:

> For as Gregory testifies, 'prayer is of the heart and not of the lips' nor, he says, does God so much pay attention to the words of the one asking, but, [rather, that God] looks upon the heart of the one praying.' Therefore Wisdom says: *Son, prepare your heart before prayer and do not wish to be like the person who tempted God.* For then the one praying is said to tempt God when without any preparation of the heart, he runs to vocal prayer and seeks divine speculation for himself. But he will hardly or never receive [divine speculation], because such a person is said not to be a devout supplicant, but, rather, a barker of words.[36]

3. 1. 2. Desire for the Good

The second form of continual prayer which Bonaventure mentions in the exegesis of Lk. 18: 1-8 is: ". . . in the *heart* by means of desire."[37]

---

[36] "Nam, teste Gregorio, 'oratio est cordis, non labiorum; nec, inquit, verba deprecantis tantum Deus intendit, sed orantis cor aspicit;' et ideo dicit Sapiens: *Fili, ante orationem praepara animam tuam, et noli esse tanquam homo, qui tentat Deum.* Tunc enim orator dicitur tentare Deum, quando absque ulla cordis praeparatione currit ad vocalem orationem et petit sibi divinam speculationem; sed vix, aut nunquam poterit impetrare, quia talis non dicitur devotus orator, sed potius verborum latrator." *Reg nov,* c. 2, n. 1 (VIII, 477a). The reference to Gregory the Great is from *Moralia in Iob,* Liber 22, c. 17, n. 43, *CChr* 143 A, 1122. See also: *Moralia in Iob,* Liber 33, c. 23, n. 43, *CChr* 143 B, 1712. The Scripture reference is to Sir. 18: 23. The question of prayer and divine speculation is taken up in section 4. 2. of Chapter Four.

[37] ". . . in *corde* per desiderium." *Comm Lc*, c. 18, n. 2 (VII, 448b). See also: *Comm Lc,* c. 11, n. 26 (VII, 285a). On desire in the theology of St. Bonaventure, see: Raymond

Bonaventure, like Augustine and Gregory the Great, holds that desire can properly be called prayer for prayer concerns the affective, as well as the cognitive, dimension of human experience.[38] Prayerful desire, which is essentially the desire of the heart for the good, constitutes unceasing prayer as long as it remains constant. Bonaventure makes this point in the *Commentary on Luke* when he quotes from the *Gloss*: ". . . indeed a good desire is itself prayer. If the desire is continuous, the prayer is continuous."[39]

Desire, as prayer, can be directed toward all of God's gifts which are the objects of human longing since it is natural to desire God's gifts and to pray for them.[40] Desire is also of fundamental importance for the efficacy of the request for those gifts. While discussing the role of angels in the life of

Johnston, "Une question d'équilibre: le rôle du désir dans la pensée primitive de saint Bonaventure," *EF* 21 (Supplément annuel 1971): 75-86; Jacques Bougerol, "L'aspect original de l'Itinerarium mentis in Deum et son influence sur la spiritualité de son temps," *Ant* 52 (1977): 310-315; and Ephrem Longpré, *La théologie mystique de saint Bonaventure*, (Quaracchi: Collegium S. Bonaventurae, 1921): 52-54. On desire and prayer, see: Jean-Claude Sagne, "Du besoin à la demande, ou la conversion du désir dans la prière," *MD* 109 (1972): 87-97 and Ann and Barry Ulanov, *Primary Speech. A Psychology of Prayer* (Atlanta: John Knox Press, 1982) 13-25.

[38] "Ad illud vero quod primo obiicitur in contrarium, quod synderesis est spiritus rationalis, qui postulat et interpellat; dicendum, quod sicut dicit Gregorius super Iob primum, non tantum loquimur ad Deum cogitationibus et exterioribus verbis, sed etiam affectibus et desideriis; et propterea, dum synderesis continue stimulando nos facit bonum desiderare, dicitur *gemitibus inenarrabilibus ad Deum interpellare*." *II Sent,* d. 34, a. 2, q. 1, concl. ad 1 (II, 910b). The theme of desire in Augustine's theology of prayer is treated in Antonio Cacciari, intro., *S. Agostino d'Ippona La Preghiera,* intro., trans. and notes Antonio Cacciari (Roma: Edizioni Paoline, 1981) 47-53 and by Gervase Corcoran, *Prayer and St. Augustine,* vol. 25 of the *Living Flame Series.* ed. Thomas Curran (Dublin: Carmelite Centre of Spirituality, 1983) 12-14. For Gregory the Great's teaching on desire in the life of prayer, see: Jean Leclercq, *The Love of Learning and the Desire for God. A Study of Monastic Culture,* trans. Catharine Marsh (London: SPCK, 1978) 36-41.

[39] ". . . ipsum enim desiderium bonum oratio est; et si continuum est desiderium, continua est oratio." *Comm Lc,* c. 18, n. 2 (VII, 448b). Once again the Quaracchi editors refer to the version of the *Gloss* found in the *Biblia Sacra cum Glossa* (see note 15 above). They quote this text from the *Biblia Sacra cum Glossa* in note 4 of *IV Sent,* d. 15, p. 2, a. 1, q. 4, concl. (IV, 368a).

[40] *IV Sent,* d. 33, dub. 6 (IV, 764a).

prayer in the *Commentary on the Sentences,* Bonaventure states that just as those who are unable to speak publicly before a civil magistrate bring in an advocate to handle their case, so the angels serve as advocates of humanity before God. Their closeness to God makes them the ideal intercessors. Angels take the multitude of human desires expressed in petitionary prayer and make them their own desires. As a result, the angels desire what humanity desires and present these desires to God. Even tepid, human desires, when inflamed by the desire of the angels, have a possibility of being heard by God.[41]

The use of the concept "desire," in relation to requesting something from God, draws the unceasing prayer of the heart into the wide realm of petitionary prayer.[42] Bonaventure's definition of prayer indicates the link between desire and petition. Desire is considered prayer in its own right, as well as the source of petition. He says in the *Commentary on the Sentences:* ". . . our prayer is the desire for something or a petition formed according to desire . . . ."[43] This identification of desire with petitionary prayer leads into the question of the nature of desire and what should be sought after in prayer.

---

[41] *IV Sent,* d. 45, dub. 7 (IV, 953a). The angels also help reconcile humanity to God by facilitating constant prayer: "Tertio liberat [Raphael] nos a *contrarietate Dei,* quam incurrimus per offensam Dei, et hoc inducendo nos ad instantiam orationis . . . ." *De sancti Angeli,* 5 (IX, 626b). On the intercession of the angels, see also: *Comm Lc,* c. 11, n. 3 (VII, 278a) and *Comm Lc,* c. 14, n. 64 (VII, 379b-380a).

[42] Unceasing prayer, as a request for something, is linked with desire in a sermon where Bonaventure describes one of the characteristics of prayer by making reference to the petition of the widow before the judge: "Tertio orationem debet *subsequi sedulitas studii* in continuatione; unde Lucae decimo octavo: *Oportet semper orare et non deficere,* dicens eis exemplum *cuiusdam viduae,* quae ratione suae importunitatis exaudita est apud iudicem. Ad litteram illi, exemplo illius viduae, merentur exaudiri in oratione, qui non impediuntur aliqua superflua occupatione; sed semper *sine intermissione* et cum importunitate debent orare, quousque obtineant quod desiderant." *Dom 9 post Pent,* 1 (IX, 389b).

[43] ". . . oratio nostra est desiderium alicuius rei vel petitio formata secundum desiderium . . ." *IV Sent,* d. 46, dub. 7 (IV, 953a).

Humanity is attracted to the good and does what it can to possess it; prayer is a common way to obtain the desired good. Although all desires are directed toward a good, they do not necessarily lead to God. In the *Collations on John,* Bonaventure points out that corporal desires, along with secular and carnal desires, lead to spiritual death:

> These desires must be *detested* because they *attack* the soul; in chapter two of the first letter of Peter: 'I implore you to abstain from carnal desires which wage war against the soul.' They *crucify* the soul; in the twenty-first chapter of Proverbs: 'Desires kill the lazy.' They *imprison* the soul; consequently that statement of the Psalm: 'God has handed them over to the desires of their hearts; they will walk according to their own intentions.'[44]

The reality of the destructive side of desire necessitates a discernment process within the movement from desire to petition. What would divert the soul in anyway from the possession of the spiritual good should not be requested or even desired. Consequently, corporal goods should be sought after only to the degree they facilitate the divine good: ". . . a *corporal* good should not be desired except for the sake of a *spiritual* [good] . . . ."[45]

---

[44] "Desideria ista *detestanda sunt,* quia animam *impugnant*; primae Petri secundo: 'Obsecro vos abstinere a carnalibus desideriis, quae militant adversus animam.' Animam *cruciant*; Proverbiorum vigesimo primo: 'Desideria occidunt pigrum.' Animam *captivant*; unde illud Psalmi: 'Tradidit eos Deus in desideria cordis eorum; ibunt in adinventionibus suis.'" *Coll Jn,* c. 8, coll. 35, an. 36 (VI, 577b). See also: *Comm Jn,* c. 8, n. 61 (VI, 366b) and *Comm Lc,* c. 12, n. 50 (VII, 324a). The Scriptures referred to are: 1 Pet. 2: 11; Pr. 21: 25 and Ps. 81: 12.

[45] ". . . *corporale* bonum non debet desiderari nisi propter *spirituale* . . . ." *Comm Lc,* c. 11, n. 8 (VII, 279b). Concerning the properness of prayer for temporal goods and the Franciscan school, see: *De orat,* membrum 3, a. 1, 691a - 692b. The fact that prayer for temporal goods is subordinate to the spiritual needs of those praying helps to ensure the proper relationship between material goods and those who seek them. It also enables

An example of prayer and the desire for corporal goods, as well as spiritual goods, is found in the *Commentary on John*. Here the Samaritan woman asks Jesus for the water which will rid her of thirst forever and free her from the burden of her work. She is speaking in terms of bodily or corporal thirst. Corporal thirst, which is a form of desire defined in terms of the lack of water, begins on the level of corporal need and leads to temporary satisfaction when the sought-after water is obtained. Despite the satisfaction of thirst afforded by the water from the well, the Samaritan woman will once again grow thirsty and be forced to return to the well. The living water Jesus offers to her is intended for her spiritual thirst. While spiritual thirst implies an implicit need, it is not characterized by the lack of something. Instead, it is defined by the possession of the gift of grace and an ever-growing thirst for grace.[46]

Bonaventure's distinction between corporal and spiritual thirst follows the insights of both Augustine and Gregory the Great who recognized two diametrically opposed principles at work in corporal and spiritual desires. Bonaventure alludes to these two principles in the *Commentary on the Sentences,* when he says that spiritual desire, as opposed to corporal and temporal desire, is experientially grounded in the ever deepening enjoyment and possession of the most high Good:

. . . the desire of the highest Good is the desire which

---

human desires to be expressed in prayer with the realization that not all desires should be actualized. As Barth notes, there is a discernment process embedded in the structure of medieval petitionary prayer; it facilitates the acceptance of human desires without giving full vent to them. For a discussion of prayer in this light, with reference to both Eastern and Western approaches to the question of human desires, see: Barth, *Wohin - woher mein Ruf,* 89-90. For another view of prayer for temporal goods in medieval thought, see: Heiler, *Das Gebet,* 307-309.

[46] *Comm Jn*, c. 4, n. 27-28 (VI, 293b-294a).

necessarily has delight and a type of actual possession already joined to it and therefore produces joy. Thus he who desires the highest Good more, is more delighted therein. Indeed in this the desire of temporal and corporal things is different from the desire of spiritual things, as Augustine indicates in the book Of Eighty Three Questions. And that truth is held most of all when God dwells in the soul by means of charity. [47]

While the desire for the most high Good includes an implicit recognition of need, it, more importantly, entails the possession and enjoyment, albeit, imperfect, of God. The primary emphasis of the desire is on what is already enjoyed instead of on that which is missing.[48] As a gift of divine grace, it is a gratuitous form of love which needs to be distinguished from natural and acquired love. This form of love, spoken of as charity, yearns to cling to God. In the positive sense of the word, it is a "concupiscent" type of love exemplified in the Apostle Paul who longed with desire to depart from the world and to be united with Christ.[49]

Bonaventure's development of spiritual desire indicates that prayer

---

[47] ". . . desiderium summi Boni est desiderium, quod habet necessario iunctam secum fruitionem et aliquam realem possessionem; et ideo parit gaudium, unde qui plus desiderat summum Bonum magis ibi delectatur. In hoc enim dissimile est desiderium temporalium et corporalium a desiderio spiritualium, ut ostendit Augustinus in libro Octoginta trium Quaestionum. Et illud veritatem habet maxime, cum Deus inhabitat per charitatem in anima." *IV Sent,* d. 20, p. 1, au., q. 2, concl. (IV, 520b). The section of the *De diversis quaestionibus octoginta tribus* Bonaventure refers to is found in c. 35, n. 1 of *CChr* 44 A, 50-52. Gregory the Great's teaching on the difference between corporal and spiritual desires appears in *Homilia* 36, n. 1, *PL* 76, 1266.

[48] *III Sent,* d. 27, dub. 1 (III, 616b-617a) and *III Sent,* d. 26, dub. 5 (III, 585b).

[49] *III Sent,* d. 27, a. 2, q. 2 concl. (III, 606b). The reference to Paul is from Phil. 1: 23. The distinction between charity and the other forms of love can be traced back to Augustine's theology of grace; see: Burns, "Grace," 348.

153

looks far beyond the temporary fulfillment of corporal desires. Spiritual desire is love, which in its longing, yearns to possess completely the beloved.[50] Whereas corporal desire can be said to push toward a temporal good, spiritual desire, as an expression of both the possession of and yearning for the divine good, pulls those who pray into the arms of God. In the *Collations on John*, Bonaventure describes this dynamic in terms of the heart being drawn upward to God. He points out that God has taken the initiative by planting the spiritual desire in the heart and that by means of such desire God draws the heart to himself: "The Lord likewise draws upward by the *hidden strength of spiritual desires*. Indeed, God infuses the spiritual desire and draws the human heart to himself by means of the hidden desire of the heart."[51]

The upward movement toward God brought about by the spiritual desires planted within the heart echoes a dynamic found in the Pseudo-Dionysian understanding of prayer: in prayer, the poor believe they draw God to themselves, but it is actually God who is drawing them to himself.[52] Bonaventure makes use of the Areopagite's teaching in the *Commentary of*

---

[50] *III Sent,* d. 27, dub. 1 (III, 616b).

[51] "Trahit etiam Dominus sursum *occulta virtute spiritualium desideriorum.* Immittit quidem Deus spirituale desiderium et trahit ad se occulto cordis desiderio cor humanum . . . ." *Coll Jn,* c. 6, coll. 28, n. 6 (VI, 567b-568a).

[52] The Pseudo-Dionysian aspect of the preceding text from the *Coll Jn* is also mentioned by Bougerol; see: "L'aspect originale de l'Itinerarium," 312. The teaching of Pseudo-Dionysian, which ties prayer with the upward movement of the soul towards God, is found in *De divinis nominibus* c. 3, § 1, *PG* 3, 679. Bonaventure refers to this teaching in *I Sent.* d. 15, p. 2, dub. 5 (I, 275b) and *Comm Lc,* c. 18, n. 63 (VII, 471b). See also: *De orat,* membrum 3, a. 2, resp., 686b. On Bonaventure's use of Pseudo-Dionysian texts in general, see: Bougerol, "Saint Bonaventure et le Pseudo-Denys l'Aréopagite," 33-80. The anagogical, upward movement of the soul in the Areopagite's theology is studied by Paul Rorem, *Biblical and Liturgical Symbols within the Pseudo-Dionysian Synthesis,* (Toronto: Pontifical Institute of Mediaeval Studies, 1984) 99-116, esp. 108 in reference to prayer.

Luke to illustrate how Christ takes the initiative in responding to the cry for mercy from the blind man near Jericho. Here the desire for the corporal good is not seen in opposition to the desire for the spiritual good; instead, the two intersect with each other. The beggar's desire to see, which strictly speaking would not normally be considered a spiritual good, is equated with the spiritual longing for the light of wisdom. Because the beggar asks for light in the name of Christ, the petition goes beyond the request for a temporal good to include the desire for a spiritual good leading to salvation. Through this desire, Christ draws the beggar to himself and heals him physically and spiritually.[53]

The spiritual desire for wisdom plays a deciding role in Bonaventure's teaching on prayer. Desire is, in fact, the first step toward receiving the divine light of wisdom.[54] As the *Journey of the Soul into God* reveals, Bonaventure longed ardently for such wisdom. In that work he maintains that only those, who, like the prophet Daniel are filled with desire, will be able to make the contemplative ascent into God[55] which culminates in the experience of divine wisdom. Those poor who follow the example of Daniel are drawn upward into a mystical rest or peace, identified with the Sabbath, where God is known in the radiant darkness of divine wisdom.[56] Their corporal desires are to be silenced, however, as they are united with Christ and pass over with him to find their ultimate and total fulfillment in God:

---

[53] *Comm Lc*, c. 18, n. 61-64 (VII, 471b-472a).

[54] *Hex*, coll. 2, n. 2 (V, 336a); *Hex*, coll. 22, n. 29 (V, 441b-442a); *Itin*, prol., n. 3 (V, 296b); and *Sabbato Santo,* 1 (IX, 269a).

[55] *Itin*, prol., n. 3 (V, 296a). The desire for wisdom, which Bonaventure equates with estatic peace, is treated in Chapter Four.

[56] *Itin*, c. 7, n. 1-6 (V, 312a-313b).

Let us therefore die and enter into the darkness. Let us impose silence on our cares, desires and imaginings. Let us pass over with Christ Crucified *from this world to the Father,* so that when the Father has been shown to us we may say with Philip: *It is enough for us;* Let us hear with Paul: *My grace is enough for you;* Let us exalt with David saying: *My flesh and my heart have grown faint. The God of my heart, and the God [who is] my portion forever. Blessed be the Lord forever. And all the people will say: So be it; so be it.* Amen.[57]

3. 1. 3. Good Deeds and Just Action

The third expression of unceasing prayer singled out in the Bonaventurian exegesis of Lk. 18: 1-8 is: ". . . in *work* by means of preparation."[58] The exegesis of Lk. 18: 1-8, which links "work" with doing good deeds and acting justly, contains two distinct, but related, ideas regarding the question of good actions, justice, and unceasing prayer. The first is that good and just actions can be considered prayer in their own right. The second is that they assure the efficacy of prayer. As Bonaventure says in the *Commentary on Luke:* "And this is what Bede says here in the Gloss: 'He

---

[57] "Moriamur igitur et ingrediamur in caliginem, imponamus silentium sollicitudinibus, concupiscentiis et phantasmatibus; transeamus cum Christo crucifixo *ex hoc mundo ad Patrem,* ut, ostenso nobis Patre, dicamus cum Philippo: *Sufficit nobis;* audiamus cum Paulo: *Sufficit tibi gratia mea;* exultemus cum David dicentes: *Defecit caro mea et cor meum, Deus cordis mei et pars mea Deus in aeternum. Benedictus Dominus in aeternum, et dicet omnis populus: Fiat, fiat.* Amen." *Itin,* c. 7, n. 6 (V, 313b).

[58] ". . . in *opere* per praeparationem." *Comm Lc,* c. 18, n. 2 (VII, 448b).

who always does good things prays always, nor does he cease to pray except when he ceases to be just . . . .'"[59] Thus, doing what is good and acting justly is a legitimate expression of prayer. It also determines the efficacy of prayer inasmuch as those who do good order their lives in such a way that a positive reception of their prayer is assured:"For the one who does good things so disposes himself toward this that his prayer deserves to be heard . . . ."[60]

Bonaventure mirrors the traditions of both the Eastern and Western Fathers when he teaches that good and just actions are a legitimate and praiseworthy expression of prayer. He, like them, sees such actions as the natural, concrete result of the desire for good found in the hearts of those seeking the kingdom of God.[61] This identification of doing good and acting justly with prayer keeps prayer from being hermetically separated from the various dimensions of life which lie outside the realm of what is normally considered prayer. Thus, since all good works are in accord with the

---

[59] "Et hoc est quod hic dicit Beda in Glossa: 'Semper orat qui semper agit bona, nec desinit orare, nisi cum desinit iustus esse . . . .'" *Comm Lc*, c. 18, n. 2 (VII, 448b). See also: *IV Sent*, d. 15, p. 2, a. 1, q. 4, concl. (IV, 368a). The text above is found in the *Biblia Sacra cum Glossa* and is quoted by the Quarrachi editors in note 4 of *IV Sent*, d. 15, p. 2, a. 1, q. 4, concl. (IV, 368a). A similar text is found in Bede's commentary on Lk. 18: 1; see: Bede, *In Lucam, CChr* 120, 322. This idea can be traced back at least as far as to Origen: "Si vero omnis actus justi, quem secundum Deum agit et secundum mandatum divinum, oratio reputatur, quia justus sine intermissione quae justa sunt agit, per hoc sine intermissione justus orabit, nec unquam ab oratione cessabit: nisi justus esse desistat." *Selecta in primum librum Regnorum I*, *PG* 12, 1005. On the theme of unceasing prayer in Origen's theology of prayer, see: *De oratione*, n. 12, *PG* 11, 451. See also: Wilhelm Gessel, *Die Theologie des Gebetes nach 'De Oratione' von Origenes* (München: Verlag Ferdinand Schöningh. 1975) 244-249.

[60] "Qui enim bona agit ad hoc se disponit, ut eius oratio debeat audiri . . . ." *Comm Lc*, c. 18, n. 2 (VII, 448b).

[61] According to Hausherr, the three major representatives of the early Christian teaching on prayer, Origen, Aphraates and Augustine, concur in holding that those who perform good or just actions manifest an authentic form of prayer. The origins of the teaching can be found in Origen and is later developed by Aphraates and Augustine. See: Hausherr, *The Name of Jesus*, 130-131 and 157.

scriptural admonition to pray always,[62] the call to pray cannot be understood fully without reference to the call to love others. These two aspects of prayer are linked together in Bonaventure's exegesis of Lk. 11: 9: "knock and it will be opened to you."[63] He writes that doing good, understood as charitable actions, is an unceasing form of petitionary prayer which supplements the words and desires of prayer. To knock then, with outstretched arms, is to reach out to God through good deeds.[64] These deeds, rooted as they are in charity, also serve to render prayer efficacious: ". . . *we knock* with charity when we sweat over [our] labors so that we may obtain that which we ask and seek."[65]

The connection between good works, charity, and the efficacy of prayer leads to a consideration of charitable actions as a crucial element of efficacious prayer. Bonaventure develops the relationship between the two within the context of discipleship and prayer. In both the *Commentary on John* and the *Collations on John*, he writes that the efficacy of prayer hinges on the relationship of the disciples with Christ since God hears the prayer of those who do his will and remain in him, and the disciples remain in God to the degree that they remain in Christ:[66] *"If you will have remained in me and my words will have remained in you, then whatever you will have wished,*

---

[62] "Tamen de illo quod dicit, quod orandum est sine intermissione; intelligendum est, quod nomine *orationis* omnis bonus actus intelligitur secundum Glossam. Unde dicit ibi: ' Non cessat orare qui non cessat bene facere.'"*IV Sent,* d. 32, dub. 5 (IV, 744b).

[63] *Comm Lc,* c. 11, n. 26-27 (VII, 285a-b).

[64] *Comm Lc,* c. 11, n. 26 (VII, 285a).

[65] ". . . *pulsamus* caritate, dum laboribus insudamus, ut quod petimus et quaerimus consequamur. *Comm Lc,* c. 11, n. 27 (VII, 285b).

[66] *Comm Jn,* c. 9, n. 37 (VI, 379a-b) and *Coll Jn,* c. 15, an. 62 (VI, 604b-605a).

you will ask, and it will be done for you . . . . Here the *fruit* of remaining in him, which is the hearing of our petitions, is described."[67] One certain way of remaining in Christ is through a life marked by charity.[68]

Bonaventure's insistence on abiding in Christ as a prerequisite for the hearing of prayer offers an insight which helps to explain what is intended in the *Commentary on Luke* when constant prayer is described as a type of preparatory action. Abiding in Christ prepares or disposes the disciple to the reception of God's grace. Petitions are heard because of the merit of those attempting to remain in God by walking as Christ walked: "Note therefore that a petition is usually granted . . . . on account of the *merit of the one petitioning;* whence here it is said: *If you will have remained in me* etc.."[69] Such abiding in Christ is not summed up in the implementation of an ethical imperative, but, rather, lived out in the disciples' fidelity to the revelation of God's love made known in Christ.[70] Remaining in Christ is demonstrated, therefore, by a loving obedience to the commands originating in the will of the Father. Adherence to the Father's commands is not, however, a passive acceptance of a series of laws; instead, it is an active willingness to walk as Christ walked in faith, love, and obedience:

> *Remain in me and I in you.* Note that one must abide in

---

[67] "*Si manseritis in me, et verba mea in vobis manserint, quodcumque volueritis petetis, et fiet vobis.* . . . describitur hic *fructus* manendi in eo, qui est petitionum nostrarum exauditio." *Coll Jn,* c.15, an. 62 (VI, 604b). On the hearing of petitionary prayer in John's Gospel, see: Hans Freiherr von Campenhausen, "Gebetserhörung in den überlieferten Jesusworten und in der Reflexion des Johannes," *KD* 23 (1977): 157-171.

[68] *Coll Jn,* c. 15, an. 61 (VI, 604b).

[69] "Nota igitur, quod petitio solet exaudiri . . . propter *meritum petentis;* unde hic dicitur: *Si manseritis in me* etc.." *Coll Jn,* c. 15, an. 62 (VI, 604b-605a).

[70] *Comm Jn,* c. 15, n. 11 (VI, 448a-b).

159

Christ through *faith*, through *charity,* and through *work.*

For he who *believes* in Christ abides in God; in chapter four of first John: 'Whoever will have confessed that Jesus is the Son of God, God abides in him and he in God.' Likewise he who *loves* him abides in God; in chapter four of first John: 'He who abides in love abides in God and God in him.' He who *obeys* him remains in God; in the fifteenth chapter of John: 'If you will have kept my commands you will abide in my love;' and in the second chapter of first John: 'He who says that he abides in him, he himself must walk, as he walked.'[71]

Filial love should be the ideal which inspires the disciples' attempt to live out God's commandments in fidelity to Christ. Those whose actions are motivated by fear are not friends but slaves. Those who act out of fear alone will never be numbered among the friends of God.[72] God pays no heed to their prayers because they are motivated by servile fear. Instead, he looks kindly upon those who cry out lovingly for mercy.[73] Those who persevere in love are not slaves, or even servants, as much as friends of Christ. Friendship with Christ, manifested in the struggle to keep the command of mutual love,

---

[71] "*Manete in me, et ego in vobis.* Nota, quod manendum est in Christo per *fidem*, per *caritatem* et per *operationem.* - In Deo enim manet qui in Christum *credit*; primae Ioannis quarto: 'Quisquis confessus fuerit, quoniam Iesus est Filius Dei, Deus in ipso manet, et ipse in Deo.' - Item, in Deo manet qui ipsum *diligit*; primae Ioannis quarto: 'Qui manet in caritate in Deo manet, et Deus in eo.' - In Deo manet qui ipsi *obedit*; Ioannis decimo quinto: 'Si praecepta mea servaveritis, manebitis in dilectione mea;' et primae Ioannis secundo: 'Qui dicit, se in ipso manere, debet, sicut ille ambulavit, et ipse ambulare.'" *Coll Jn.,* c. 15, an. 61 (VI, 604b).

[72] *Comm Jn,* c. 15, n. 28, resp. (VI, 452b).

[73] *IV Sent,* d. 20, p. 1, dub. 2 (IV, 527b).

creates a favorable atmosphere for prayer. In this atmosphere of love, the friends of Christ can pray confidently in his name to the Father, knowing that all the gifts needed for salvation will be theirs.[74]

3. 2. Unceasing Prayer and the Struggle against Concupiscence

Friendship with Christ eventually brings his disciples into confrontation with evil. It is not surprising, therefore, that the early Christian understanding of unceasing prayer as spiritual warfare against the forces of evil finds ready acceptance and further development in Bonaventure's teaching on prayer.[75] He maintains that concupiscence, an inordinate or illicit desire manifested in pleasure, curiosity, and vanity, is an evil which needs to be overcome since it is the root of all sin.[76] An important way of withstanding the onslaught of concupiscence is an unceasing prayer for mercy directed toward Christ.[77] The forces of concupiscence are to be

---

[74] *Comm Jn,* c. 15, n. 23 (VI, 451b).

[75] Prayer, as the struggle against evil, permeates the early Christian theology of prayer. Stanley speaks of constant prayer as a "spiritual weapon" in the "holy war" waged by Saint Paul in *Boasting in the Lord,* 102. For a discussion of prayer as a struggle against demons in the desert spirituality of Anthony and Pachomius, see: Derwas J. Chitty, *The Desert a City: An Introduction to the Study of Egyptian and Palestinian Monasticism under the Christian Empire* (London: Mowbrays, 1977) 3 and 10, respectively. A succinct description of prayer as a constant struggle against evil appears in a story from the life of Abba Agathon: "Interrogaverunt eum [Abba Agathon] adhuc fratres, dicentes: Quae virtus, Pater, inter caeteras majorem exigit laborem? Dicit eis: Ignoscite mihi, existimo nullum laborem aequari precibus ad Deum. Quotiescunque enim homo voluerit orare, inimici seu daemones nituntur eum avertere. Sciunt quippe non aliter impediri se, nisi per orationem ad Deum. Certe quidquid aliud boni operis homo aggressus fuerit, in eo perseverans, requiem obtinet; at oratio ad ultimum usque spiritum eget certamine." *Apophthegmata Patrum, PG* 65, n. 9, 111.

[76] *Trip via,* c. 1, n. 5 (VIII, 4b-5a) and *Perf vitae,* c. 1, n. 3 (VIII, 108b).

[77] *Feria 5 post prima Dom in Quad* (IX, 213a-214b). The removal of evil, as well as the acquisition of the good, are two facets of Bonaventure's theology of prayer; see: *Comm*

resisted because they draw the heart away from God by encouraging it to embrace lesser, transistory goods, instead of ultimate, divine goods. The result of concupiscence is spiritual blindness which impedes the growth in self-knowledge necessary to come to a knowledge of God:

> Oh my God, from whence [comes] such blindness in a religious? Behold the reason is evident. Listen: because the mind of a person, distracted by *cares*, does not enter into itself through the *memory*; because darkened by *images* it does not return to itself through *intelligence*; because attracted by *illicit desires,* it never turns back to itself through the *desire* of internal sweetness and spiritual happiness, lingering therefore completely in these sense objects, it is unable to enter into itself as to the image of God. And so, completely miserable, it is ignorant of itself and does not know its very self. Therefore, after all these things have been disregarded, acquire the memory and the knowledge of yourself. Blessed Bernard use to pray for this saying 'May God give to me to know nothing other than that I may know my very self.' [78]

Lc, c. 11, n. 3 (VII, 278a)

[78] "O Deus meus, unde in religioso tanta caecitas? Ecce, in promptu ratio est, audi: quia mens hominis *sollicitudinibus* distracta, non intrat ad se per *memoriam*; quia *phantasmatibus* obnubilata, non redit ad se per *intelligentiam*; quia *concupiscentiis illicitis* illecta, ad se nequaquam revertitur per *desiderium* suavitatis internae et laetitiae spiritualis; ideo totaliter in his sensibilibus iacens, non potest ad se tanquam ad Dei imaginem intrare, et sic totus miser se ipsum ignorat et nescit. Omnibus ergo postpositis, tui ipsius habe memoriam et notitiam. Hoc etiam beatus Bernardus orabat, dicens: 'Deus det mihi non aliud scire, quam ut me ipsum cognoscam.'" *Perf vitae,* c. 1, n. 6 (VIII, 109b). For a study on the question of self-knowledge and knowledge of God in the Western Christian tradition, see: Bernard McGinn, "The Human Person as Image of God II. Western

3. 2. 1. The Poor Man of Jericho

Bonaventure's exegesis of Lk. 18: 35-42, the healing of the poor, blind mendicant on the road near Jericho, presents constant prayer within the context of the bitter struggle against the blinding power of concupiscence. At the same time, it draws special attention to the correlation between poverty and prayer. The beggar, who symbolizes all of humanity, is blinded in the depths of his heart and unable to understand the mysteries of salvation. He lacks the light of wisdom, which alone makes possible the knowledge of truth. God alone is the source of light capable of restoring sight to those blinded to eternal truth.[79] The blind man is mired hopelessly in the poverty of sin. Without justice or grace, he has been reduced to begging.[80]

Cupidity, a particular form of concupiscence, is what blinds the heart of the mendicant and of all humanity. It is a manifestation of the will's refusal to love the greatest good above all others. Where cupidity is operative, temporal goods become the focus of the heart's desire, and the result is a debilitating blindness and foolishness curable by the light of divine wisdom alone.[81] The decision to choose lesser goods leads to anxious mendicancy instead of peaceful rest since peace is inaccessible outside of union with the

---

Christianity" in vol. 16 of *WS*, 312-330.

[79] *Comm Lc,* c. 18, n. 57 (VII, 469b). For an English translation of Bonaventure's exegesis of this section of the Gospel of Luke with a commentary, see: Thomas Reist, *Saint Bonaventure as a Biblical Commentator* (Lanham, Md.: University Press of America, 1985) 97-102 and 164-168.

[80] *Comm Lc,* c. 18, n. 58 (VII, 470a).

[81] *Comm Lc,* c. 18, n. 58 (VII, 470a).

greatest good, which is God. Although humanity has fallen away from the greatest good, the remembrance and desire for this eternal good remains etched indelibly into the foundation of its being.[82]

Bonaventure stresses the poverty of the blind man by drawing attention to his close physical proximity to Jericho. He interprets "Jericho" to mean "moon," hence, a symbol of instability in juxtaposition with the sun, which is a symbol of stability.[83] The instability of the blind man, seen in the inordinate love of changeable things, is a bitter witness to human poverty. However, it is paradoxically the reality of human poverty which opens up an avenue to salvation by leading the mendicant to reflect on his own defects and weaknesses. The experiential acknowledgement and subsequent acceptance of poverty is the door to wisdom which opens in the redemptive encounter between the poor and the poor Christ. Quoting the *Gloss*, Bonaventure teaches that the Lord's acceptance of human poverty in the Incarnation renders humanity capable of returning to the knowledge of divine matters:

> . . . the blind man sits *along the road*, when he *draws near* to the light of truth from the consideration of his deficiency and inconsistency. Whence the Gloss: 'Jericho is interpreted as the moon by which the feebleness of humanity is understood. Therefore as the Word of God assumes the weakness of our flesh, humanity returns to know divine things.'[84]

---

[82] *II Sent,* prooem. (II, 5b-6a).

[83] *Comm Lc,* c. 18, n. 58 (VII, 470a-b).

[84] ". . . caecus sedet *secus viam,* quando ad lumen veritatis *appropinquat* ex consideratione suae defectibilitatis et variabilitatis; unde Glossa: *'Iericho* luna interpretatur, per quam defectus mortalitatis intelligitur. Dum ergo Verbum Dei infirmitatem nostrae carnis suscipit,

The blind man's acceptance and acknowledgment of his poverty leads to a corresponding cry for mercy. His prayer, which Bonaventure holds up as a model worthy of imitation, is marked by three spiritual movements common to unceasing prayer: "seeking," "asking" and "knocking."[85] As Jesus draws near, the mendicant "seeks" in prayer by inquiring into the cause or significance of the multitude passing by along the road. The passing crowd represents the movement of creatures, who, when questioned, point to God as the source of all things, visible and invisible. The crowd tells the mendicant, just as creatures tell all of humanity, that Jesus of Nazareth is near.[86] The recognition of Jesus' presence leads the mendicant to "ask" in a devout prayer for mercy sealed by spiritual desire:

> He *asks* likewise *devoutly* and therefore it follows: *And he*
> *cried out saying: Jesus, Son of David, have mercy on me.*
> In the fact that he cries out, he shows that he has a
> superabundance of desire. On account of which it is said
> in the eighth chapter of Romans: 'It is the Spirit who asks
> for us with indescribable groans.'[87]

As the mendicant asks for mercy, he faces once again the reality of poverty which threatens to hold him imprisoned in the darkness of concupiscence. On hearing the plea of the mendicant, the crowd turns on him in order to silence him. Bonaventure says the crowd here represents various

---

homo ad cognoscenda divina redit.'" *Comm Lc,* c. 18, n. 58 (VII, 470b).

[85] *Comm Lc,* c. 18, n. 59 (VII, 470b). See also: *Comm Lc,* c. 11, n. 25 (VII, 284b-285a).

[86] *Comm Lc,* c. 18, n. 59-60 (VII, 470b-471a).

[87] "*Petit* etiam *devote,* et ideo sequitur: *Et clamavit dicens: Iesu, fili David, miserere mei.* In hoc, quod *clamat,* ostendit, se habere *excedentiam desiderii;* propter quod dicitur ad Romanos octavo: ' Spiritus est, qui postulat pro nobis gemitibus inenarrabilibus.'" *Comm Lc,* c. 18, n. 61 (VII, 471a). The reference to Scripture is Rom. 8: 26.

images of material things. Originally leading into God, they have since become an obstacle exercising a disruptive effect on the reflection necessary for prayer. These mental images, understood as the tumult of carnal desires, threaten to suffocate the cry for mercy, thereby, keeping Jesus from illuminating the darkness of the heart.[88] Despite the power of the desires, the beggar does not succumb to them, but, instead, cries out more insistently for mercy. Just as the resistance of the crowd serves as a catalyst for the mendicant's prayer, the negative images and desires hindering prayer move the poor to call out more insistently than before to the Lord. Thus, in the face of the images of concupiscence, prayer should become an unceasing knock on the door of divine mercy. The door of mercy is no other than Jesus, the Son of David:

> Consequently, images of this kind, [which are] holding us back from prayer by their confusing din, are nothing other than a kind of obstacle between us and Christ according to that third chapter of Lamentations: 'You have placed a cloud before you so that prayer may not pass;' therefore there is need for a troublesome *knocking*. On account of which the blind man *knocks continually* when it is added: *'He was crying out all the more: Son of David, have mercy on me;* [according to] the Psalm: 'Lord God of my salvation, in the day and night I have called out before you.'[89]

---

[88] *Comm Lc,* c. 18, n. 62 (VII, 471a). See also: *Dom 13 post Pent,* 1 (IX, 405a-b).

[89] "Unde huiusmodi imaginationes, retrahentes nos ab oratione per strepitum suum, nihil aliud sunt quam quoddam obstaculum inter nos et Christum, secundum illud Threnorum tertio: 'Opposuisti nubem tibi, ne transeat oratio;' et ideo opus est importuna *pulsatione.* -

The prayerful struggle against the desires and images equated with concupiscence inflames faith and results in a continuous prayer which is heard and answered by Christ.[90] Immersed once again into the redemptive aspect of poverty, the poor man's plea for mercy is heard and answered because of Christ's participation in human poverty. As Bonaventure says, Christ looks with great compassion on those cries for mercy originating in the blindness of concupiscence because he, too, has embraced the poverty of human flesh.[91] His compassion is evidenced in the outpouring of grace into the life of the poor man who calls out for mercy. Christ responds to this prayer by having him brought forward and then generously answers his request by restoring his sight. On the spiritual plane, the mendicant's reception of sight is matched with the infusion of the divine light of wisdom, which as a gift of grace, heals the intellect and the will,[92] illuminates the heart, and reveals the way of justice.[93] Once without both grace and justice, the mendicant is left rich in grace and justified in faith after his encounter with Christ in prayer.

Propter quod caecus *pulsat continue,* cum subiungitur: *Ipse vero multo magis clamabat: Fili David, miserere mei*; Psalmus 'Domine Deus salutis meae, in die clamavi et nocte coram te.'" *Comm Lc,* c. 18, n. 62 (VII, 471a-b). The Scriptural references are Lam. 3: 44 and Ps. 77: 2.

[90] " . . . qui vult a Iesu illuminari spiritualiter, cum tumultus 'carnalium vitiorum dissipant cogitationes hominis et perturbant vocem orationis, ne Iesus ad illuminandum venire possit cor hominis, sed iam credens, sentiens, se gravari phantasmate priorum vitiorum et vocem orationis suae impediri, ardentius clamet, quia, dum vehementius insistit orationi, ducitur ad *Iesum stantem* et recipit lumen . . . .'" *Dom 13 post Pent,* 1 (IX, 405b). See also: *Comm Lc,* c. 18, n. 62 (VII, 471b).

[91] *Comm Lc,* c. 18, n. 63 (VII, 471b).

[92] *Comm Lc,* c. 18, n. 64 (VII, 471b-472a). See also: *De donis,* coll. 9, n. 5 (V, 500a-b) and Mariani, note 1 in *San Bonaventura, I sette doni dello spirito santo,* 240-241.

[93] *Comm Lc,* c. 18, n. 64-66 (VII, 471b-472b)

3. 2. 2. Concupiscence and the Solitude of the Heart

The unceasing prayer of the poor man outside of Jericho underlines the importance of the struggle against concupiscence. It also draws attention to the central position of the heart in Bonaventure's teaching on prayer.[94] For Bonaventure, the human heart is the battleground where manifestations of concupiscence both provoke and threaten to smother the cry for divine mercy. The heart is also the sanctuary where God is encountered through the reception of divine grace. To foster this encounter with God, the poor must learn to turn inward and enter into the solitude of the heart where they can focus their thoughts and desires on God. To enter into the heart requires the renunciation of those imperfect loves characteristic of concupiscence. Only then will the heart be set aflame with the love of God. [95]

Bonaventure's view of solitude vis-à-vis prayer and the struggle against concupiscence emerges in his interpretation of three biblical images identified commonly with prayer: the desert, the mountain, and the temple.

---

[94] As Châtillon indicates, the medieval concept of "cor" is both rich and complex. It is often identified with other concepts such as "mens," "animus," "intellectus," and "ratio." The biblical idea of the heart as the spiritual center of humanity, which was developed further by Augustine and Gregory, was employed throughout the Middle Ages. Bonaventure makes use of the word in the traditonal fashion. He considers the heart to be the seat of intelligence and love, with a decided emphasis on the love or affective aspect. On the medieval understanding of heart, see: Jean Châtillon, "Cor et cordis affectus" in vol. 2 of DS, 2289-2300; and esp. 2298 for Bonaventure's use of the word.

[95] Perf vitae, c. 5, n. 4-7 (VIII, 118b-119b) and Dom 17 post Pent, 1 (IX, 421a). It should also be noted that Bonaventure does not ignore the question of physical solitude and prayer. When writing to religious, he does not hesitate to remind them of the necessity of such solitude. See: Perf vitae, c. 4, n. 3 (VIII, 116b); Reg nov, c. 2, n. 6 (VIII, 478b) and Ep off, 1, n. 4 (VIII, 469b).

Unceasing prayer, as witnessed in the life of Christ, requires a special, secret place if it is to flourish: " . . . *And it came to pass while he was in a certain place praying;* a *certain* [place], that is to say in a solitary and secret [place], because such places are suitable for prayer . . . ."[96] In Bonaventure's geography of prayer, the desert, mountain, and temple are all such places of prayerful solitude found by following along the path of resistance to the insistent pull of concupiscence on the heart. The prayer which God desires from the poor is not to be offered publicly, but, rather, privately in the hidden regions of the heart which can be identified with all three biblical symbols.

The *Commentary on Luke* draws attention to the link between solitude and the desert. According to the Gospel, Jesus was led into the wilderness by the Spirit after having been baptized in the Jordan (Lk. 4: 1-13). The wilderness, or solitary place, signifies the desert. It is a privileged place because God is accustomed to speaking intimately with the heart drawn into solitude.[97] The desert is a place where the heart is purified.[98] It is also the arena of spiritual combat where Jesus struggled against the evil of concupiscence. As Bonaventure says, Jesus was led into the desert by the powerful attraction of the good since, in spiritual terms, "to be led" in Luke's

---

[96] " . . . *Et factum est, dum esset in quodam loco orans; quodam,* id est solitario et secreto, quia talia loca sunt orationi apta . . . ." *Comm Lc,* c. 11, n. 2 (VII, 277a). See also: *Comm Lc,* c. 22, n. 51 (VII, 555b-556a) and *Reg nov,* c. 2, n. 1 (VIII, 476b). On the question of places of prayer, see: *Comm Jn,* c. 4, n. 43, resp. (VI, 296a-b) and also: *De orat,* membrum 3, a. 7, resp., 720a-721b.

[97] *Comm Lc,* c. 4, n. 3 (VII, 89b). On Bonaventure's use of the word "desert," see: Werner Dettloff, "Incipit speculatio pauperis," *FS* 66 (1984): 61-62 and 67. On the symbolism of the desert in the Christian tradition, see: Forstner, "Wüste," *Die Welt der christlichen Symbole,* 85-87.

[98] *De trans S. Franc* (IX, 534a-b).

Gospel means to be moved by the love of goodness.[99] The love of goodness drew Jesus into a direct confrontation with evil. The Devil enticed him to sin by tempting him to choose temporal goods over divine goods. Each temptation which Jesus overcame presented a different face of concupiscence.[100] The challenge to change stones into bread concerned the flesh which is an inferior good. The offer of authority and glory entailed the exterior good of the world. The questioning of Jesus' divinity touched upon the interior good of the soul. Given the exemplary nature of Jesus' solitary struggle in the desert,[101] it can be said that his experience offers an insight into the link between solitude and the battle against concupiscence: the love, or desire, for the good leads into the solitude of the desert where the poor are called to abandon all lesser goods and cling to the eternal good alone.

The turning away from concupiscence and turning toward God takes place when the decision is reached to enter into prayerful solitude. Commenting on Lk. 5: 16, "he went into the desert and prayed," Bonaventure points out that Jesus left the multitudes for the desert because he was desiring neither worldly fame nor glory. This action, together with his leaving to pray on the mountain after the miracle of the loaves and fishes (Mt. 14: 23), shows how the poor are to abandon the world and draw near to God, as God does not desire public prayer in the marketplace, but, rather, hidden prayer in the desert.[102] Although physical withdrawal from the world can be helpful in the facilitation of solitary prayer, it is not always possible or necessary.

---

[99] *Comm Lc,* c. 4, n. 5 (VII, 90a).

[100] *Comm Lc,* c. 4, n. 8 (VII, 90b).

[101] *Lig vit,* fr. 3, n. 10 (VIII, 73a-b).

[102] *Comm Lc,* c. 5, n. 35 (VII, 122a)

Thus, the desert can also represent the hidden room of the heart where the soul encounters the divine spouse. Entrance into this interior, secret room calls for the abandonment of everything that could possibly hinder the meeting between the soul and the spouse. Quoting Bernard of Clairvaux, Bonaventure illustrates how the movement into prayerful solitude includes the abandonment of what is obviously sinful and many good things which, when compared with the divine good, are to be considered inferior:

> . . . thus in the sixth chapter of Matthew: 'You however, when you pray, go into your bedroom.' And this is what Bernard says on the Canticles: 'Oh holy soul! Be alone so you may keep yourself for the one of all people whom you have chosen from all people. Avoid the public and flee from family members themselves. Withdraw from friends and intimates and from that one who serves you. Or perhaps you not know that you have a shy spouse who wishes by no means to grant his presence to you when others are present? Withdraw therefore, but in mind, not body; but in intention, but in devotion, but in spirit; although not in vain do you separate yourself physically, now and then, especially in the time of prayer.'[103]

The image of the mountain also holds a significant place in the

---

[103] "unde Matthaei sexto: 'Tu autem, cum oraveris, intra cubiculum tuum.' Et hoc est quod dicit Bernardus in Cantica; 'O sancta anima! sola esto, ut soli omnium serves te ipsam, quem tibi ex omnibus elegisti. Fuge publicum, fuge et ipsos domesticos, secede ab amicis et intimis et ab illo qui tibi ministrat. An nescis, te verecundum habere sponsum, et qui nequaquam velit tibi suam indulgere praesentiam, praesentibus ceteris? Secede ergo, sed mente, non corpore; sed intentione, sed devotione, sed spiritu; quamquam et corpore interdum non otiose te separas, praesertim in tempore orationis.'" *Comm Lc,* c. 5, n. 35 (VII, 122a). The reference to Matthew's Gospel is Mt. 6: 6 and that to Bernard's work is *Sermo 40,* n. 4 in vol. 2 of *Sancti Bernardi Opera,* 27.

discussion of solitude and concupiscence. Bonaventure makes a point of drawing out the symbolic meaning embedded in Christ's practice of solitary prayer on the mountains. Before choosing the apostles, Christ left the company of the crowd to find a quiet place suitable for prayer. He ascended a mountain where he passed the night in constant prayer, thereby, giving example to those who wish to live by the Spirit.[104] His ascent up the mountain is, itself, analogous to praying since prayer by definition is the ascent of the mind into God. It is also a reminder of the need of all who pray to withdraw from earthly concerns:

> ... *he went out onto the mountain,* namely by ascending,
> so he might demonstrate that prayer must be *elevated* and
> that the one who prays must be elevated from earthly
> matters because as [John] of Damascus says, 'prayer is the
> ascent of the intellect into God.'[105]

The mountain is a proper place for both constant prayer and contemplation because, suspended between heaven and earth, it extends in symbolic fashion from the depths of earthly matters to the heights of celestial concerns. When Peter, James and John ascended Mount Tabor with Christ, they separated themselves from the earth and turned their attention to the divine. As the experience on Mount Tabor indicates, the mountain is one of the privileged locations of divine revelation, provided those who ascend lift their minds continually to God in prayer and abandon the concerns of the

---

[104] *Comm Lc,* c. 6, n. 25-27 (VII, 140b-141a).

[105] "... *exiit in montem,* scilicet ascendendo, ut ostenderet, quod oratio debet esse *elevata,* et orans elevatus a terrenis; quia sicut dicit Damascenus, 'oratio est ascensus intellectus in Deum.'" *Comm Lc,* c. 6, n. 25 (VII, 141a).

world.[106] This ascent of the mountain presupposes the movement into solitude, for Christ had to leave the crowds before he could pray in secret. At the same time, it is clear that prayer in solitude does not necessitate physical aloneness. Bonaventure does not limit his reflection on Christ's prayer in solitude to a literal interpretation. Even though the apostles are present with Christ as he prays, he is still considered to be alone in prayer.[107]

Solitude is necessary to avoid the occasion of pride and to foster an atmosphere free of restlessness in which reverent prayer can be offered to God. A secret place is to be found far removed from view, thereby eliminating a prideful form of prayer which seeks human recognition. The crowds are to be dismissed because they are a source of disturbance to prayer. The apostles are permitted to remain with Christ because they approve of his prayer. Just as Abraham dismissed his servant and allowed Isaac to join him in prayer on the mountain, Jesus allows his disciples, as sons of faith, to accompany him while dismissing the crowds who would hinder his prayer.[108] For Bonaventure, Christ's dismissal of the crowd symbolizes the struggle against the images and phantasms of concupiscence which blinded the heart of the Jericho beggar to the light of divine wisdom. He makes this point in a homily based on Lk. 19: 46 where he says that the dismissal of the crowds is to be understood as a withdrawal into the inner reaches of the heart.[109] Such spiritual solitude is analogous to Christ's solitude

---

[106] *Comm Lc,* c. 9, n. 46 (VII, 231a). For an insight into the mountain as a religious symbol, see: De Champeaux and Sterckx, *I simboli del medievo,* 188-207 and Forstner, "Berg," *Die Welt der christlichen Symbole,* 87-89.

[107] *Comm Lc,* c. 9, n. 30 (VII, 225a-b).

[108] *Comm Lc,* c. 9, n. 30 (VII, 225a-b) and *Comm Lc,* c. 22, n. 51 (VII, 556a).

[109] *Dom 9 post Pent,* 2 (IX, 391a).

on the mountain, and it facilitates prayer by removing the cloud of images and phantasms which envelop the heart and obscure the divine light from view. Thus, just as Christ left the crowds to pray in solitude, those who wish to pray are counseled by Bonaventure to leave the crowds of concupiscence behind and enter into spiritual solitude:

> Our mind, therefore, must be cleansed from things of this
> type which indeed takes place by means of the solitude of
> religion; that is to say, by receding from the crowd of the
> senses, of the sense objects, and images. That which was
> well represented in chapter fourteen of Matthew where it
> is said the Saviour *ascended the mountain to pray alone*
> *after the crowd had been sent away.* This solitude of
> religion is, however, more fully attended to through a
> spiritual retreat into the interior things of the conscience,
> than through physical separation from the company of the
> crowd.[110]

The image of the temple, like that of the desert and mountain, is employed at various times in the context of solitude and concupiscence.[111] Bonaventure uses it to symbolize the universal Church, a place where God is encountered in prayer. The Church of God, like the Temple of Solomon,

---

[110] "Debet igitur mens nostra ab huiusmodi purgari; quod quidem fit per solitudinem religionis, recedendo scilicet a turba sensuum et sensibilium et imaginabilium. Quod bene figuratum est Matthaei decimo quarto, ubi dicitur, quod Salvator, *dimissa turba, ascendit in montem solus orare.* Haec autem solitudo religionis magis attenditur per spiritualem recessum in interiora conscientiae quam per corporalem separationem a consortio turbae." *Dom 9 post Pent,* 2 (IX, 391a). The reference to Matthew's Gospel is Mt. 14: 23.

[111] For a general overview of the temple as a religious symbol, see: De Champeaux and Sterckx, *I simboli del medievo,* 133-164 and Forstner, "Tempel und Kirche," *Die Welt der christlichen Symbole,* 350-352.

should be respected because God dwells within it. The avaricious, that is to say those who have surrendered to concupiscence, abuse the Church for their own monetary profit; therefore, they should be expelled from the Church just as Christ drove the money-changers from the Temple. The gift of grace, which had been received through prayer, is not a commodity to be bought and sold. As a gift of God which has been received in prayer, grace should be shared with others as freely as it has been received in prayer. Prayer then is the activity proper to the temple; for the temple is not a place dedicated to business, but, rather, to the imploration of grace.[112]

The temple, which is also symbolic of interior prayer, is entered only by those who are willing to take part in a purification from the power of concupiscence. Bonaventure's exegesis of the healing of the lame man at the pool of Bethzatha, found in Jn. 5: 1 ff., indicates the degree to which the entrance into the temple, that is into interior prayer, requires a struggle against concupiscence and facilitates the encounter with Christ. After his healing, the man was unable to find Christ as long as he remained in the crowd. Upon leaving the crowd and entering the Temple, Christ found him. Here, once again, a crowd of people represents the multitude of affections and evils impeding the relationship with the Lord. According to the *Commentary on John,* the crowd of affections must be left behind so that Christ can be encountered in the interior temple of prayer:

Jesus later found him [the lame man] *in the temple,*
namely when he [the lame man] had left from the crowd.
Augustine says: 'Situated in the crowd, he did not

---

[112] *De purif B.V.M,* 4 (IX, 650b). On the question of prayer and money, see: *IV Sent,* d. 45, dub. 4 (IV, 952a)

175

recognize Jesus, but afterwards in the temple [he did];' in which fact we are taught that whoever wishes to arrive at the vision of God should flee the crowd of his affections and human wickedness and approach the temple of inner prayer. Whence, in the ninth chapter of Matthew, he [Jesus] commanded that the tumultuous crowd be driven away during the resuscitation of the young girl.[113]

As the text above indicates, concupiscence is dangerous; it has sufficient power in itself to draw the heart away from God. In the face of this power, Bonaventure teaches that purity is needed to keep the heart oriented toward God instead of toward idols. Impurity, which violates the dignity of the body as the temple of God, floods the heart with shameful images. These images, generated as they are by concupiscence, become idols within the heart, rendering the temple unfit for the Holy Spirit. Therefore, both the heart, as the temple of God, and the exterior senses, as the entrance way into the temple of the heart, are to be guarded with the upmost vigilance.[114] When the senses are left unguarded, they may serve the forces of concupiscence and, ultimately, foster spiritual death. Bonaventure mentions this possibility in a homily drawn from life in Paris: just as everyone would close the

---

113 "*Postea invenit eum Iesus in templo,* quando scilicet a turba recesserat. Augustinus: 'In turba positus non cognovit Iesum, sed post in templo'; in quo docemur, ut, quisquis ad visionem Dei vult pervenire, fugiat turbam suorum affectuum et nequitiam hominum et adeat internae orationis templum. Unde in suscitatione puellae praecepit, eiici turbam tumultuantem, Matthaei nono." *Comm Jn,* c. 5, n. 26 (VI, 307a). The reference to Augustine is from *In Joannis Evangelium Tractatus 124,* tractatus 17, n. 11, *CChr* 36, 176 and to the Gospel of Matthew, Mat. 9: 24.

114 *De purif B.V.M.,* 4 (IX, 652b). Concerning the "guarding of the heart," see: Pierre Adnès, "Garde du cœur" in vol. 6 of *DS,* 100-117, esp. 111 in regards to Bonaventure's teaching. The theme of the "guarding of the senses" is covered by the same author in "Garde des sens" in vol. 6 of *DS,* 117-122.

176

windows of their homes if "death" was roaming the streets of Paris, so, too, the exterior senses must be closed and guarded lest they allow death to enter.[115]

The guarding of the senses is not merely an action taken up in fear of the power of concupiscence; instead, it is an integral part of the overall movement into interior solitude which closes the heart to concupiscence and opens it to God. According to the *Perfection of Life,* those who guard their hearts from concupiscence foster the centering of all their affections, thoughts, and desires upon God.[116] As a result, devotion is inflamed and their hearts enter into the house of God. It is here, in the house or tabernacle of God, that the poor encounter the Lord and are embraced by him with love:

> You should not relax the spirit from prayer, but for so
> long a time rise above by means of the ardor of devotion
> until you enter *in the place of the admirable tabernacle,*
> *up to the house of God.* And there, after your love in
> whatever way has been seen by the eye of the heart, and
> [you have in] whatever way *tasted, how pleasant is the*
> *Lord and how great is the magnitude of his sweetness,*

---

[115] *De S. Barth* (IX, 571a) and *De purif B.V.M.,* 5 (IX, 652b). In both homilies, Bonaventure quotes the text from Jer. 9: 21 :"Mors intravit per fenestras nostras." In the homily on St. Bartholomew, he adapts it to the congregation by referring to Paris. This is the classical text used in the Eastern and Western Church in the elaboration of the teaching on the guarding of the senses according to Pierre Adnès, "Garde des sens," 118.

[116] "Debet enim famula Dei tempore orationis cor suum ab omnibus exterioribus curis, ab omnibus mundanis desideriis, ab omnibus carnalibus amoribus revocare ad interiora et illi soli in toto corde et tota mente intendere, ad quem suam orationem dirigit. Et hoc consuluit tibi Sponsus tuus Iesus in Evangelio, dicens: *Tu autem, cum oraveris, intra in cubiculum tuum, et clauso ostio, ora Patrem tuum.* Tunc *cubiculum es ingressa,* quando omnes cogitationes, omnia desideria, omnes affectiones tuas in secretum cordis tui revocasti; tunc *clausisti ostium tuum,* quando sic diligenter cor tuum custodis, ut per nullas cogitationes tuas phantasticas possis in devotione impediri." *Perf. vitae,* c. 5, n. 4 (VIII, 118b).

may you rush into his loving embrace, with the pressed lips of intimate devotion may you kiss, so that completely outside of yourself, completely carried away into heaven, completely transformed in Christ, you will not be able to contain your spirit, instead you will exclaim with the prophet David and say: *My soul refused to be comforted; I remembered God and I was delighted.*[117]

3. 3. Summary

At first glance, Bonaventure's teaching on unceasing prayer may appear to be disjointed. This impression arises from the very nature of the many-faceted reality of unceasing prayer. Vocal prayer, interior desire, and exterior action are all included together under the broad heading of "unceasing prayer." A closer examination of Bonaventure's writings, however, brings to light a unifying thread found throughout his teaching on unceasing prayer. From his point of view, the unceasing prayer of the poor is the expression of their desire for God and their fierce determination to resist anything that would hinder the fulfillment of that divine longing.

According to Bonaventure, the Scriptural call to "pray always" finds a voice in what he terms "vocal prayer." He writes that the practice of vocal

---

[117] "Nec debes ab oratione spiritum relaxare, sed tamdiu per devotionis ardorem sursum ascendere, donec ingrediaris *in locum tabernaculi admirabilis usque ad domum Dei,* et ibi utcumque cordis oculo dilecto tuo viso et utcumque *degustato, quam suavis est Dominus, et quam magna multitudo dulcedinis eius,* in amplexus eius ruas, impressis labiis intimae devotionis oscula figas, ut sic tota a te alienata, tota in caelum rapta, tota in Christum transformata, non valeas cohibere spiritum tuum, sed exclames cum propheta David et dicas: *Renuit consolari anima mea; memor fui Dei et delectatus sum." Perf vitae,* c. 5, n. 5 (VIII, 119a).

prayer, which includes the Liturgy of the Hours, as well as other formal and less formal expressions of prayer, is both therapeutic and pedagogical. Vocal prayer is therapeutic in that it affects those praying; that is to say, it helps them to focus their thoughts and affections on God and what they are asking from God in prayer. It is pedagogical because it serves as an audible model of prayer to be copied by those wishing to learn how to pray. The therapeutic and pedagogical aspects of vocal prayer enable the poor to fervently seek out the Lord with the interior prayer of the heart. This intimate expression of prayer, which Bonaventure terms "mental prayer," is the culmination and end of vocal prayer.

Like vocal prayer, the desire for the good, which is ultimately a spiritual desire for the goodness of God, is another way the poor pray without ceasing. Such desire is incarnated not only in the specific words proper to prayer, but, also, in the attempt to do good and to live justly. For Bonaventure, good and just actions are the exterior expression of the interior orientation of the poor towards God. When rooted in charity, these actions become a continuous prayer, an unceasing cry for divine mercy. This orientation of the poor towards God, which both constitutes a particular type of prayer and renders all other types of prayer efficacious, finds specific form in the pattern of discipleship revealed by Christ. By acting charitably, the poor take to heart Christ's example and follow the same path he walked. Those who follow Christ and abide in him by following his commandments can pray with confidence. They are assured of receiving all that is needed for salvation because they are disciples of Christ.

The decision of the poor to follow Christ entails a continous struggle against the destructive power of concupiscence. In the battle with the corporal desires equated with concupiscence, the poor find encouragement by looking to Christ, for his own confrontation with evil in the Judean desert indicates how they can also fight against those desires which would lead them away from God. It is ultimately in the solitude of the heart, symbolized by Bonaventure at different times by the desert, mountain, and temple, where the poor are called to resist the forces of concupiscence and foster those spiritual desires which carry them upward into God, the source of mercy and fulfillment of every desire.

Chapter Four: The Way of Peace

The prayer of the poor is ultimately the yearning for the peace proclaimed by Christ and witnessed in the life of Francis of Assisi who: ". . . in every contemplation was sighing for ecstatic peace . . . ."[1] Bonaventure reveals in the *Journey of the Soul into God* his own profound longing for the contemplative peace marking Francis' experience on Mount La Verna.[2] In the same work, he describes the path along which the poor ascend into the peace of God in terms of prayer.[3] As Bonaventure indicates, prayer and the experience of peace are inseparably intertwined; for God's mercy, manifested in the grace poured into the hearts of those invoking him, finds its culmination in ecstatic peace.[4]

---

[1] ". . . in omni contemplatione ad ecstaticam pacem suspirans . . . ." *Itin*, prol., n. 1 (V, 295a). A distinction should be made between the contemplative activities such as prayer, indicated by the phrase "in omni contemplatione," and the culminating experience of ecstatic peace. The activities leading to ecstatic peace are described among other places in *Trip via*, c. 3, n. 1-14 (VIII, 11a-18b) and *Comm Lc*, c. 9, n. 47-49 (VII, 231a-232a). These activities are the grades of contemplation leading to the fullnes of contemplation which is spoken of in the *Journey of the Soul into God* as ecstatic peace. This distinction in the *Itin* is mentioned in Alfonso Pompei, "Amore ed esperienza di Dio nella mistica bonaventuriana," *DtS* 33 (1986): 6-7. For a selection of Bonaventurian texts on contemplation with bibliography, see: Jacques Guy Bougerol, "Contemplatio," *LSB* 40-41.

[2] "Cum igitur exemplo beatissimi patris Francisci hanc pacem anhelo spiritu quaererem . . . ." *Itin*, prol., n. 2 (V, 295a). On Bonaventure's and Francis' search for peace, see: Gilson, *The Philosophy of St. Bonaventure,* 66-80. On some of the difficulties facing Bonaventure as he undertook his pilgrimage to Mount La Verna, see: Johnston, "Une question d'équilibre: le rôle du désir dans la pensée primitve de saint Bonaventure," 75-77.

[3] The six meditations or considerations, which Bonaventure proposes in the *Itin*, fall into the general category of prayer since they concern the act of contemplation. Contemplation is, itself, prayer as he points out in the *Commentary on the Sentences: "Communiter* oratio dicitur, secundum quod comprehendit omnem actum contemplativae ad Deum relatum." *IV Sent,* d. 15, p. 2, a. 1, q. 4, concl. (IV, 368a).

181

This concluding chapter looks at the pathways of prayer which the poor ascend on the road to peace. They are outlined in the *Commentary on Luke* were the Transfiguration of Jesus on Mount Tabor gives Bonaventure cause to examine both the conditions and nature of the contemplative experience. The different paths open to the poor who wish to follow Christ up the mountain are mapped out by spiritually interpreting the companions of Jesus – the apostles Peter, James, and John – in the light of the Christian mystical tradition: the Augustinian "way of splendor" is represented by Peter and the Pseudo-Dionysian "way of love" by John. Although not mentioned by name, the third "way of sorrow and lamentation" is similar to the Eastern Christian way of compunction[5] and is represented by James (Jacob):

> . . . the *three ways of ascending* to the peak of contempla-
> tion are understood by means of these three people. For
> instance, in one manner the ascent is made by means of the
> way of *splendor*, and Augustine teaches this way of
> ascending, and it is represented here by Peter. The ascent
> is made in another manner by means of the way of *sorrow*

---

[4] The bond between the prayer for mercy and peace is seen in the *Itin* where Bonaventure describes a path that the poor follow in order to arrive at the ecstatic peace which Francis experienced on Mount La Verna. Peace is identified here with the contemplative state marked by divine wisdom. On the identification of peace with wisdom in the *Itin*, see: Edgar Sauer, *Die religiöse Wertung der Welt in Bonaventuras Itinerarium Mentis in Deum* (Werl/Westfalen: Franziskus Druckerei, 1937) 1-7. Bonaventure contends that Francis of Assisi invited everyone to pray for this peace with the words from Ps. 122: 6: " . . . *Rogate quae ad pacem sunt Ierusalem.*" *Itin*, prol. 1 (V, 295a). On contemplation, peace, and Jerusalem, see also: *Comm Lc*, c. 2, n. 56 (VII, 57b). In this context, it should be noted that the prayer for the peace of Jerusalem is also a prayer for God's grace. The poor cannot begin the ascent to God, which culminates in the experience of divine wisdom, without the assistance of grace; see: *Itin*, c. 1, n. 8 (V, 298a). Divine mercy determines both the beginning and end of the ascent because it is the principle of grace, as well as, of peace, see: *Trip via*, c. 2, n. 12 (VIII, 11b).

[5] For a study on the theme of compunction in the Christian East, see: Irénée Hausherr, *Penthos. The Doctrine of Compunction in the Christian East,* trans. Anselm Hufstader (Kalamazoo, Mich.: Cistercian Publications, 1982).

and lamentation, and this [way is pointed out] here in Jacob, and this manner is common to all who pray. [The ascent is made] in the third manner by means of the way of *love,* Dionysius teaches this [way], and it is represented here by John . . . .[6]

4. 1. The Way of James (Jacob)

The apostle James, whom Bonaventure identifies with the Old Testament figure of Jacob, represents the way of contemplation open to all who embrace the painful struggle of prayer. James, like Jacob, means "wrestler,"[7] and as the account of Gen. 32: 22-32 attests, Jacob received a blessing only after having passed the night wrestling in painful combat with a mysterious assailant. At the outcome of the battle, Jacob was given both a

---

[6] ". . . per has tres personas intelliguntur *tres modi ascendendi* in apicem contemplationis. Uno enim modo ascenditur per viam *splendoris,* et hunc modum ascendendi docet beatus Augustinus, et hic designatur per Petrum. Alio modo ascenditur per viam *doloris et gemitus,* et hic in Iacobo, et iste modus est communis orantibus. Tertio modo per viam *amoris,* et hunc modum docet Dionysius, et hic designatur per Ioannem . . . ." *Comm Lc,* c. 9, n. 49 (VII, 232a). This text refers to the three-fold way of purification, illumination and union outlined in the *Trip via;* see: Jean de Dieu, "Contemplation et contemplation acquise d'après S. Bonaventure," *EF* 43 (1931): 423. For a study of the *Trip via,* see: Jean Bonnefoy, *Une somme bonaventurienne de théologie mystique: Le 'De triplici via'* (Paris: Librairie Saint-François, 1934). The three ways are also examined in Werner Dettloff, "Das officium praelationis" in *Ius Sacrum. Klaus Mörsdorf zum 60. Geburtstag,* ed. Audomar Scheurmann and Georg May (München: Verlag Ferdinand Schöningh, 1969) 209-226. Dettloff notes (219) that the three ways are not mutually exclusive; they are different ways of accenting and illustrating the one way to God. Bonaventure also interprets Peter, James and John as representing the priestly, active and contemplative lives in *Dom 2 in Quad,* 1 (IX, 215a-219a).

[7] *Comm Lc,* c. 6, n. 36 (VII, 143b); *Comm Lc,* c. 6, n. 39 (VII, 144b); *Comm Lc,* c. 8, n. 91 (VII, 214b) and *Comm Lc,* c. 9, n. 49 (VII, 232a). On the interpretation of the name James (Jacob) as well as Peter and John, see: note 9 of *Comm Lc,* 8, n. 91 (VII, 214b). On the medieval interpretation of the patriarch Jacob, see: Paul-Marie Guillaume, "Jacob" in vol. 8 of *DS,* 15-16.

blessing and a new name from the departing adversary. Jacob became "Israel," which can be interpreted as "the one who sees God." As Gen. 32: 30 relates, Jacob named the site of his struggle, "Peniel," saying, "For I have seen God face to face, yet my life is preserved."[8]

Bonaventure sees Jacob's struggle as connected to the blessing of contemplation: the new name "Israel" is based on Jacob's contemplative experience of God; it is Jacob: " . . . who because of the contemplation of celestial realities was called *Israel*, that is to say, the one seeing God."[9] The interplay between struggle and blessing is underscored by the description of Jacob's way of contemplation as a mixture of human effort and divine grace. On the other hand, the Augustinian way, symbolized by Peter, relies to a great extent on human activity, while the Pseudo-Dionysian route of John arises primarily through grace.[10] Until Jacob was blessed, he refused to break off the battle with his assailant which demonstrates an insistent effort in prayer. This becomes for Bonaventure a concrete example of a form of prayer assuring God's grace:

> The second principal way of acquiring a blessing is the
> constancy of prayer; and this was expressed well in
> chapter thirty-two of Genesis in Jacob *wrestling with the*

---

[8] For an examination of the historical backround and theological/spiritual significance of the Peniel pericope with a bibliography, see: Lothar Ruppert, *Das Buch Genesis*, vol. 6/2 in *Geistliche Schriftlesung. Erläuterungen zum Alten Testament für die geistliche Lesung*, ed. Hermann Eising and Hans Lubsczyk (Düsseldorf: Patmos Verlag, 1984)121-128.

[9] " . . . qui propter contemplationem caelestium vocatus est *Israel*, id est videns Dominum." *De sanctis Angelis*, 1 (IX, 609b).

[10] *Comm Lc,* c. 9, n. 49 (VII, 232a). On grace and human effort in contemplation, see also: *Hex*, coll. 22, n. 24-27 (V, 441a-b). For a look at the relation between human effort and divine grace in Bonaventure's theology of contemplation, with reference to the question of acquired and infused contemplation, see: Jean de Dieu, "Contemplation et contemplation acquise d'apres S. Bonaventure," 401-429.

angel, to whom he said *'let me go,* it is *dawn'* and he [said]: *'I will not let you go, unless you will have blessed me'* and it follows that he blessed *him in that same place.* For indeed that struggle, by which a person acquires the Holy Spirit and the tears of devotion, is through prayer and lamentation.[11]

4. 1. 1. Tears of Misery and the Promise of Hope

A distinguishing characteristic of prayer in Jacob's way of "pain and lamentation" is the tears of compunction shed by those immersed in the painful reality of sin.[12] It is not a spontaneous outpouring of emotion, but, rather, a gift which is to be sought after in continuous prayer.[13] Bonaventure, reflecting a teaching also found in the Eastern Church, considers tears to be necessary in the ascent to contemplation: ". . . that is the duty of the contemplative soul, namely to devote [itself] to tears of compunction and devotion."[14] For Bonaventure, this teaching on tears was enfleshed in an

---

[11] "Secunda via principalis acquirendae benedictionis est *instantia precis;* et hoc bene significatum fuit Genesis trigesimo secundo in Iacob *luctante cum Angelo,* cui dixit: *Dimitte me, aurora* est; et ille: *Non dimittam te, nisi benedixeris mihi;* et sequitur, quod *benedixit ei in eodem loco.* Ista namque colluctatio est per orationem et gemitum, per quam acquirit homo Spiritum sanctum et devotionis irriguum . . . ." *De annun B.V.M.,* 6 (IX, 686a-b). On the meaning of the word "irriguum," which Albert Blaise identifies with "la grâce des larmes," see: "Irriguum" in Blaise, *Lexicon latinitatis medii aevi,* 510.

[12] On the role of tears in prayer, with reference to the teaching of both the Eastern and Western Church, see: Anselm Grün, *Gebet und Selbsterkenntnis* (Münsterschwarzach: Vier Türme Verlag, 1984) 25-39.

[13] *Dom in Sexagesima* (IX, 199a-b). See also: *IV Sent,* d. 14, p. 2, dub. 3 (IV, 341a) and *De annun B.V.M.,* 3 (IX, 669b).

[14] ". . . illud est officium animae contemplativae, vacare scilicet lacrymis compunctionis et devotionis." *Comm Lc,* c. 10, n. 67 (VII, 273a). On tears and the ascent to peace in the

exemplary fashion in the life of Francis of Assisi, the new "Jacob-Israel,"[15] who out of zeal for divine righteousness, weeped for his own sins and the sins of others.[16]

Tears of compunction arise during reflection on the misery common to all humanity as a result of sin. As Bonaventure sees it, reflection on this misery is bound to tearful prayer. He tells novices in the *Rule of Novices,* for example, to make the consideration of their sins and their rightful punishment as the starting point of a prayer flowing ultimately into a contemplative encounter with the Lord. Tears are an element of their reflection. Unless the novices descend humbly to look with tears at their spiritual state, they will never be able to ascend to the contemplation of God.[17] Bonaventure, likewise, reminds sisters, in the *Perfection of Life,* to begin prayer by reflecting on the manifestations of sin found in their lives

---

teaching of the Eastern Church, see: Hausherr, *Penthos,* 148-149. Peace is not identified by Hausherr as synonymous to ecstatic peace but, rather, as the prelude to the highest contemplation in which the heavenly mysteries are revealed and the faithful are transformed.

[15] *Itin,* c. 7, n. 3 (V, 312b).

[16] *De S. P. Franc,* 2 (IX, 581a). On Francis' weeping, see also: *Leg maj,* c. 5, n. 8 (VIII, 518b); *Leg min,* Lectio tertia (VIII, 570a); *De S. Maria Magdalena,* 1 (IX, 557a); *De sanctis Angelis,* 5 (IX, 626a) and *De S. P. Franc,* 2 (IX, 576b). On Francis' weeping and medieval piety, see: Keith Hanes, "The Death of St. Francis of Assisi," *FS* 58 (1976): 43-45.

[17] *Reg nov,* c. 2, n. 3 (VIII, 477b). The seemingly contradictory nature of the ascent to God is seen in the use of the words "descend" and "ascend". To "descend" by reflecting upon human misery is, itself, a part of the ascent to God. Bonaventure teaches: ". . . qui vult cum Christo in caelum ascendere, oportet, eum exemplo Christi primo descendere dupliciter, scilicet per *recognitionem* propriae *iniquitatis,* per *revisionem propriae fragilitatis.* Talis enim est qui ascendit dupliciter, scilicet ad *contemplationem* altitudinis divinae *maiestatis,* ad *obsecrationem* condescensionis divinae *pietatis,* ut *impleat omnia* interiora sua dono sapientiae et abundantia gratiae." *In Ascen,* 3 (IX, 319b). On the theme of descent and ascent in Bonaventure's theology, see: Jacques Guy Bougerol, "Ascensus" and "Descensus," *LSB,* 21 and 52, respectively. On Bonaventure's theology as "Aufstiegstheologie," see: Fischer, *De Deo trino et uno,* 23-67. On the ascension theme in general, see: Louis Beirnaert, "Le symbolisme ascensionnel dans la liturgie et la mystique chrétiennes," *EJ* 19 (1950): 41-63.

prior, and subsequent, to their entrance into religious life, as well as on the ramifications of their sins. In this reflection, which spans the past, present, and future, the past sins of omission and commission, the present separation from God, and the justified, future punishment become sufficient grounds for tearful compunction.[18]

Bonaventure refers to the recognition of sin and its attendant consequences in the *Triple Way* as being among the initial steps on the road to peace.[19] He sees this reflection on past sins and future punishment as having positive ramifications: it gives rise to shame, fear, sorrow, and prayer for divine assistance. Furthermore, it encourages the struggle against the vices of sloth, malice, concupiscence, and pride.[20] When speaking of this struggle against vice, the struggle against concupiscence is especially significant, for it is a specific component of Jacob's way of contemplation. As the *Commentary on Luke* points out, those poor wishing to ascend Mount Tabor with Christ must overcome concupiscence.[21] In this struggle against concupiscence, the poor can learn something from the example of Jacob, who was crippled as he wrestled with the assailant at Peniel. According to Bonaventure, the crippling

---

[18] *Perf vitae,* c. 5, n. 2 (VIII, 117b-118a). See also: *Trip via,* c. 2, n. 2 (VIII, 8a-b).

[19] *Trip via,* c. 3, n. 2 (VIII, 12a-b). According to Longpré, Bonaventure is referring to the peace of conscience which is a condition for mystical peace; see: Longpré, "Bonaventure" 1792-1293. Peace in the way of Jacob resembles to some extent the peace of the Eastern Christian way of compunction mentioned in note 14.

[20] As *Trip via,* c. 3, n. 2 (VIII, 12b) indicates, the desire for martyrdom is another step on the way to peace. On martyrdom and the ascent to God in Bonaventue's theology, see: E. Randolph Daniel, "The Desire for Martyrdom: A Leitmotiv of St. Bonaventure," *FSt* 32 (1972): 74-87.

[21] "Vel per tres personas intelligimus *tres dispositiones* necessarias animae contemplativae, scilicet *industriam, disciplinam* et *gratiam:* prima in Petro, secunda in Iacobo, tertia in Ioanne. Oportet enim, *intelligentiam* illuminari, *concupiscentiam* domari et *affectum* inflammari, ut possimus sursum cum Domino ferri." *Comm Lc,* c. 9, n. 49 (VII, 232a).

of Jacob's thigh is symbolic of the mortification of the flesh necessary for those wishing to deaden their own sensitivity to concupiscence.[22]

The tears of sorrow, which are evoked by the reflection on sin and accompany the struggle against vice,[23] signal the beginning of the contemplative search for peace and the abandonment of anything capable of obstructing or destroying the relationship with God, who is the source of true peace. Such weeping is certainly not a useless display of emotion; it is, in fact, a salient element of penance which reveals exteriorly the interior conversion of the heart.[24] When these tears find expression in prayer, they foster the efficacy of prayer.[25] Bonaventure makes this point in the *Commentary on Luke*. In regard to Mary Magdalene, who bathed the feet of Christ with her tears of penance, he writes: "And therefore the perfect penitent was devoting the *eyes* to crying so Christ might say to her that which is written in the fourth chapter of the Fourth Book of Kings: 'I have heard your prayer, I have seen your tears.'"[26]

For Bonaventure, the reality of human misery gives rise to the tears of sorrowful penance and forms a fertile humus for contemplation. Jacob, traveling along the path to peace in sorrowful, tearful prayer, shares the same point of departure with the poor, who yearning for peace, cry out for

---

[22] *Dom 2 post Pent,* 3 (IX, 364b) and *De S. P. Franc,* 2 (IX, 578a-b).

[23] *De S. P. Franc,* 5 (IX, 591b-592a).

[24] On penance and tears, see: *IV Sent,* d. 14, p. 2., dub. 1-4 (IV, 340a-341b); *IV Sent,* d. 15, p. 2, a. 2, q. 3 (IV, 373a-375b); *IV Sent,* d. 15, p. 2, dub. 11 (IV, 379b-380a); *Dom 3 post Pent,* 1 (IX, 368b); and *De S. Magdalena,* 1 (IX, 556b).

[25] *Comm Jn,* c. 11, n. 43 (VI, 402a).

[26] "Et ideo perfecta poenitens *oculis* serviebat ad lacrymandum, ita ut posset ei Christus dicere illud quarti Regum vigesimo: 'Audivi orationem tuam: vidi lacrymam tuam . . . .'" *Comm Lc,* c. 7, n. 67 (VII, 183b). The Scripture text is from 2 Kg. 20: 5.

God's mercy. Both are filled with sorrow before the profound suffering entailed in human poverty; yet, they both find common ground in an unshakable hope in God,[27] which already renders the poor rich in the present life.[28] It is not surprising, therefore, to see that Jacob's way is identified with the virtue of hope,[29] one of the theological virtues facilitating the contemplative ascent of the soul into God. In the *Commentary on the Sentences,* Bonaventure underlines the crucial role of hope in contemplation:

> Likewise, a theological virtue is a virtue which is of the greatest service to contemplation and which makes one to rise upward; yet hope is such [a virtue], because as the Apostle to the Hebrews says in chapter six, hope advances *all the way up to the hidden places of the veil:* therefore hope is a theological virtue.[30]

---

[27] On hope and the ascent into God in Bonaventure's theology, see: Jacques Guy Bougerol, *La théologie de l'espérance aux XII et XIII siècles,* vol. 1 of *Études* (Paris: Études Augustiniennes, 1985) 263-277, esp. 276-277 on hope and poverty; Jean Pierre Rézette, "L'espérance, vertu du pauvre, selon S. Bonaventure," in vol. 2 of *La speranza. Atti del Congresso promosso dal Pontificio Ateneo "Antonianum" 30 maggio-2 giugno 1982,* ed. Bruno Giordani (Roma: Ed. Antonianum, 1984) 357-380, esp. 376-380; Cornelio del Zotto, "Gesù Cristo senso e speranza della storia in San Bonaventura," vol. 2 of *La speranza,* 483- 547, esp. 531-537 and Schalück, "Armut und Heil. Die theologischen Implikationen des Armutsgedankens bei Bonaventura," 682-683.

[28] *Comm Lc,* c. 12, n. 31 (VII, 318b-319a).

[29] "Per *tres* autem *personas assumtas* dantur intelligi *tres virtutes* ad contemplandum necessariae, scilicet *fides, spes, caritas . . . spes* [is signified] per Iacobum luctatorem . . .." *Comm Lc,* c. 9, n. 49 (VII, 232a). On Jacob and hope, see also: *Dom II in Quad,* 1 (IX, 218b).

[30] "Item, virtus, quae maxime subservit contemplationi et facit sursum tendere, est virtus theologica; sed spes est huiusmodi, quoniam, sicut dicit Apostolus ad Hebraeos sexto, spes incedit *usque ad interiora velaminis:* ergo spes est virtus theologica." *III Sent,* d. 26, a. 1, q. 3, fund. 3 (III, 560b-561a). See also: *III Sent,* d. 26, a. 2, q. 4, concl. ad 3 (III, 577b) and *Hex,* coll. 18, n. 15 (V, 417a).

A further insight into Bonaventure's understanding of hope, which he considers to be a most essential virtue in the contemplative ascent to God,[31] is found in the *Commentary on the Sentences* where the object of hope is described as the great, good things which God has promised. In explaining the dynamic of hope, Bonaventure draws from human experience to make the point that hope begins with trust, which in turn engenders expectation. People are mistaken when they look to trust another who is a questionable source of support. The only one who can withstand the test of trust is God, who is most powerful and generous. Those who, like the patriarch Abraham, put their trust in God, should, likewise, expect great things from God.[32]

Hope, like the other two theological virtues of faith and love, plays a particular role in the contemplative ascent into God.[33] Like an unmovable stone, hope offers a steady foothold to the unstable soul, thereby, enabling it to reach out for spiritual gifts which go far beyond the horizons of human expectation. Just as faith brings about assent to the first Truth, and love brings adherence to the highest Good, so hope engenders a complete trust and resting in God, who is the source of the highest and greatest liberality. As the soul reaches out[34] in the expectation of God's generosity, it is raised above

---

[31] "Item, licet omnes virtutes gratuitae quodam modo elevent mentem, et hoc maxime faciant virtutes theologicae; elevatio tamen et erectio ipsius animi propriissime competit ipsi spei . . . ." *III Sent,* d. 26, a. 2, q. 4, fund. 5 (III, 576a).

[32] *III Sent,* d. 26, a. 2, q. 4, concl. (III, 577a).

[33] *Brev,* p. 5, c. 4 (V, 256b).

[34] This "reaching out" proper to hope is defined by Bonaventure as "tentio." Just as "visio" belongs to faith and "dilectio" to love, "tentio" belongs to hope; see: *III Sent,* d. 26, a. 1, q. 3, concl. (III, 561b-562a); *III Sent,* d. 26, a. 2, q. 5, concl. (III, 580a); *III Sent,* d. 31, a. 2, q. 2, concl. (III, 684b-685a); *IV Sent,* d. 4, p. 2, a. 2, q. 2, fund. 4 (IV, 114a) and *IV Sent,* d. 49, p. 1, au., q. 5, concl. (IV, 1009a-b). On "tentio," "visio" and "dilectio" as constituent elements of contemplation, see: *II Sent,* d. 9, praenota (II, 240b).

itself and made acceptable to God.[35] The ultimate fulfillment of hope is found not in any specific divine gift, but in God, the source of all good things: "... all the things which hope itself expects, not only does it expect to receive *from God;* but, indeed, it [hope] expects to obtain those things *in God himself,* so that by possessing God, it may possess every good."[36]

4. 1. 2. Ascension and Intercession

Jacob's way of painful struggle in prayer is shared by all of humanity weighted down by the oppressing burden of poverty. Christ, as Bonaventure insists against the objections of some, also confronted the poverty of human suffering and sought to alleviate it by calling out for mercy in prayer. Yet, as the *Commentary on the Sentences* indicates, some would argue Christ never actually prayed; that is, if prayer is understood according to the classical definition of John of Damascus as the ascent of the intellect into God. How could the Lord have prayed, it is asked, if he was continuously united with the Father during his days in the flesh? There would have been no ascent of the intellect in his case because it was always present to the Father.[37]

Bonaventure affirms the reality of Christ's prayer by making a distinction between the ascent of the intellect seen in the prayer for mercy, which includes the attempt to alleviate misery, and prayer as the speculative

---

[35] *III Sent,* d. 26, a. 1, q. 1, concl. (III, 556b).

[36] "... ipsa spes omnia quae exspectat, non solum exspectat *a Deo,* sed etiam exspectat illa obtinere *in ipso Deo,* ut habendo Deum habeat omne bonum." *III Sent,* d. 26, a. 1, q. 2, concl. (III, 559b). See also: *III Sent,* d. 26, a. 1, q. 1, concl. ad 5 (III, 557b) and *III Sent,* d. 26, a. 1, q. 3, concl. ad 3 and 4 (III, 562b).

[37] *III Sent,* d. 17, a, 2, q. 1, con. 3 (III, 371a). This argument and the following response also appear in *De orat,* membrum 1, a. 1, resp., 671b.

reflection on Creation leading to the Creator. While on earth, Christ enjoyed the beatific vision; therefore, he did not pray in the strict sense. Although he withdrew at times to pray, he was not obliged to follow the path of speculative prayer, which leads through nature from Creation to the Creator.[38] On the other hand, he prayed in the broad sense when seeking to relieve misery and by raising his voice in a plea for mercy:

> In regard to that which is objected, that prayer according to [John of] Damascus is the ascent of the intellect into God; it should be stated that the *ascent* is able to be spoken of *broadly* or *strictly*. According to how it is understood *broadly*, the intellect can be said to thus ascend into God when it is carried into him who is above itself by imploring mercy, which is *above itself*, or by alleviating the misery, which is *below itself;* and by understanding [the ascent] in this way, it fits not only us, but also Christ; and in such a manner falls under the definition of prayer.[39]

---

[38] *III Sent*, d. 17, a. 2, q. 1, concl. ad 3 (III, 372a-b). It should be noted that the text does say Christ prayed in the strict sense in that he withdrew in times of prayer from the active life to devote himself totally to contemplation. On the relation between the active and contemplative life in Bonaventure's theology, see: Bernardo Aperribay, "La vida activa y la vida contemplativa según San Buenaventura," *VV* 2 (1944): 655-689 and "Prioridad entre la vida activa y la vida contemplativa según San Buenaventura," *VV* 5 (1947): 65-97.

[39] "Ad illud quod obiicitur, quod oratio est ascensus intellectus in Deum, secundum Damascenum; dicendum, quod *ascensus* potest dici *large*, vel *stricte*. Secundum quod *large* dicitur, sic potest dici intellectus ascendere in Deum, quando fertur in eum qui *supra se* est, implorando misericordiam, quae est *supra se,* aut relevando miseriam, quae est *infra se;* et hoc modo accipiendo, non tantum competit nobis, verum etiam Christo; et sic cadit in definitione orationis." *III Sent*, d. 17, a. 2, q. 1, concl. ad 3 (III, 372a). The phrase "aut revelando miseriam, quae *infra se*" once again reveals the paradoxical nature of the ascent into God mentioned above in note 17. The downward movement, or descent, suggested by the attempt to "alleviate the misery below" belongs to the movement into God, as does the upward movement or ascent seen in the imploration of divine mercy "which is above." The

192

The raising of Lazarus is an example of Jesus' prayerful effort to alleviate human misery. Bonaventure's exegesis of Jn. 11: 1-44 in the *Commentary on John* underlines Jesus' compassionate love for Lazarus and his sisters while offering an insight into the intercessory nature of Jacob's way to peace. The news of Lazarus' illness induced Jesus to set out for Bethany; but, before arriving at the burial site, he was met by Martha and then Mary. Both sisters implore the Lord's mercy by insinuating that his presence alone would have prevented the death of their brother. Of the two sisters, Mary's prayer is the most efficacious because it is accompanied by tears.[40]

Mary's weeping, along with that of the others present, brings Jesus himself to weep tears of pain and compassion. He is shaken once again by the force of compassion at the entrance to Lazarus' tomb. Compassion draws Jesus to the tomb and moves him to raise Lazarus from the dead. His strong emotional response to the suffering around him is more than clear proof of

descent to alleviate misery is exemplified in the descent of Christ; he descended as God's merciful response to human misery; see: *Dom 20 post Pent*, 1 (IX, 430a-433a). One way for others to descend is to follow Christ's example of humility; see: *Hex*, coll. 22, n. 33, (V, 442a-b). Those who do not descend by showing mercy to others are not worthy to receive the Lord, who for their sake, descended mercifully from heaven; see: *Hex*, coll. 23, n. 24 (V, 448a-b). Love is the force behind the descent to others and the ascent into God; see: *Hex*, coll. 23, n. 31 (V, 449b). On the theme of ascent and descent in the mystical theology of another Franciscan, Rudolf von Biberach (with reference to Bonaventure), see: Margot Schmidt, "Gottförmiges Wirken als Vollendung der "contemplatio," in *Grundfragen christlicher Mystik*, 226.

[40] "Et subditur *fidelis* confessio: *Et dixit ei: Domine, si fuisses hic, frater meus non fuisset mortuus;* in quo insinuat virtutem Domini, ut soror prius fecerat; sed illa amplius dixit, quod adhuc resuscitaret, si vellet; et haec ob reverentiam tacuit et ob devotionem flevit et amplius Dominum movit, sicut infra patebit. In quo innuitur, quod Dominus magis audit gemitum cordis quam sonum oris . . . ." *Comm Jn,* c. 11, n. 43 (VI, 402a). Mary and Martha's intimation that Lazarus would not have died had the Lord been present can be termed a "prayer of insinuation." See: *Comm Jn,* c. 11, n. 13 (VI, 396b-397a). In his descripton of the prayer of insinuation, Bonaventure relies on Hugh of St. Victor's work *De modo orandi, PL* 176, 980-981. On the Franciscan school's interpretation of Hugh's prayer of insinuation, see: *De orat,* membrum 3, a. 2 resp., 688a-b.

his humanity. The fact that Jesus is touched so deeply by the suffering around him indicates he has already answered Mary and Martha's plea for mercy. Compassion in Christ becomes the synthesis of misery and mercy because it encompasses the embrace of suffering along with the effort to alleviate it.[41]

Bonaventure notes that it is human misery, signified in the death of Lazarus, which gives rise to Jesus' weeping.[42] Jesus' alleviating of this manifestation of suffering is in full accord with the will of the Father. When Jesus prays in thanksgiving at the tomb of Lazarus for the wonder which is about to take place, he does not ask for the power to raise his friend from the dead. Such a prayer would suggest that he was inferior to the Father, or that his prayer might not be heard. Instead, he gives thanks that his prayer has been heard; he knows the Father hears him because they are one in all their works.[43]

The extent of Jesus' compassionate attempt to enter into the depths of human suffering is definitively revealed to the world in the Paschal Mystery. At the close of his public ministry, Jesus is described as troubled by the coming hour of suffering; he chooses, however, not to pray that he be freed from suffering, but, instead, that the Father's name be made known through the Passion to the entire world.[44] In the Garden of Gethsemane, he showed his

---

[41] *Comm Jn,* c. 11, n. 46-51 (VI, 402b-403b).

[42] *Comm Jn,* c. 11, n. 57, resp. (VI, 404b) and *Lig vit,* fr. 4, n. 14 (VIII, 74b). In these texts, Bonaventure emphasizes that Jesus cried because Lazarus' death is symbolic of human misery. In a homily on Mary Magdalene, however, he underlines Jesus' personal sorrow and love for his friend Lazarus. Jesus' compassion serves as a model for those called to suffer with others in their time of corporal and spiritual need: "Sumus enim nos homines, debemus compati unus alii, tam infirmitati spirituali quam corporali." *De S. Maria Magdalena,* 1 (IX, 557a)

[43] *Comm Jn,* c. 11, n. 54-55 (VI, 404a) and *Comm Jn,* c. 11, n. 58, resp. (VI, 405a).

[44] *Comm Jn,* c. 12, n. 39-40 (VI, 418b).

own fears in prayer as he was confronted by the stark reality of approaching death. His example of suffering in prayer discloses his compassion and encourages the poor to prayerfully deepen the virtues of faith, hope and love in their own lives.[45] As high priest, he intercedes from the Cross with tearful prayer for the welfare of his people and consummates this desire with his own sacrifice.[46] While suffering on the Cross, Christ reveals his merciful goodness in a prayer for peace offered for his executioners.[47] This exemplary, priestly prayer of Christ,[48] together with the promise of redemption made to the repentant thief, offers hope to those yearning for pardon and emboldens them to pray for mercy.[49]

After the resurrection, Christ continues to intercede for those who call out for mercy.[50] His intercessory prayer is shared by the communion of saints

---

[45] *Lig vit,* fr. 5, n. 18 (VIII, 75b-76a).

[46] *Comm Lc,* c. 23, n. 56 (VII, 581b-582a).

[47] "Cum enim ostenditur *benignitas* Christi, quod scilicet pro peccatoribus et etiam pro crucifixoribus suis passus est et pro eis oravit pacem . . . ." *De S. Andrea,* 1 (Collatio) (IX, 467b).

[48] *Comm Lc,* c. 23, n. 41 (VII, 576b-577a). On Christ's intercessory prayer as high priest, see: *III Sent,* d. 17, a. 2, q. 1, concl. (III, 371a-b); *IV Sent,* d. 11, p. 1, dub. 4 (IV, 253b); *Comm Lc,* c. 23, n. 41 (VII, 576b-577a) and *Comm Lc,* c. 23, n. 56 (VII, 581b-582a)

[49] "O verbum totius dulcoris et veniae: *Pater, ignosce illis!* O verbum totius amoris et gratiae: *Hodie mecum eris in paradiso!* Respira nunc in spem veniae, anima, quantumcumque peccatrix, si tamen patientis pro te Domini Dei tui vestigia sequi non abhorres, 'qui in omnibus pressuris suis nec semel os suum aperuit, ut aut querelae aut excusationis aut comminationis aut maledictionis sermonem adversus maledictos illos canes vel leviter diceret; quin potius novae benedictionis verbum, quale *a saeculis non est auditum,* super inimicos suos effudit.' Dic ergo cum multa fiducia: *Miserere mei, Deus, miserere mei, quoniam in te confidit anima mea;* si forte more confitentis latronis audire merearis in mortis articulo: *Hodie mecum eris in paradiso."* *Lig vit,* fr. 7, n. 27 (VIII, 78a-b).

[50] *IV Sent,* d. 45, a. 3, q. 1, fund. 1 (IV, 947a-b) and *IV Sent,* d. 45, a. 3, q. 1, concl. ad 3 (IV, 948b-949a).

who look upon the misery of those still on pilgrimage. Their desire to help those still in the world reveals the communal dimension of Jacob's way to peace. Although they have entered into eternal beatitude, the saints are, nevertheless, concerned for those in need of divine assistance. The prayer of the blessed, like that of Christ, constitutes an ascent of the intellect into God because it seeks divine mercy for the sake of alleviating human misery.[51] The Mother of God is the preferred intercessor[52] among the blessed because of her compassion and decisive role in salvation history. She is the Mother of Mercy, looking with love upon those who suffer, interceding for them, and providing a sure sanctuary for them in time of distress.

---

[51] On the intercession of the saints, see: *IV Sent,* d. 45, a. 3, q. 1-3 (IV, 947a-951b). A difference between the intercession of the saints and Christ is seen in that the saints only ask for help to alleviate misery, while Christ asks both for help and alleviates misery; see: *IV Sent,* d. 5, dub. 4 (IV, 132b); *IV Sent,* d. 45, a. 3, q. 1, concl. ad 2 (IV, 948b) and *III Sent,* d. 17, a. 2, q. 1, concl. ad 1 (III, 371b) and ad 4 (III, 372b). The definiton applied to the intercessory prayer of the saints is the same one found in regard to the general prayer for mercy: they both are considered as the "ascensus intellectus in Deum," see: *III Sent,* d. 27, a. 2, q. 1, concl. ad 3 (III, 372a-b) and *IV Sent,* d. 45, a. 3, q. 1, concl. ad 2 (IV, 948b). The prayer of the saints for those still in the world indicates that Jacob's way of prayer reaches beyond the present peace of contemplation to include the future enjoyment of eternal beatitude with God in the communion of saints. Jacob's prayer for mercy is "viae et patriae;" see: *IV Sent,* d. 45, a. 3, q. 1, concl. ad 2 (IV, 948b).

[52] On Mary's intercessory role, see: *IV Sent,* d. 5, dub. 4 (IV, 132b); *De donis,* coll. 7, n. 3 (V, 489b-490a); *Comm Jn,* c. 2, n. 13 (VI, 271a); *Coll Jn,* coll. 53, n. 4 (VI, 603a); *Comm Lc,* c. 1, n. 45 (VII, 22a); *Comm Lc,* c. 1, n. 70 (VII, 27a-b); *Comm Lc,* c. 1, n. 81 (VII, 30a); *Trip via,* c. 3, n. 2 (VIII, 12a); *Solil,* c. 1, n. 28 (VIII, 38b); *Dom 20 post Pent,* 1 (IX, 432a), *De annun B.V.M.,* 2 (IX, 665a), *De annun B.V.M.,* 4 (IX, 673b), *De annun B.V.M.,* 5 (IX, 680a), *De assum B.V.M.,* 1 (IX, 690b-691a); *De nat B.V.M.,* 2 (IX, 710b-711a) and *De nat B.V.M,* 5 (IX, 718a). The text *Comm Lc,* c. 1, n. 70 (VII, 27a-b) is of notable interest because Mary herself is considered to be like Jacob's ladder, a way of ascent into God. It should also be noted that Bonaventure refers to works attributed to Bernard of Clairvaux in all the homilies listed here as well as in *Solil,* c. 1, n. 28 (VIII, 38b) and *Comm Lc,* c. 1, n. 45 (VII, 22a). On the sources for Bonaventure's Mariology, see: Emanuele Chiettini, *Mariologia S. Bonaventurae* (Romae: Officium Libri Catholici, 1941). On intercessory prayer and the teaching of the early church, see: Gerhard Ludwig Müller, *Gemeinschaft und Verehrung der Heiligen. Geschichtlich-systematische Grundlegung der Hagiologie* (Freiburg: Herder, 1986) 249-259. On the intercession of Mary and the saints in medieval theology, see: Jaroslav Pelikan, *The Growth of Medieval Theology (600-1300)* in vol. 3 of *The Christian Tradition. A History of the Development of Doctrine* (Chicago: The University of Chicago Press, 1978) 173-176.

Bonaventure considers the intercession of the blessed to be an integral dimension of the ascent to divine peace.[53] He sets out on his own personal search for peace in the *Journey of the Soul into God* with a prayerful acknowledgment of this fundamental role of intercessory prayer: he requests the intercession of the Mother of God and Francis of Assisi[54] so that he, and all those willing to imitate Francis, the new "Jacob-Israel,"[55] might also be led through divine assistance into the way of peace:

> In the beginning I invoke the First Beginning, from whom all illuminations descend as *from the Father of Lights* from whom there is *every good and perfect gift,* namely the Eternal Father through his Son, our Lord Jesus Christ so that by the intercession of the most holy Virgin Mary, mother of this same God, our Lord Jesus Christ and the blessed Francis, our guide and father, *he may illuminate the eyes* of our mind *to direct our feet into the way of that peace which surpasses all understanding . . . .* [56]

---

[53] *Trip via,* c. 3, n. 2 (VIII, 12a).

[54] That Bonaventure turns to Francis to intercede for him is based on more than his own Franciscan background. As he writes in the prologue of the *Leg maj,* he experienced, as a child, the power of Francis' intercession. This experience was one of the factors which induced him to write his biography of Francis: "Ad huius tam venerabilis viri vitam omni imitatione dignissimam describendam indignum et insufficientem me sentiens, id nullatenus attentassem, nisi me Fratrum fervens incitasset affectus, generalis quoque Capituli concors induxisset instantia, et ea quam ad sanctum Patrem habere teneor devotio compulisset, utpote qui per ipsius invocationem et merita in puerili aetate, sicut recenti memoria teneo, a mortis faucibus erutus, si praeconia laudis eius tacuero, timeo sceleris argui ut ingratus; et haec penes me causa praecipua hunc assumendi laborem, ut ego, qui vitam corporis et animae a Deo mihi conservatam recognosco per ipsum, et virtutem eius in me ipso expertus, ... " *Leg maj,* prol., n. 3 (VIII, 505a).

[55] *Itin,* c. 7, n. 3 (VII, 312b).

4. 2. The Way of Peter

The prayer for divine illumination at the beginning of the *Journey of the Soul into God* introduces a second way of peace in Bonaventure's theology of prayer. It is symbolized by the apostle Peter and characterized by a form of intellectual speculation[57] leading the soul to a progressively deeper knowledge of God.[58] The name "Peter," which Bonaventure interprets like Jerome to signify "the one who knows,"[59] underscores the importance of knowledge in the ascent along the Augustinian "way of splendor,"[60] in which

[56] "In principio primum principium, a quo cunctae illuminationes descendunt tanquam *a Patre luminum,* a quo est *omne datum optimum et omne donum perfectum,* Patrem scilicet aeternum, invoco per Filium eius, dominum nostrum Iesum Christum, ut intercessione sanctissimae Virginis Mariae, genitricis eiusdem Dei et domini nostri Iesu Christi, et beati Francisci, ducis et patris nostri, *det illuminatos oculos* mentis nostrae *ad dirigendos pedes nostros in viam pacis* illius, *quae exsuperat omnem sensum* . . . ." *Itin,* prol., n. 1 (V, 295a). On this prayer and the ascent to God, see: Fischer, *De Deo trino et uno,* 33 ff.. See also: Michael Schmaus, "Die Trinitätskonzeption in Bonaventuras Itinerarium Mentis in Deum," *WissWb* 15 (1962): 231-232.

[57] When the word "speculation" is used in this section, it is intended, unless otherwise stated, in the contemplative sense described by Boehner: "The terms *consideratio* and *contemplatio* are practically synonymous with *speculatio* when occurring in the *Itinerarium.* Thus, speculation is not merely an intellectual activity, but an intellectual activity of the contemplative soul, and only as such is it a means of enkindling desire for union with God." See: Boehner, *Saint Bonaventure's Itinerarium,* 107, note 12.

[58] "Uno enim modo ascenditur per viam *splendoris*, et hunc modum ascendendi docet beatus Augustinus, et hic designatur per Petrum." *Comm Lc,* c. 9, n. 49 (VII, 232a). On the ascent of the intellect into God which is symbolized by the apostle Peter, see: Longpré, "Bonaventure" 1819-1823. Longpré describes Peter's way of contemplative ascent as "La contemplation intellectuelle." (1819). Bonaventure's understanding of the intellect and divine illumination is treated by Gilson in *The Philosophy of St. Bonaventure,* 309-364.

[59] *Comm Lc,* c. 9, n. 49 (VII, 232a). In his work *Liber interpretationis hebraicorum nominum, CChr* 72, Jerome says the name Peter means "agnoscens" (141), or "agnoscens, sive dissolvens" (147). Some readings (note 16, 147) also include "cognoscens." That reading is found in the same work of Jerome's in *PL* 23, 849.

198

the soul passes from the visible, material world through the invisible, spiritual world upward toward the Highest Truth of the Trinity. This manner of contemplative ascent, in which the poor consider the reflection of the Trinity in Creation, can also be described as the ascent "through the way of affirmation".[61]

Bonaventure teaches that the contemplative ascent along the "way of splendor" requires the disciplined and ordered use of the intellect if God, the Highest Truth, is to be known. Although the role of grace is in no way diminished, it is not accented to the degree found in the way of love taught by Pseudo-Dionysius. Peter's way is defined in terms of intellectual activity:[62] through the systematic investigation of the world, both within the human soul and outside in the realm of the senses, the intellect comes to discover the divine truths reflected in the cosmos. Discernment needs to be exercised together with intellectual speculation so that the intellect will remain firmly fixed on those eternal truths leading to illumination.[63] Presumptuous

---

[60] *Comm Lc,* c. 9, n. 49 (VII, 232a). Bonaventure refers to the Augustinian ascent in *Comm Lc,* c. 9, n. 48 (VII, 231b) and *Trip via,* c. 3, n. 11-12 (VIII, 16b-17b) For a treatment of the Augustinian ascent to God, see: Andrew Louth, *The Origins of the Christian Mystical Tradition. From Plato to Denys* (Oxford: Clarendon Press, 1983) 132-158. The classic example of Bonaventure's teaching on the ascent of the soul along the "way of splendor" appears in the *Itin.* Not suprisingly, the word "splendor" appears several times in this work; see: Jacqueline Hamesse, *Itinerarium mentis in Deum. De reductione artium ad theologiam,* in vol. 1 of *Thesaurus Bonaventurianus* (Louvain: CETEDOC, 1972), 72.

[61] Bonaventure describes the Augustinian "way of affirmation" in *Trip via,* c. 3, n. 11-12 (VIII, 16b-17a).

[62] Bonaventure says that in Peter's way of contemplative ascent: "Oportet enim, intelligentiam illuminari . . . multa valet industria vel scientia" *Comm Lc,* c. 9, n. 49 (VII, 232a). This indicates that Peter's way of illumination is proper to those who are drawn naturally to intellectual investigation; see: Jean de Dieu, "Contemplation et contemplation acquise d'après S. Bonaventure," 424. The phrase "industria vel scientia" is described as "la recherche naturelle de l'espirit" by Longpré; see: Longpré, "Bonaventure," 1826, note 1.

[63] *Dom 14 post Pent,* 1 (IX, 407a-408a); *Brev,* p. 2, c. 8 (V, 226a); *Plant par,* n. 7 (V,

---

curiosity and careless research, which operate without the assistance of faith, should be avoided because they only blind the intellect to the divine splendors:

> For the thoughtless and presumptuous *seeker of the* [divine] *Majesty,* who as it were so relies on the darkness of common reasonings that he wishes to fix [his] gaze in the eternal splendors, *will be kept from glory* because of the darkness of imagination which the Sun of wisdom suffers. *He appears, however, to those* who, with the support of faith, raising themselves higher above their very selves in the transports of contemplation, contemplate God in a penetrating manner; whence Richard in the first book of On Contemplation [writes]: 'Contemplation is the unimpeded, penetrating look of the mind which has been raised up with admiration into the wonders of wisdom.'[64]

576b); *Hex,* coll. 20, n. 23 (V, 429a-b); coll. 22, n. 30 (V, 442a); and coll. 22, n. 39 (V, 443b). See also: Longpré "Bonaventure," 1821, note 3.

[64] "Nam praesumtuosus et temerarius *scrutator Maiestatis,* qui quasi tenebrositati pedestrium ratiocinationum sic innititur, ut velit figere aspectum in splendoribus aeternis, prae phantastica tenebrositate, quam Sol sapientiae patitur, *opprimetur a gloria. Apparet autem eis,* qui fidei adminiculo per excessus contemplationis altius se supra se ipsos elevantes, Deum perspicaciter contemplantur; unde Richardus de Contemplatione, libro primo: 'Contemplatio est libera mentis perspicacia in sapientiae spectacula cum admiratione suspensa.'" *Dom 14 post Pent,* 1 (IX, 408a). Richard of St. Victor's definition of contemplation is found in *De gratia contemplationis,* Liber 1, c. 4, *PL* 196, 67.

4. 2. 1. Grace and the Knowledge of God as Trinity[65]

Intellectual speculation without divine assistance is mere curiosity ending in sterility,[66] for ". . . grace is the foundation . . . of the penetrating illumination of reason . . . ."[67] Bonaventure holds that the highest truth, that God is a Trinity of Persons, is inaccessible to those who, like the ancient philosophers, lack the illumination of faith, for it is impossible for the intellect to ascend through creatures to the knowledge of the Trinity by the unaided application of human reason.[68] While philosophers can come to a knowledge of God, they, nevertheless, remain like ostriches; they have wings but are unable to fly.[69] The wings of faith allow the soul to rise to the heights of contemplation.[70] The grace of faith enables those searching with natural

---

[65] Bonaventure lists three levels of the knowledge of God which are determined by grace: "Dicendum, quod cognitio de Deo sub ratione veri potest haberi secundum triplicem modum: uno modo habetur cognitio de Deo per *simplicem assensum;* alio modo per *rationis adminiculum;* tertio modo per *simplicem contuitum.* Primum est virtutis fidei, cuius est assentire; secundum est doni intellectus, cuius est credita per rationem intelligere; tertium est beatitudinis munditiae cordis, cuius est Deum videre." *III Sent,* d. 35, au., q. 3, concl. (III, 778a).

[66] On the difference between "speculatio" as the activity of contemplatives and "speculatio" as "curiositas," see: Boehner, comm., *Saint Bonaventure's Itinerarium,* 107, note 12.

[67] ". . . gratia fundamentum est . . . illustrationis perspicuae rationis . . . ." *Itin,* c. 1, n. 8 (V, 298a).

[68] *I Sent,* d. 3, p. 1, au., q. 4, concl. (I, 76b) and *III Sent,* d. 24, a. 2, q. 3, concl. ad 4 (III, 524b). On the question of faith and the knowledge of God in Bonaventure's theology, see: Elisabeth Gössmann, *Glaube und Gotteserkenntnis im Mittelalter* in vol. 1 (Faszikel 2b) of *HDG,* 72-83 and Schlosser, "Lux Inaccessibilis. Zur negativen Theologie bei Bonaventura," *FS* 68 (1986): 83-98.

[69] *Hex,* coll. 7, n. 12 (V, 367a).

[70] *Comm Lc,* c. 9, n. 49 (VII, 232a).

reason to acquire a knowledge of God surpassing that found in their own philosophical investigation.[71]

The virtue of faith, which Bonaventure identifies with the apostle Peter,[72] is of primary importance in the "way of splendor;" it is the solid rock upon which the speculative ascent into God is built. As the foundation of the spiritual life, faith guides the intellect and opens the door to illumination: "For *as long as we journey far from the Lord,* faith is itself the stabilizing *foundation,* the guiding *lamp,* and the opening *door* of all supernatural illuminations . . . ."[73] Faith is also the light of divine truth which purges, purifies and sanctifies the poor.[74] In the practice of faith, seen in the assent to, and belief of, divine truth, the soul is ordered to God as the highest Truth and carried upward into the Trinity.[75]

As an assent to the articles of belief,[76] faith is considered to be infused, rather than acquired, when the assent is based on divine illumination and not on mere human motives such as respect or love. Those who are divinely illuminated voluntarily assent to the truth of faith and trust in God as the source of Truth.[77] By means of such illumination, their faculty of reason is

---

[71] *Sent III,* d. 24, a. 2, q. 3, concl. ad 4 (III, 524b).

[72] "Per *tres* autem *personas assumtas* dantur intelligi *tres virtutes* ad contemplandum necessariae, scilicet *fides, spes, caritas; fides,* per Petrum . . . ." *Comm Lc,* c. 9, n. 49 (VII, 232a). See also: *Comm Lc,* c. 8, n. 91 (VII, 214b) and c. 22, n. 11 (VII, 543a).

[73] "Est enim ipsa fides omnium supernaturalium illuminationum, quamdiu *peregrinamur a Domino,* et *fundamentum* stabiliens et *lucerna* dirigens et *ianua* introducens . . . ." *Brev,* prol. (V, 201b).

[74] *De purif B.V.M.,* 2 (IX, 643a). See also: *I Sent,* d. 2, dub. 1 (I, 59a-b); *III Sent,* d. 23, a. 1, q. 1, fund. 2 (III, 470a) and *Hex,* coll. 7, n. 13 (V, 367b).

[75] *Brev,* p. 5, c. 4 (V, 256b).

[76] On the articles of faith, see: *Brev,* p. 5, c. 7 (V, 260a-261b).

202

said to be raised above itself.[78] This does not mean, however, that they have arrived at a full knowledge of the Trinity. While the virtue of faith facilitates the assent to God in the articles of belief and acknowledges the reflection of the Trinity in creatures which are vestiges of the divine, it cannot readily perceive the image of the divine within the human soul without the help of the gift of understanding. [79]

The gift of understanding affords the poor a depth of knowledge far superior to that possible with faith. As Bonaventure says in the *Commentary on the Sentences* : ". . . a clearer and more excellent contemplation pertains to the gift *of understanding* than to the knowledge of faith . . . ."[80] The particular object of the gift of understanding is the eternal Truth as intelligible. In the act of understanding, the contemplative soul considers the divine truth present within rational, spiritual creatures and is able to perceive

---

[77] *III Sent,* d. 23, a. 2, q. 2, concl. (III, 491a-b).

[78] "Quidam autem assentiunt veritati fidei *propter divinam illustrationem,* sicut illi qui innituntur primae Veritati super omnia et propter se, sicut multi Christiani, qui caritatem non habent; et in talibus fides est *per infusionem.* Voluntarie enim assentiunt, concomitante divina illuminatione, illuminatione, inquam, quae rationem elevat in his quae sunt supra ipsam." *III Sent,* d. 23, a. 2, q. 2, concl. (III, 491b).

[79] *III Sent,* d. 35, au., q. 3, concl. ad 4 and 6 (III, 779a-b). For a discussion of this point with reference to these texts, see: Bonnefoy, *Le Saint-Esprit,* 180-181, esp. 181, note 1. It should be noted that Bonaventure also says: "Ad illud quod obiicitur de imagine, dicendum, quod est cognoscere animam secundum id quod *est*; et cognitio ista est rationis; vel secundum quod *imago*; et cognito ista est solius fidei." *I Sent,* d. 3, p. 1, au., q. 4, concl. ad 4 (I, 76b). Faith, in this context, most probably means the faith which is enlightened by the gift of understanding since Bonaventure stresses the superior role of the gift of understanding as opposed to faith in discerning the image and similitude of the divine in spiritual creatures: "Ad illud quod obiicitur, quod sicut contingit Deum cognoscere in imagine, sic et in vestigio; dicendum, quod non est omnimoda similitudo. In *imagine* enim, quia magis appropinquat, magis clare habet cognosci; in *vestigio* vero, quia multum distat, sub maiori obscuritate et aenigmate. Et quia ad donum *intellectus* spectat contemplatio clarior et excellentior, quam sit cognitio fidei; hinc est, quod ad donum illud non spectat cognoscere Deum in *quacumque* creatura, sed in ea, quae est eius *imago* et similitudo expressa . . . ." *III Sent,* d. 35, au., q. 3, concl. ad 4 (III, 779a-b).

[80] ". . . ad donum *intellectus* spectat contemplatio clarior et excellentior, quam sit cognitio fidei . . . ." *III Sent,* d. 35, au., q. 3, concl. ad 4 (III, 779a).

the trinitarian properties which they reflect as images of God.[81] The consideration of the divine truth equated with this gift is not undertaken for the sake of knowledge; but, instead, so that the eternal truths mirrored in the splendor of rational creatures can be believed more devoutly and loved more ardently than before.[82] Thus, the soul not only knows the truth in a speculative way, but to a certain extent, even delights and takes pleasure in it.[83]

The gift of understanding finds perfection in the purity of heart needed for a deeper knowledge of God. In the systematic consideration of divine truth, the gift of understanding purifies the heart, thereby, preparing the intellect for the simple contuition of God.[84] Contuition marks the height of contemplative knowledge which the intellect can acquire through the systematic reflection particular to the Petrine "way of splendor."[85] As the *Journey of the Soul into God* reveals, contuition is present at every stage of reflection as the intellect ascends from the vestiges of material creatures to

---

[81] *III Sent,* d. 35, au., q. 3, concl. ad 6 (III, 779b).

[82] *III Sent,* d. 35, au., q. 3, concl. (III, 778b).

[83] *III Sent,* d. 35, au., q. 3, concl. ad 3 (III, 778a).

[84] *Brev,* p. 5, c. 6 (V, 259b). On the meaning of contuition, Gilson says: "Intuition is just the direct vision of God which is refused us; 'contuition,' in the proper sense, is only the apprehension in a perceived result of the presence of a cause which we cannot discover intuitively; divine light therefore cannot be immediately perceived, although it acts upon us immediately; between it and ourselves there are intermediaries in the order of knowledge which have no counterpart in the order of influence or in that of being, and for that reason, in spite of all our efforts, we reach only 'contuitions' of God, in things, in our souls, or in the transcendent principles we apprehend." See: Gilson, *The Philosophy of St. Bonaventure,* 362-363.

[85] Concerning contuition as both the result and reward of the intellectual ascension associated with the gift of understanding, see: Bonnefoy, *Le Saint-Esprit,* 182-183. For an overview of Bonaventure's teaching on contuition, along with a summary of various scholarly opinions on the subject, see: Louis Prunières, "Contuitio," *LSB,* 41- 46.

the image and similitude of the soul upward toward the eternal truths of the Trinity.[86] When the intellect arrives at the point of contuition of the divine Trinity, it can go no further; instead, it is called to rest from all speculative labor.[87]

4. 2. 2. Speculative Prayer as Ascension

The ascent of the intellect along the "way of splendor" into the truth of God as Trinity is a contemplative form of speculative investigation. Bonaventure teaches that such speculation falls under the definition of prayer. As he writes in the *Commentary on the Sentences*, the systematic reflection on the splendors of Creation is, like Jacob's prayer for mercy, a valid example of John of Damascus' concept of prayer:[88] "In another way, the ascent into God means a new perception of God; accordingly, it means an elevation of our intellect to God, proceeding step by step from the consideration of Creation to the consideration of the Creator."[89]

Speculative prayer begins the ascent to peace in the midst of Creation; for Bonaventure, as well as Augustine, teaches that the visible world is the

---

[86] *Itin*, c. 7, n. 1 (V, 312a).

[87] *Itin*, c. 7, n. 6 (V, 312a).

[88] ". . . oratio est ascensus intellectus in Deum, secundum Damascenum . . . ." *III Sent*, d. 17, a. 2, q. 1, concl. ad 3 (III, 372a).

[89] "*Alio* modo ascensus in Deum dicit *novam* Dei considerationem, prout dicit elevationem intellectus nostri ad Deum, procedentem gradatim a consideratione creaturae ad considerationem Creatoris." *III Sent*, d. 17, a. 2, q. 1, concl. ad 3 (III, 372a). The importance of grace is underscored by Bonaventure's use of the adjective "novam" to describe the perception of God proper to speculative prayer. In ecclesiastical Latin "novum" conveys the idea of being "renewed by grace;" see: Lewis and Short, *A Latin Dictionary*, 1220.

privileged point of departure for anyone yearning to know the living God.[90] The desire to begin the ascent in the world is rooted in the conviction that all of created reality reveals the causative, creative wisdom of God[91] and shares an analogical relationship with Him.[92] The reality of poverty also dictates the necessity of learning about God through creatures; the intellect by nature is incapable of directly perceiving the spiritual light of God. Because of its material composition, it must depend on creatures who reveal, albeit, in a darkened, imperfect manner, the light of the Creator.[93]

The splendors of Creation serve as an appropriate matrix for speculative prayer because knowledge of God, like all knowledge of the intelligible, begins in contact with sense objects.[94] While it would be a mistake to remain fixed on the level of sense objects by treating them as if they were more than vestiges of the Creator, the intellect cannot ignore them if it wishes to be illuminated. As Bonaventure points out, a painting can be known in two ways, either as a simple picture or as an image. To refuse to consider the painting as an image is to remain fixed in the beauty of the object without being drawn to the source of the beauty. On the other hand, to attribute the beauty to the source is an excellent way of knowing about God because all noble properties observed in creatures speak of the Most High Creator.[95]

---

[90] On the Augustian understanding of created world vis-a-vis the ascent of the intellect to God and the Bonaventurian ascent found in the *Itin*, see: Sauer, *Die religiöse Wertung der Welt*, 39-42.

[91] *I Sent*, d. 3, p. 1, au., q. 2, concl. (I, 72a).

[92] *I Sent*, d. 3, p. 1, au., q. 2, concl. ad 3 (I, 72b).

[93] *I Sent*, d. 3, p. 1, au., q. 2, concl. and ad 3 (I, 72a-b). On this point, see: Gilson, *The Philosophy of St. Bonaventure*, 112-113.

[94] *I Sent*, d. 3, p. 1, au., q. 2, fund. 3 (I, 72a).

Francis of Assisi's appreciation of creatures as witnesses to the Most High God also stands behind Bonaventure's decision to begin the ascent into God amidst the beauty of Creation.[96] He points out in the *Major Life of St. Francis,* that the Poor Man of Assisi was neither deaf to the joyful testimony of creatures nor blind to their beauty. Attentive to God's glory throughout Creation, he delighted in creatures, raised his voice with them in prayer, and ascended through them toward the Beloved. In the midst of nature, Francis perceived the divine harmony reflected in the various qualities of creatures. Filled with spiritual joy, he presided over the cosmic liturgy of praise; he prayed with creatures and responded to their antiphons with his own. Like King David, he invited them, his fellow friars, along with all the rest of humanity to praise the Most High.[97]

Bonaventure writes that Francis saw all of Creation as a ladder

---

[95] *I Sent,* d. 3, p. 1, au., q. 2, concl. ad 1 (I, 72b). On the concept of beauty in Bonaventure's theology, see: Hans Urs von Balthasar, *Studies in Theological Styles: Clerical Styles* in vol 2 of *The Glory of the Lord. A Theological Aesthetics.* trans. Andrew Louth, Francis McDonagh, and Brian McNeil, ed. John Riches (San Francisco: Ignatius Press, 1984) 260-362. See also: Emma Jane Marie Spargo, *The Category of the Aesthetic in the Philosophy of Saint Bonaventure* (St. Bonaventure, N. Y.: The Franciscan Institute, 1953) and Karl Peter, *Die Lehre von der Schönheit nach Bonaventura* (Werl/Westfalen: Dietrich Coelde Verlag, 1964).

[96] On the influence of Francis of Assisi, as well as of Augustine, on the symbolic understanding of Creation in Bonaventure's theology, see: Werner Dettloff, "Die Geistigkeit des hl. Franziskus in der Theologie der Franziskaner," *WW* 19 (1956): 201-203.

[97] *Leg Maj,* c. 9, n. 1 (VIII, 530a); c. 4, n. 3 (VIII, 513b); and c. 8, n. 6 (VIII, 527b). On Francis' contemplation of God in creatures, see: Thomas of Celano *Vita Secunda S. Francisci Assisiensis,* ed. PP. Collegii S. Bonaventurae (Quaracchi: Collegium S. Bonventurae, 1927) n. 165, 163-165. Creation's role in Francis' spirituality is evident in his prayers, especially in the *Canticle of Creatures.* The text of this prayer, along with critical apparatus, is found in Eßer, *Die Opuscula,* 122-133. For a study of the *Canticle of the Creatures* with bibliography, see: Leonard Lehmann, *Tiefe und Weite. Der universale Grundzug in den Gebeten des Franziskus von Assisi* (Werl/Westfalen: Dietrich Coelde Verlag, 1984) 279-324.

allowing him to ascend to the Most High God.[98] This ladder, leading from creatures upward to the Creator, has three principal steps[99] which are revealed to those praying for the grace of divine illumination.[100] The first

[98] *Leg maj*, c. 9, n. 1 (VIII, 530a). On the symbolism of the ladder and the ascent into God in Bonaventure's theology, see: Bernard McGinn, "Ascension and Introversion," in vol. 3 of *SB*, 541. On the ladder symbol, see also: Bernard McGinn, *The Golden Chain. A Study in the Theological Anthropology of Isaac of Stella* (Washington, D.C.: Cistercian Publications, 1972) 93-97 and Forstner, *Die Welt der Symbole*, 573-575.

[99] ". . . mens nostra tres habet aspectus principales. Unus est ad corporalia exteriora, secundum quem vocatur *animalitas* seu sensualitas; alius intra se et in se, secundum quem dicitur *spiritus*; tertius supra se, secundum quem dicitur *mens*." *Itin*, c. 1, n. 4 (V, 297a-b). See also: *Itin*, c. 1, n. 2 (V, 297a) and *Hex*, coll. 22, n. 34 (V, 442b). On this three-fold division which indicates an Augustinian influence, see: Sauer, *Die religiöse Wertung der Welt*, 21-24. Bonaventure goes on to say in the *Itin* that the three steps should be multiplied to six; see: *Itin*, c. 1, n. 5 (V, 297b). The six steps are also mentioned in *Brev*, p. 5, c. 6 (V, 260a) and, with reference to Richard of St. Victor, in: *Comm Lc*, c. 9, n. 47 (VII, 231a-b). Concerning the six steps of the *Itin* and the six steps of Richard of St. Victor's work, *De gratia contemplationis*, PL 196, 63-192, see: Friedrich Andres, "Die Stufen der Contemplatio in Bonaventuras Itinerarium Mentis in Deum und im Benjamin maior des Richard von St. Viktor," *FS* 8 (1921): 189-200. On the historcal backround of both the three-step and six-step framework, see: Bernard Mc Ginn, "Ascension and Introversion," 542-549.

[100] *Itin*, c. 1, n. 2 (V, 297a). The *Itin* shows how Bonaventure uses prayer, not only to seek the grace of ascent, but also as a pedagogical tool to outline the steps on the path of illumination leading to peace. He begins by stating the importance of prayer in the ascent to God and then offers a prayer to that end: "Oratio igitur est mater et origo sursum-actionis. . . . Oremus igitur et dicamus ad Dominum Deum nostrum: *Deduc me, Domine, in via tua, et ingrediar in veritate tua; laetetur cor meum, ut timeat nomen tuum*." *Itin*, c. 1, n. 1 (V, 297a) The prayer opens the poor to an understanding of the steps of ascent into God: "In hac oratione orando illuminamur ad cognoscendum divinae ascensionis gradus. Cum enim secundum statum conditionis nostrae ipsa rerum universitas sit scala ad ascendendum in Deum . . . ." *Itin*, c. 1, n. 2 (V, 297a) The structure of the prayer itself indicates the steps of ascent. The following diagram based on *Itin*, c. 1, n. 2 (V, 297a) shows how Bonaventure uses Ps. 86: 11 as an outline for the three steps proper to speculative prayer. The diagram is found in Boehner, comm., *Saint Bonaventure's Itinerarium*, 109, note 2.

Psalm text	Our movement	In reference to us	Objects
deduci in via	transire per vestigium	extra nos	corporalia-temporalia
ingredi in veritate	intrare in mentem (imago)	intra nos	spiritualia-aeviterna
laetari in Dei notitia et reverentia	transcendere ad aeternum	supra nos	spiritualissima-aeterna

208

step consists in the consideration of external, visible, sense objects which are given the technical term "vestige," meaning "footstep." These divine vestiges, or "footsteps," are the discernible traces of God's creative action in creatures. They disclose God in a distinct, yet distant, way and are found in all creatures, be they material or spiritual. Creatures, as vestiges, display the ternary properties of causality attributable to God as efficient, exemplary, and final cause.[101]

In the *Journey of the Soul into God,* Bonaventure divides the first step of ascent into two meditations since divine vestiges can be perceived both through, and in, creatures.[102] The reflection of God is seen through creatures as the contemplative makes use of the exterior and interior senses to rise from visible things to the consideration of the power, wisdom, and goodness of God.[103] With the grace of divine illumination, the intellect sees that creatures everywhere reveal the glory of God; each creature stands both as witness and challenge to those not yet on the "way of splendor" lest they fail to join their voice to the cosmic song of praise.[104] Bonaventure, like Francis, was attuned to the voice of Creation and invites his readers to respond with a prayer of praise to the splendors of the Lord disclosed in the seven-fold qualities of creatures. Each quality speaks of God's power, wisdom, and goodness.[105]

---

maiestatis

[101] *I Sent,* d. 3, p. 1, au., q. 2, concl. ad 4 (I, 73b); *Brev,* p. 2, c. 1, (V, 219a) and *Itin,* c. 2, n. 12 (V, 302b-303a).

[102] *Itin,* c. 2, n. 1 (V, 299b-300a). See also: *I Sent,* d. 3, p. 1, au., q. 3, concl. (I, 74b-75a); *III Sent,* d. 31, a. 2, q. 1, concl. ad 5 (III, 682a-b) and *Itin,* c. 1, n. 5 (V, 297b). On the difference between the two modes of perception, see: Grünewald, *Franziskanische Mystik,* 90-92.

[103] *Itin,* c. 1, n. 10-13 (V, 298b-299a).

[104] *Itin* c. 1, n. 15 (V, 299b).

While the divine vestiges are weaved into the fabric of creatures, not everyone recognizes them; those who do, and praise God, are numbered among the wise, and those who refuse are fools:

> Therefore, whoever is not enlightened by such great splendors of created things is blind; whoever does not awaken from such great outcries is deaf; whoever on account of all these effects does not praise God is dumb; whoever does not perceive the First Principle from such great signs is a fool. – Open your eyes, therefore, direct the ears of your spirit, free your lips and apply your heart so that you may see, hear, praise, love and worship, magnify and honor your God in all creatures lest perhaps the whole world rise up against you. For because of this *the whole world will fight against* the senseless, but on the contrary it will be a matter of glory for the intelligent, who can say according to the Prophet: *O Lord, you have delighted me in your work and in the works of your hands I will rejoice. How exalted are your works, O Lord: you have done all things in wisdom, the earth has been filled with your possessions.*[106]

---

[105] "Haec autem consideratio [of creatures as vestiges] dilatatur secundum septiformen conditionem creaturarum, quae est divinae potentiae, sapientiae et bonitatis testimonium septiforme, si consideretur cunctarum rerum *origo, magnitudo, multitudo, pulcritudo, plentitudo, operatio* et *ordo." Itin,* c. 1, n. 14 (V, 299a). Boehner sees an influence of Hugh of St. Victor's *Eruditionis Didascalicae (PL* 176, 811-822) on Bonaventure's development of the seven-fold property of creatures; see: Boehner, comm., *St. Bonaventure's Itinerarium,* 114, note 19. For a comparison of Francis' prayer of praise, exemplified in his *Canticle of the Creatures,* and that of Bonaventure's seen in the seven-fold consideration of creatures, see: Cousins, intro., *Bonaventure,* 27-30.

[106] "Qui igitur tantis rerum creaturarum splendoribus non illustratur caecus est; qui tantis clamoribus non evigilat surdus est; qui ex omnibus his effectibus Deum non laudat mutus

Bonaventure comes to consider God in creatures by reflecting on the intellectual process by which sense data from the exterior world or "macrocosm" is apprehended, enjoyed, and judged by the soul or "microcosm."[107] The generation of similitudes by sense objects, which the soul then apprehends as they are impressed upon the sense organs, suggests the generation of the Son by the Father and his redemptive union with humanity.[108] Delight in the generated similitudes, insomuch as they are proportional to the five senses of sight, smell, hearing, taste, and touch, mirror the supreme delight found in Christ, who is the eternal similitude generated by the Father.[109] Finally, judgment, which discerns by abstraction why objects are pleasurable, requires the assistance of the eternal reasons existing in God and, thereby, points to God.[110] This process, by which knowledge of the exterior world is acquired, reflects the divine exemplarity seen in mathematics.[111] Numerical proportion, apprehended, enjoyed and

---

est; qui ex tantis indiciis primum principium non advertit stultus est. - Aperi igitur oculos, aures spirituales admove, labia tua solve et cor tuum appone, ut in omnibus creaturis Deum tuum videas, audias, laudes, diligas et colas, magnifices et honores, ne forte totus contra te orbis terrarum consurgat. Nam ob hoc *pugnabit orbis terrarum contra insensatos*, et econtra sensatis erit materia gloriae, qui secundum Prophetam possunt dicere: *Delectasti me, Domine, in factura tua, et in operibus manuum tuarum exsultabo. Quam magnificata sunt opera tua, Domine! omnia in sapientia fecisti, impleta est terra possessione tua." Itin,* c. 1, n. 15 (V, 299b).

[107] *Itin,* c. 2, n. 2 (V, 300a). The consideration of God in creatures, which Bonaventure proposes by means of a reflection on the way the soul apprehends, enjoys, and judges the sense data of the exterior world, is examined in Sauer, *Die religiöse Wertung der Welt,* 145-161. On the concepts of "macrocosm" and "microcosm" in Bonaventure's theology, see: James McEvoy, "Microcosm and Macrocosm in the Writings of St. Bonaventure," in vol. 2 of *SB,* 309-343, esp. 332-336 on their use in the *Itin.*

[108] *Itin,* c. 2, n. 7 (V, 301a-b). See also: *Red art,* n. 8 (V, 322a-b).

[109] *Itin,* c. 2, n. 8 (V, 301b). Concerning the five senses and the perception of divine beauty in the world, with reference to the *Itin,* see: Balthasar, *Studies in Theological Style: Clerical Styles,* 340-343.

[110] *Itin,* c. 2, n. 9 (V, 301b-302a).

employed in judgment, leads to God because: ". . . 'number is the principal exemplar in the mind of the Creator'. . . ."[112]

The second step in the ascent along the "way of splendor" outlined in the *Journey of the Soul into God*, is the consideration of the image of God first seen in the natural powers of the soul and then in the soul reformed by divine grace.[113] At this point, the exterior light of creatures is left behind and the light of the sciences is employed.[114] The contemplative enters within to seek out the divine image shining through the mirror of the soul,[115] and in doing so, ascends to a knowledge of God as Father, Word, and Love.[116] The soul, as "image," manifests God in a close and distinct way.[117] It is spoken of

---

[111] *Itin*, c. 2, n. 10 (V, 302a-b). Concerning Bonaventure's use and development of the Augustinian teaching on mathematics, see: Boehner, comm., *Saint Bonaventure's Itinerarium*, 119, note 11.

[112] ". . . 'numerus est praecipuum in animo Conditoris exemplar'. . . ." *Itin*, c. 2, n. 10 (V, 302b). Bonaventure makes use here of Boethius' *De arithmetica*, Liber 1, c. 2., *PL* 63, 1083.

[113] *Itin*, c. 3, n. 1-7 (V, 303a-306a). The second step in the speculative ascent to God, the contemplation of the image of God within the soul, comprises two moments in the *Itin*: the first is the reflection on the image of God seen through the mirror of the soul's three natural powers (memory, intelligence and will), and the second concerns the image of God in the mirror of the soul reformed by grace. Both movements "ad intra" are summed up in *Itin*, c. 4, n. 7 (V, 307b-308a).

[114] *Itin*, c. 3, n. 6-7 (V, 305b-306a). Concerning the sciences and the ascent into God, see: *Red art* (V, 319a-325b).

[115] *Itin*, c. 2, n. 13 (V, 303a) and *Itin*, c. 3, n. 1 (V, 303a). This stage of ascent in the *Itin* is examined in Sauer, *Die religiöse Wertung der Welt*, 161-183. Both the above texts use the verb "reintrare" in describing the ascending movement away from the exterior sense world of creatures into the interior microcosm of the soul. On the dialectic of ascension to God and the entrance into the soul, see: McGinn, "Ascension and Introversion," 535-552. Concerning the entrance into the soul and the contemplative ascent according to Augustine, see: Louth, *The Origins of the Christian Mystical Tradition*, 141-158; and with reference to Bonaventure, see: Russo, *La Metodologia del Sapere*, 86 and Bougerol, "L'aspect original de l'Itinerarium mentis in Deum et son influence sur la spiritualité de son temps," 320.

[116] *Itin*, c. 3, n. 5 (V, 305b).

[117] *I Sent*, d. 3, p. 1, au., q. 2, concl. ad 4 (I, 73b). For the principal texts and bibliography on Bonaventure's idea of image, see: Jacques Guy Bougerol, "Imago" *LSB*,

as an image because its natural powers of memory, intellect, and will suggest analogically the relationship of persons proper to the Trinity. Just as memory is the source of intelligence, so the Father can be perceived as the source behind the emanation of the Word. As the will binds the intelligence to the source, the Holy Spirit binds the Father and the Word as the mutual expression of love.[118]

Continuing the inward ascent, the poor come to an even deeper knowledge of the Trinity when they carefully consider the image of God in the soul reformed by grace.[119] Whereas, the triad of the natural powers of the soul reflect by analogy the relationship of the Father, Son, and Spirit within the Trinity, the soul transformed by the theological virtues of faith, hope and love discloses the intimate relationship of the soul itself with the Triune God:

> Filled with all these intellectual lights [which include the gifts of grace], our mind like the house of God is inhabited by divine Wisdom; it has been made a daughter, spouse and friend of God; it has been made a member, sister and co-heir of Christ the Head; it has been made nonetheless the temple of the Holy Spirit . . . ."[120]

84-86.

[118] *Itin*, c. 3, n. 5 (V, 305a-b). On this analogical relationship, see: Hayes, intro., *Saint Bonaventure's Disputed Questions*, 77.

[119] *Itin*, c. 4, n. 1-8 (V, 306a-308b). The deeper knowledge of God rests on the similarity of the deified soul with the Trinity; a closer resemblance to God is not possible; see: Boehner, *Saint Bonaventure's Itinerarium*, 110-111, note 3 and Gilson, *The Philosophy of St. Bonaventure*, 206-207.

[120] "Quibus omnibus luminibus intellectualibus mens nostra repleta, a divina Sapientia tanquam domus Dei inhabitatur, effecta Dei filia, sponsa et amica; effecta Christi capitis membrum, soror et coheres; effecta nihilominus Spiritus sancti templum . . . ." *Itin*, c. 4, n. 8 (V, 308a). See also: *Brev*, p. 5, c. 4 (V, 256b). Concerning the natural image (imago creationis), and the reformed image (imago recreationis), see: *III Sent*, d. 27, a. 1, q. 1, concl. (III, 592a). See also: Gilson, *The Philosophy of St. Bonaventure*, 198-207.

The relationship of the soul with the indwelling Trinity is anchored in the redemptive action of Christ, both revealed and interpreted, throughout the pages of Sacred Scripture.[121] Only the love of Christ can render the soul a divine "similitude,"[122] which is clothed with the theological virtues, healed through the restoration of the spiritual senses, prepared for spiritual transport, and conformed in hierarchical fashion to the heavenly Jerusalem.[123] Only the love of Christ, poured out by the Holy Spirit into the willing hearts of the faithful, enables those ascending into God to comprehend the mysteries of the Trinity.[124]

The ascent of speculative prayer arrives at the heights of contemplation in the *Journey of the Soul into God* when the soul transcends itself in a two-fold metaphysical consideration of God as Being and Good.[125] Bonaventure grounds both meditations in biblical revelation. The first meditation concerns the contemplation of the essential attributes of God, which were revealed in Moses' encounter with God on Mount Horeb. The second meditation treats the proper attributes of the Persons in the Trinity, which were revealed in the teaching of Christ.[126] The Old Testament

---

[121] *Itin*, c. 4, n. 5-6 (V, 307a-b).

[122] On the meaning of similitude in Bonaventure's theology, see: Jean Pierre Rézette, "Grâce et similitude de Dieu chez saint Bonaventure," *ETL* 32 (1956): 46-64.

[123] *Itin*, c. 4, n. 8 (V, 308a). The effects of grace, which Bonaventure here identifies with the love of Christ, are described in *Itin*, c. 4, n. 3-4 (V, 306b-307a).

[124] *Itin*, c. 4, n. 8 (V, 308a).

[125] *Itin*, c. 5 - 6 (V, 308a-312a). For a commentary on these two chapters, with reference to other works of Bonaventure, see: Boehner, intro. and comm., *St. Bonaventure's Itinerarium,* 27 and 126-129, notes 1-7 and 129, notes 1-4. With regard to metaphysics, see: 126-127, note 2.

[126] *Itin*, c. 5, n. 2 (V, 308b).

214

revelation of God as "He Who is" underscores the unity of the divine essence which Bonaventure interprets using the metaphysical category of being. God as Being Itself is first, eternal, most simple, most actual, most perfect, and supremely one.[127] As the *Schema* (Dt. 6: 4) proclaims: "*Hear, therefore, Israel, your God is one God.*"[128] To hear the testimony of Scripture and perfectly contemplate the one Lord who is all-good is to be blessed; it is to partake in the promise made to Moses on Mount Horeb for God is: "*all-powerful, all-knowing,* and *in every way good,* which to see perfectly is to be blessed, as it was said to Moses: *I will show you all good.*"[129]

The promise to Moses culminates in Christ's revelation of God as the highest good.[130] Goodness is the particular, exclusive name for God, which, when examined, offers an insight into the Trinity of Persons. According to Bonaventure, the good is necessarily self-diffusive, and the highest good must be most self-diffusive. While the good of Creation speaks of the Creator, it only faintly reflects the most self-diffusive good seen in the eternal processions of the Trinity. The highest good, as the First Principle, fully communicates substance and nature to another in a love of the greatest diffusion by way of the Word and the Gift.[131] A consideration of the proper attributes of the three Persons, Father, Son and Holy Spirit, lifts the soul in

---

[127] *Itin,* c. 5, n. 5 and 6 (V, 309a-b).

[128] "*Audi* igitur, *Israel, Deus tuus Deus unus est.*" *Itin,* c. 5, n. 6 (V, 309b).

[129] ". . . *omnipotens, omnisciens* et *omnimode bonum,* quod perfecte videre est esse beatum, sicut dictum est Moysi: *Ego ostendam tibi omne bonum.*" *Itin,* c. 5, n. 8 (V, 310b).

[130] *Itin,* c. 5, n. 2 (V, 308b).

[131] *Itin,* c. 6, n. 2 (V, 310b-311a).

admiration to the contemplation of the Truth.[132] When the attributes of God as Trinity and as Divine Being are compared with the coincidence of opposites manifested in Christ,[133] the soul is lifted again in admiration.[134]

The ascent along the "way of splendor" reaches the limits of intellectual investigation as the soul gazes upon Christ:[135] ". . . who is the *image of the invisible God* and the *splendor of [his] glory* . . . ."[136] Afterwards, the soul is called to rest from intellectual activity as the efforts of speculative prayer give way to the unitive power of love; for the most intimate knowledge of God comes only when the poor pass over with the Crucified beyond the horizon of intellectual speculation into the darkness of the consuming fire of the living God.[137] Since the passing over, or "transitus," is brought about only in and through prayer,[138] Bonaventure teaches the poor to pray with the words of the Pseudo-Dionysius to the Triune God for divine assistance:

. . . 'O Trinity, supreme essence, highest divinity, most

---

[132] *Itin*, c. 6, n. 3 (V, 311a-b). On the importance of admiration in the ascent toward ecstatic peace, see: Boehner, comm., *St. Bonventure's Itinerarium,* 108-109, note 13.

[133] On the coincidence of opposites in Bonaventure's theology, see: Ewert Cousins, *Bonaventure and the Coincidence of Opposites;* regarding the *Itin* in general, 69-95, and on Christ and the coincidence of opposites, 91-93. Cf. Schlosser, "Lux Inaccessibilis. Zur negativen Theologie bei Bonaventura," 76-79.

[134] *Itin*, c. 6, n. 4-6 (V, 311b-312a).

[135] *Itin*, c. 6, n. 7 (V, 312a).

[136] ". . . qui est *imago invisibilis Dei et splendor gloriae* . . . ." *Itin,* c. 2, n. 7 (V, 301b).

[137] *Itin*, c. 7 (V, 312a-313b).

[138] *Hex,* coll, 2, n. 32 (V, 342a). See also: *Comm Lc,* c. 9, n. 55 (VII, 234b). On the transitus theme in Bonaventure's theology, see: Werner Hülsbusch, "Die Theologie des Transitus bei Bonaventura" and André Ménard, "Spiritualité du Transitus," in vol. 4 of *SB,* 533-565 and 607-635, respectively.

optimal overseer of the divine wisdom of Christians, direct us into the supremely unknown, superluminous and most sublime summit of mystical communications; where new, absolute, and unchangeable mysteries of theology are concealed according to the superluminous darkness of a silence teaching secretly in the utmost obscurity which is supremely manifest; a superresplendent darkness in which everything also shines, and in a darkness which supremely fills invisible intellects with the splendors of invisible goods transcending all goods.'[139]

---

[139] "'Trinitas superessentialis et superdeus et superoptime Christianorum inspector theosophiae, dirige nos in mysticorum eloquiorum superincognitum et superlucentem et sublimissimum verticem; ubi nova et absoluta et inconversibilia theologiae mysteria secundum superlucentem absconduntur occulte docentis silentii caliginem in obscurissimo, quod est supermanifestissimum, supersplendentem, et in qua omne relucet, et invisibilium superbonorum splendoribus superimplentem invisibiles intellectus.'" *Itin*, c. 7, n. 5 (V, 313a). See also: *Hex*, col. 2, n. 32 (V, 342a). On this prayer in Bonaventure's works, see: Bougerol, "Saint Bonaventure et le Pseudo-Denys l'Aréopagite," 59.

4. 3. The Way of John

The Areopagite's trinitarian prayer for mystical knowledge[140] is the point of departure for the third way of peace symbolized by the Apostle John. The Johannine way of peace is the preeminent way of contemplation taught by Pseudo-Dionysius in which the poor follow the path of love and rely almost exclusively on grace.[141] Bonaventure's identification of John with the Pseudo-Dionysian form of contemplation begins with the interpretation of the apostle's name. "John," as he relates, means "the one in whom grace resides."[142] The particular grace in question is the theological virtue of charity.[143] The testimony of Scripture reveals the profound and intimate love

---

[140] Because of the vagueness surrounding the term "mystical" it would be helpful to offer a defintion from Louth's, *The Origin of the Christian Mystical Tradition,* xv. He says of the mystical experience: "it can be characterized as a search for and experience of the immediacy with God. The mystic is not content to know *about* God, he longs for union with God. 'Union with God' can mean different things, from literal identity, where the mystic loses all sense of himself and is absorbed into God, to the union that is experienced as the consumation of love, in which the lover and the beloved remain intensely aware both of themselves and the other. . . . the search for God, or the ultimate, for His own sake, and an unwilligness to be satisfied with anything less than Him; the search for immediacy with this object of the soul's longing; this would seem to be the heart of mysticism." Bonaventure's mysticism falls in the second category mentioned above, of lover and the beloved. His writings often treat the soul's longing for the immediacy of spousal union with God. On the spousal image in his theology, see: Balthasar, *Studies in Theological Styles: Clerical Styles,* 262, 268-270, 320-326, 355-360; on Bernard of Clairvaux's influence on Bonaventure's nuptial theology, see: 262.

[141] *Comm Lc,* c. 9, n. 49 (VII, 232a). On the role of grace in the Pseudo-Dionysian ascent, see: Louth, *The Origins of the Christian Mystical Tradition,* 175.

[142] "*Ioannes,* in quo gratia." *Comm Lc,* c. 8, n. 91 (VII, 214b). See also: *Comm Lc,* c. 9, n. 49 (VII, 232a). On Jerome's interpretation of John's name, see: *Liber interpretationis, CChr* 72, 146.

[143] *Comm Lc,* c. 8, n. 91 (VII, 214b) and *Comm Lc,* c. 9, n. 49 (VII, 232a). Bonaventure also idenitifies John with the cardinal virtue of temperance and, thereby, with virginity in

---

218

uniting the Lord with the Beloved Disciple.[144] The soul's mystical ascent to union with God taught by the Areopagite[145] also hinges on the grace of charity:

> This contemplation is brought about through *grace*; still *diligence* does help, namely, so one may separate oneself from everything that is not God, and from one's very self, if that were possible. And this is the loftiest union through love. And that is brought about only by means of love [as] the Apostle says: *rooted and grounded in charity you may be able to comprehend with all the Saints what is the breath and length and height and depth.*[146]

The gratuitous nature of divine love in the Johannine way of peace is underscored by Bonaventure's comparison of Peter's and John's relationship with Jesus: although Peter loved the Lord more than John, the Lord loved John more than Peter.[147] As the beloved disciple, John enjoyed a special

---

Comm Lc, c. 6, n. 36 (VII, 143b). According to Bonaventure, John's virginity was one of the qualities making him most lovable to the Lord, see: *III Sent,* d. 32, au., q. 6, concl. (III, 708a) and *Comm Jn,* c. 21, n. 52, resp. (VI, 529a).

[144] *Comm Jn,* prooem., n. 2 (VI, 240a); *Comm Jn,* c. 13, n. 30 (VI, 429b-430a); *De S. Ioanne Evan,* 3 (IX, 496a-b); and *De S. Ioanne Evan,* 14 (IX, 500a-b).

[145] *Hex,* coll. 2, n. 28-29 (V, 340b-341a).

[146] "Haec autem contemplatio fit per *gratiam*, et tamen iuvat *industria*, scilicet ut separet se ab omni eo, quod Deus non est, et a se ipso, si possibile esset. Et haec est suprema unitio per amorem. Et quod solum per amorem fiat, dicit Apostolus: *In caritate radicati et fundati, ut possitis comprehendere cum omnibus Sanctis, quae sit longitudo, latitudo, sublimitas et profundum.*" *Hex,* coll. 2, n. 30 (V, 341a). As this quote indicates, Bonaventure can use the terms "amor" and "caritas" interchangeably. On the different meanings of "amor" and "caritas" with texts and bibliography, see: Jacques Guy Bougerol, "Amor' and Jean Pierre Rézette, "Caritas,"16-18 and 29-32, respectively, in *LSB.*

[147] *Comm Lc,* c. 22, n. 11 (VII, 543a) and *Comm Jn,* c. 21, n. 52 (VI, 528b-529a). Cf. *III Sent,* d. 32, au., q. 6 (III, 706a-708b) where Bonaventure describes the mutually excellent, but decidedly different, relationships of love between Peter, John and Christ.

relationship with Jesus affording him a profound knowledge of the divine. Bonaventure states that because of his love for John, Jesus taught John and helped him to reach an understanding of the sublime truths concerning his divinity which no one will ever surpass.[148] The image of the Evangelist leaning his head upon Christ's chest denotes the depth of his intimacy with the Lord in whom all riches of wisdom and understanding are to be found.[149] The Johannine emphasis on both loving intimacy and knowledge is mirrored in the *Commentary on the Sentences* where Bonaventure, commenting on a text from the Areopagite, writes that the most excellent knowledge of the divine is an experiential knowledge revealed when the soul is united intimately with God in ecstatic love.[150]

4. 3. 1. The Experiential Knowledge of God

The experiential knowledge of God, which Bonaventure links with wisdom in the *Commentary on the Sentences*, is considered the most excellent example of knowledge because of the decisive role played by charity in the contemplative ascent. Although he teaches that all three theological virtues are crucial in the ascent into God, Bonaventure does say that charity is the most excellent in that it renders the soul a divine similitude through the

---

[148] *Comm Jn,* prooem., n. 3 (VI, 240b).

[149] *Comm Jn,* c. 13, n. 32 (VI, 430a).

[150] *III Sent,* d. 24, dub. 4 (III, 531b). The text in question refers to Ps. 18: 12 "Deus posuit tenebras latibulum suum" and is found in *De mystica theologia,* c. 1, § 2, *PG* 3, 999. It is also quoted in *II Sent,* d. 23, a. 2, q. 3, concl. (II, 544b). Concerning the ecstasy of love in Pseudo-Dionysius' theology, see: Louth, *The Origins of the Christian Mystical Tradition,* 175-177.

unitive power proper to love.[151] While faith and hope facilitate the union of the soul with God, charity alone brings the ascent into God to fulfillment; faith offers a vision of God as the Highest Truth, hope reaches out with trust to God as Most Generous, but only charity satisfies the contemplative's desire to embrace and cling to God as the Greatest Good.[152] The cleaving of the soul to God within the intimacy of the anagogical union affords the most excellent form of divine knowledge:

> But the knowledge [of God] in this world has many levels.
> For God is known in a *vestige*, he is known in an *image*,
> and he is known in the *effect of grace*. According to that
> which the Apostle says he is also known through the
> *intimate union* of God and the soul: He who clings to God
> is one spirit [with God]. And this is the most excellent
> knowledge which Dionysius teaches . . . .[153]

The knowledge of God in the anagogical union presupposes the virtue of charity along with the gift of wisdom because most of all it is an affective experience of the divine goodness. Bonaventure's position that the union of the soul with God is primarily affective is determined by the nature of love:

---

[151] *III Sent,* d. 27, a. 2, q. 1, concl. ad 6 (III, 604b) and *III Sent,* d. 27, a. 2, q. 1, concl. (III, 604a). On Bonaventure's theology of love, see: Zoltan Alszeghy, *Grundformen der Liebe. Die Theorie der Gottesliebe bei dem hl. Bonaventura* (Roma: Typis Pontificae Universitatis Gregorianae, 1946). Cf.: Enrique Rivera de Ventosa, "Amour personnel et impersonnel chez saint Bonaventure," *EF* 18 (Supplément annuel 1968): 191-203. On love in Bonaventure's thought, see also: Robert Prentice, *The Psychology of Love according to St. Bonaventure* (St. Bonaventure, N. Y.: The Franciscan Institute, 1951).

[152] On the cleaving of the soul to the good, see: *I Sent,* d. 1, a. 2, q. unica, concl. and ad 2 (I, 36b-37b); *III Sent,* d. 26, a. 1, q. 1, concl. (III, 556b) and *Red art,* n. 25 (V, 325a).

[153] "Sed cognitio viae multos habet gradus. Cognoscitur enim Deus in *vestigio,* cognoscitur in *imagine,* cognoscitur et in *effectu gratiae,* cognoscitur etiam per *intimam unionem* Dei et animae, iuxta quod dicit Apostolus: *Qui adhaeret Deo unus spiritus est.* Et haec est cognitio excellentissima, quam docet Dionysius . . . ." *III Sent,* d. 24, dub. 4 (III, 531b).

"For *love* means the cleaving of the affection with regard to the one loved. Whence Dionysius [says]: 'We call love unitive.'"[154] Consequently, love can be spoken of as an affective power bringing about the union of the lover and the beloved. This affective, unitive power of love, which is evidenced in charity, penetrates deeply into the divine mystery and brings with it delight as the soul cleaves to God.[155] The affective pleasure charity discovers in God is deepened by the gift of wisdom since the role of the gifts is to build on the virtues; wisdom enables the soul to more easily taste the goodness of the Lord.[156]

Wisdom is a fuller expression of the affective union begun in love and deepened by charity; as Bonaventure states, quoting a work attributed to Bernard of Clairvaux: "'Love advances into charity, charity into wisdom.'"[157] The hallmark of the gift of wisdom as the fullness of love is an interior affective "tasting" or "delighting" in the divine.[158] Although there is

---

154 "*Amor* enim dicit affectus adhaesionem respectu amati; unde Dionysius: 'Amorem unitivum dicimus.'" *I Sent,* d. 10, dub. 1 (I, 205a). See also: *I Sent,* d. 10, a. 2, q. 2, fund. 2 (I, 202a). For the text from the Areopagite, see: *De divinis nominibus,* c. 4, § 15, *PG* 3, 714.

155 *I Sent,* d. 1, a. 2, q. unica, concl. and ad 2 (I, 36b-37b); *II Sent,* d. 23, a. 2, q. 3, concl. ad 4 (II, 545b); and *III Sent,* d. 27, a. 2, q. 2, concl. (III, 606b).

156 *III Sent,* d. 34, p. 1, a. 1, q. 3, concl. ad 1 (III, 742b). See also: *I Sent,* d. 17, p. 1, dub. 4 (I, 305a-b).

157 "'Amor proficit in caritatem, caritas proficit in sapientiam.'" *III Sent,* d. 34, p. 1, a. 1, q. 3, fund. 1 (III, 742a). This text, which is actually from William of Saint-Thierry, is found in *De natura et dignitate amoris,* c. 2, n. 5, *PL* 184, 383. On this text, see: Jacques Guy Bougerol, "Saint Bonaventure et Guillaume de Saint-Thierry," *Ant* 46 (1971): 306-307; and on Bonaventure's teaching on love in light of the influence of Pseudo-Dionysius, Augustine, Bernard and William of Saint-Thierry, 313- 321.

158 *III Sent,* d. 35, au., q. 1, fund. 1 (III, 773a); concl. (III, 774a-b); ad 5 (III, 775 a-b); *III Sent,* d. 35, au., q. 3, concl. ad 5 (III, 779b); and *II Sent,* d. 9, au., q. 4, concl. ad 7 (II, 249b). On the affective experience of God and the spiritual senses, such as that of "tasting" as well as others, see: Longpré, "Bonaventure," 1832-1833. The eucharist offers the poor the unique opportunity to "taste" the Lord. Bonaventure says that Francis often

both an affective and cognitive element at work when the soul experiences the delightfulness of God, the element most proper to the gift of wisdom is without a doubt the affective. The cognitive dimension refers to taking hold of the the desired object, and the affective dimension refers to the union of the subject with the object; for the soul ascending along the Johannine way of love, the knowledge of God commences with cognition but is consumed in affection.[159]

The experiential knowledge of wisdom extends far beyond the speculative knowledge equated with the gift of understanding in the Petrine "way of splendor." Whereas, the gift of understanding considers God as Truth reflected in the mirror of Creation, the gift of wisdom delights in God as Good revealed in the interior of the soul; whereas, the intellect relies on the assistance of creatures to ascend into God, the affections are free to enter directly into the contemplation of spiritual realities.[160] The affective power of love plays a deciding role in determining the superiority of wisdom over and against understanding; the contemplative rises into a closer union with God through the influence of the affective dimension of wisdom than with the support of reason.[161] The knowledge of God in speculative contemplation should not in any way be denigrated; however, it can never surpass the

---

went into esctasy while tasting the sweetness of the Lord present in the eucharist: "Saepe communicabat et tam devote, ut alios devotos efficeret, dum ad immaculati Agni degustationem suavem, quasi spiritu ebrius, in mentis ut plurimum rapiebatur excessum." *Leg maj,* c. 9, n. 2 (VIII, 530b). The place of the eucharist in Bonaventure's spiritual theology is treated by Longpré in "Bonaventure," 1812-1814.

[159] *III Sent,* d. 35, au., q. 1, concl. (III, 774a-b); ad 3 (III, 774b) and ad 5 (III, 775a-b). See also: *III Sent,* d. 35, au., q. 3, concl. ad 1 (III, 778b).

[160] *III Sent,* d. 35, au., q. 3, concl. ad 1-6 (III, 778a-779b).

[161] *III Sent,* d. 35, au., q. 3, concl. ad 5 (III, 779b) and *III Sent,* d. 31, a. 3, q. 1, concl. (III, 689a-b).

unique affective knowledge of wisdom:

> To that which is objected, that the gift of wisdom is the most excellent [gift], it must be stated that wisdom, in accordance with it being the most excellent gift, has been named from *taste,* and not from *knowing,* and thus it includes charity. But wisdom, or rather *knowledge,* from which the Cherubim are designated, designates the knowledge of God, which even though it may be a most noble knowledge and ordered to the affection and, therefore, can be called *wisdom,* nevertheless, it is not as noble as love, from which is taste.[162]

Bonaventure emphasizes the uniqueness of wisdom's affective knowledge by speaking of it as a secret knowledge equated with darkness. As the poor are drawn into union with God, the powers of the intellect are darkened and the divine mysteries of theology are secretly revealed by the Holy Spirit to the affective powers.[163] Since the intellectual powers have been transcended, the contents of the revelation cannot be articulated in word; they remain secret, accessible only to those chosen by God to partake in such experiential knowledge.[164] Under the influence of the gift of wisdom, the

---

[162] "Ad illud quod obiicitur, quod donum sapientiae est excellentissimum; dicendum, quod *sapientia,* secundum quod est donum excellentissimum, est dicta a *sapore,* non a *sapere,* et ita includit caritatem; sed sapientia sive *scientia,* a qua denominantur Cherubim, nominat Dei cognitionem, quae etsi nobilissima cognitio et ordinata ad affectionem et ideo possit dici *sapientia,* non tamen est ita nobilis, ut dilectio, a qua est sapor." *II Sent,* d. 9, au., q. 4, concl. ad 7 (II, 249b). Bonaventure teaches that the angelic orders refer to the three acts proper to contemplation: Thrones refer "ad perfectam *tentionem,*" Cherubims "ad perfectam *cognitionem*" and Seraphims "ad perfectam *dilectionem;*" see: *II Sent,* d. 9, praenot. (II, 240b).

[163] *Hex,* coll. 2, n. 30 (V, 341b).

[164] *Hex,* coll. 2, n. 28-30 (V, 341a-b). See also: *II Sent,* d. 23, a. 2, q. 3, concl. ad 6 (II,

224

intellect is blinded by the intensity of the divine revelation and rendered incapable of the reflection previously identified with "the way of splendor." When the ray of divine light overwhelms the intellectual powers, it leaves an impenetrable darkness in its wake; however, in a paradoxical fashion, the darkness itself is nothing less than the supreme illumination of the soul:

> What is this, that this ray *blinds* when it ought rather to *illuminate?* But this blindness is the highest illumination because it is in the loftiness of the mind beyond the investigation of the human intellect. There the intellect darkens because it is not able to investigate because it transcends all investigative power. There is therefore there an inaccessible darkness which, nevertheless, illumines the minds which already have lost [their] curious investigations. And this is what the Lord has said, that he dwells *in a cloud;* and in the Psalm: that *he has made the darkness his hiding place.*[165]

The illuminating darkness of the secret encounter with God is not marked by fear, but, rather, with an intense spiritual delight, which as Bonaventure writes in the *Breviloquium* ". . . no one knows except the one who experiences [it] . . . ."[166] As the soul is drawn into God, it is overcome

---

546a); *Brev*, p. 5, c. 6 (V, 260a) and *Comm Jn,* c. 1, n. 43 (VI, 256a).

[165] "Sed quid est, quod iste radius *excaecat*, cum potius deberet *illuminare?* Sed ista excaecatio est summa illuminatio, quia est in sublimitate mentis ultra humani intellectus investigationem. Ibi intellectus *caligat*, quia non potest investigare, quia transcendit omnem potentiam investigativam. Est ergo ibi caligo inaccessibilis, quae tamen illuminat mentes, quae perdiderunt investigationes curiosas. Et hoc est quod dixit Dominus, se habitare *in nebula;* et in Psalmo: *Posuit tenebras latibulum suum." Hex*, coll. 20, n. 11 (V, 427a).

[166] ". . . nemo novit nisi qui probat . . . ." *Brev*, p. 5, c. 6 (V, 260a).

with delight and carried out of itself in ecstatic love.[167] In ecstasy the soul is so imbued with the consolation of the Spirit that it is "inebriated."[168] Such joy and delight is a clear witness to the union of the contemplative with God symbolized by the biblical imagery borrowed from the Old Testament *Song of Solomon*.[169] The soul exults with joy because it has arrived at the desired end of prayer:[170] the intimate encounter between the Bride and the Bridegroom, between the soul and Christ.

---

[167] *Hex*, col. 22, n. 39 (V, 443b). See also: *III Sent*, d. 24, dub. 4 (III, 531b) and *Perf vitae*, c. 5, n. 9 (VIII, 119b-120a). The exact nature of the ecstatic experience in Bonaventure's spiritual theology, and the respective roles of the intellect and will in that experience, have been examined at length without a satisfactory conclusion. For a discussion of the various scholarly opinions on this topic with bibliography, see: Longpré "Bonaventure,"1823-1838. See also: Titus Szabó, "Extase IV. chez les theologiens du 13e siècle," in vol. 4 of *DS*, 2120-2126.

[168] *Perf vitae*, c. 5, n. 9 (VIII, 119b-120a) and *Dom in Albis*, 1 (IX, 291b). There is a mutual inebriation of bridegroom and bride in the mystical union. Bonaventure speaks of Christ as being inebriated on the cross out of love for the bride; see: *Hex*, coll. 14, n. 19 (V, 396b) He describes Francis in ecstasy as being: "quasi spiritu ebrius;" see: *Leg maj*, c. 9, n. 2 (VIII, 530b).

[169] *Hex*, coll. 22, n. 39 (V, 443b). On the *Song of Solomon* and mystical theology, see: Ulrich Köpf, "Hoheliedauslegung, Quelle einer Theologie der Mystik," in *Grundfragen christlicher Mystik*, 50-72. On the use of Scripture in Bonaventure's mystical theology see in the same work: Helmut Riedlinger, "Zur buchstäblichen und mystischen Schriftauslegung Bonaventuras," 139-156.

[170] *Trip via*, c. 2, n. 4 (VIII, 9a). This affective aspect of the joyful encounter with Christ in prayer, which is often spoken of in terms of tasting or delighting, is the proper end of the ascent into God. As Bonaventure writes: "*Proprie* oratio est ascensus in Deum ad aliquid degustandum . . . ." *IV Sent*, d. 15, p. 2, a. 1, q. 4, concl. (IV, 368a). In the text from the *Trip via*, Bonventure uses the word "complacentia" to describe the love which is the desired end of prayer. He goes on to show in the same work (c. 2, n. 8 (VIII, 9b-10a)) that the perfection of "complacentia" is found in the love of neighbor, thereby, binding the mystical experience to the active life. A similar view of contemplative love appears in Richard of St. Victor's fourth degree of love; see: Jean Châtillon, "Richard de Saint Victor," in vol. 13 of *DS*, 646. The similarity between the teachings appears once again in the description of Francis after the stigmata. He is described as thirsting with the Crucified for the salvation of others; see: *Leg maj*, c. 14, n. 1 (VIII, 545a). To thirst according to God's thirst is also a sign of the the fourth degree of love according to Châtillon, 646.

4. 3. 2.   Spiritual Desire and Transformation

The delight of experiential knowledge, which the contemplative finds in Christ as the Bridegroom of the soul,[171] is inaccessible to those not inflamed by spiritual desire.[172] Spiritual desire is the door to wisdom, a prerequisite in the contemplative ascent leading to delight in the Lord.[173] It is a distinguishing characteristic of the contemplative soul, the necessary first step facilitating the reception of the divine light of wisdom.[174] In the prologue to the *Journey of the Soul into God,* Bonaventure reminds all would-be contemplatives of the importance of spiritual desire: nobody can enter into the way of contemplation unless they become like the prophet Daniel, a "*man of desires.*"[175] The significance of spiritual desire appears once again in the

---

[171] Bonaventure refers to Christ as the Bridegroom, or Spouse, of the soul in several works. Among others, see: *Itin,* c. 4, n. 5 (V, 307b); c. 7, n. 6 (V, 313b); *Hex,* col. 2, n. 32 (V, 342a); *Brev,* p. 5, c. 1 (V, 253a); p. 5, c. 6 (V, 259b); *Regn Dei,* n. 21 (V, 544b); *Trip via,* c. 3, n. 6 (VIII, 14a-b); *Perf vitae,* c. 5, n. 4 (VIII, 118b); c. 6, n. 3 (VIII, 120b); and *Ephip,* 4 (IX, 162b). With reference to the Apostle John, see: *De S. Ioanne Evan,* 2 (IX, 495b-496a). On Christ as Spouse of the Church, see: *Itin,* c. 4, n. 5 (V, 307b) and *Brev,* p. 6, c. 5 (V, 270a). As Balthasar notes, the spousal relationship of the soul to Christ in Bonaventure's theology is anchored in the relationship between the Church and Christ; see: Balthasar, *Studies in Theological Styles: Clerical Styles,* 358. Consequently, just as the ascent of the individual soul should be seen in the context of the Church's ascent (See note 20 of the Introduction), so also should the union of the individual soul with Christ be understood in the light of the Church's union with Christ. Concerning the use of spousal symbolism in the Middle Ages, see: Leo Scheffczyk, "Brautsymbolik" in vol. 2 of *LM,* 589-591.

[172] *Trip via,* c. 3, n. 6 (VIII, 14b). See also: *Brev,* p. 5, c. 6 (V, 260a).

[173] *Hex,* coll. 2, n. 2 (V, 336a-b). See also: *Hex,* coll. 2, n. 6 (V, 337a-b); *Sabbato Sancto,* 1 (IX, 269a-b) and *De S. Andrea,* 1 (Collatio) (IX, 467a-b).

[174] *Hex,* col. 22, n. 29 (V, 441b-442a). See also: *Hex,* coll. 20, n. 19 (V, 428b).

[175] "Non enim dispositus est aliquo modo ad contemplationes divinas, quae ad mentales

final chapter when Bonaventure exhorts his readers to pray for the gift of desire if they hope to experience the ecstatic peace of Mount LaVerna.[176]

The desire to pass over with Christ into the ecstatic peace of Mount LaVerna is brought about by the Holy Spirit. The divine knowledge hidden beyond the veil of human understanding will never be sought nor experienced unless the Holy Spirit, the gift of Christ, inflames the heart with an ardent desire for wisdom.[177] While the reception of the Holy Spirit lies outside the realm of human power alone, it can be sought for,[178] as well as nurtured, in prayer.[179] In prayer, the Holy Spirit, like a burning flame, ignites the affections and, thereby, raises the soul into the illuminated darkness associated with the most excellent, experiential knowledge of God.[180] The effect of the Holy Spirit on the affective powers[181] is crucial because in

ducunt excessus, nisi cum Daniele sit *vir desideriorum.*" *Itin*, prol., n. 3 (V, 296a). See also the version of the *Hex* found in Ferdinandus Delorme, ed., *Collationes in Hexaëmeron et Bonaventura quaedam selecta* (Quaracchi: Collegium S. Bonaventurae, 1934) coll. 2, n. 3, 21.

[176] *Itin*, c. 7, n. 6 (V, 313b).

[177] *Itin*, c. 7, n. 4 (V, 312b).

[178] *Comm Lc*, c. 11, n. 35 (VII, 288a) and *Dom 4 post Pascha,* 1 (IX, 309b-310a).

[179] *Hex*, coll. 2, n. 32 (V, 342b). Cf: *Delorme*, coll. 2, n. 32, 32 which speaks of the gift of wisdom as opposed to the gift of the Holy Spirit. See also: *Itin*, prol., n. 3 (V, 296a) which speaks of nurturing desire in prayer. This text from the *Itin* binds the prayer of desire from the Johannine way to peace with Jacob's prayer for mercy and the speculative prayer of Petrine contemplation: "Desideria autem in nobis inflammantur dupliciter, scilicet per *clamorem orationis,* quae rugire facit *a gemitu cordis,* et per *fulgorem speculationis,* qua mens ad radios lucis directissime et intensissime se convertit." The presence of these three aspects of prayer constitute the *Itin* as a synthesis of Bonaventure's theology of prayer, albeit, with a decided emphasis in the Petrine way of contemplation. In this context, it should be noted that, although the bulk of the *Itin* deals directly with the inflamation of desire through speculation, the beginning and end of the work underline the need for the "gemitum orationis." *Itin*, prol., n. 4 (V, 296a) and *Itin*, c. 7, n. 6 (V, 313b).

[180] *Itin*, c. 7, n. 6 (V, 313b) and *Hex*, coll. 2, n. 32 (V, 342a-b).

[181] The inflamming of the affections is an integral part of the Johannine way of contemplation; see: *Comm Lc,* c. 9, n. 49 (VII, 232a).

the mystical darkness only the affections have the capability of entering into union with Christ, who is the wisdom of the Father. As Bonaventure says:

> Christ *draws back* then when the mind strives with intellectual eyes to see that wisdom; because the *affection*, not the *intellect* enters there. Hence in the Canticle: *You have wounded my heart, my sister, spouse; you have wounded my heart with one of your eyes,* because the affection reaches all the way to the depths of Christ.[182]

The role of the Holy Spirit in the affective union of the soul with Christ is developed briefly, yet systematically, in the *Triple Way*.[183] In the chapter dealing with contemplation, Bonaventure outlines seven steps marking the movement toward the mystical encounter with the Bridegroom which is effected by the the Holy Spirit. The first step on the way toward the Bridegroom, solicitous vigilance, denotes the use of reason. On the other hand, all the remaining six steps reveal the effects of the Holy Spirit on the affective powers as the soul is drawn into an ever deepening relationship with the Bridegroom.[184] Those six steps are: comforting trust, inflaming desire, uplifting excess, calming pleasure, delighting joy, and binding union. The unitive effect of the Holy Spirit seen in the seven grades leading to the perfection of love is the object of prayer:

> The grades *of the unitive way* are distinguished in the

---

[182] "Tunc Christus *recedit*, quando mens oculis intellectualibus nititur illam sapientiam videre; quia ibi non intrat *intellectus*, sed *affectus*. Unde in Cantico: *Vulnerasti cor meum, soror mea, sponsa; vulnerasti cor meum in uno oculorum tuorum,* quia *affectus* vadit usque ad profundum Christi." *Hex*, coll. 2, n. 32 (V, 342a). The one eye of contemplative love is treated in: Gillebertus of Hoilandia, *Sermones in Cantica*, Sermo 30, *PL* 184, 156-157.

[183] *Trip via*, c. 3, n. 6-8 (VIII, 14a-15b).

[184] *Trip via*, c. 3, n. 6-7 (VIII, 14a-15a).

following manner: because of the Spouse's readiness let *vigilance* arouse you; because of his faithfulness let *trust* strengthen you; because of his sweetness let *concupiscence* inflame you; because of his loftiness let *excess* lift you up; because of his beauty let *pleasure* bring you rest; because of the plenitude of his love let *joy* inebriate you; because of the strength of his love let *clinging* bind you, so that at all times the devout soul may say in its heart to the Lord: I seek you, I hope in you, I desire you, I raise up in you, I accept you, I exult in you and to you I finally cling.[185]

The unitive presence of the Spirit brings consolation and great delight as the soul is joined to the most desired Spouse;[186] yet, a concomitant element of spiritual struggle and upheaval is also discerned. Bonaventure acknowledges in the *Collations on the Six Days,* that the Holy Spirit moves with tremendous force within the soul during the ascent into God: ". . . that ascent is brought about by the force and the most powerful agitation of the Holy Spirit, as is affirmed of Elijah: *Behold, the spirit overturning*

---

[185] "Gradus *viae unitivae* sic distinguuntur: te *vigilantia* sollicitet propter Sponsi promptitudinem; te *confidentia* corroboret propter eius certitudinem; *concupiscentia* te inflammet propter eius dulcedinem; *excedentia* te sublevet propter eius celsitudinem; *complacentia* te quietet propter eius pulcritudinem; *laetitia* te inebriet propter amoris eius plenitudinem; *adhaerentia* te conglutinet propter amoris eius fortitudinem, ut dicat semper devota anima in corde suo ad Dominum: Te quaero, in te spero, te desidero, in te consurgo, te accepto, in te exsulto et tibi finaliter adhaereo." *Trip via,* c. 3, n. 8 (VIII, 15a-b).

[186] *Perf vitae,* c. 5, n. 5 (VIII, 119a); *Brev,* p. 5, c. 6 (V, 260a) *Red art,* n. 26 (V, 325b) and *Sabbato Sancto,* 1 (IX, 269a). On the desire for Christ, who is the Spouse of the soul, and the affective "tasting" of wisdom, Bonaventure says: "Tertio est Christus desiderabilis propter *oblectationem sapientialis demulcentiae,* quia delectat sive dulcorat *gustum* in prefruendo. Unde Canticorum secundo: *Sub umbra illius quem desideraveram, sedi, et fructus eius dulcis gutturi meo. - Sub umbra,* refrigerantis gratiae, *illius,* scilicet Christi, *quem desideraveram,* per excessum inflammatae dilectionis, *sedi,* per mentis quietationem, non discurrendo per mentis vagationem, *et fructus eius dulcis gutturi meo,* propter degustationem sapientiae." *Dom 1 Adventus,* 2 (IX, 29a).

mountains and crushing stones . . . ."[187] The ardent desire for God, a hallmark of the Holy Spirit, serves as a fiery sword separating the soul from all terrestrial concerns[188] and inordinate loves.[189] Although this re-ordering of the affections toward the Spouse is an essential element of Johannine contemplation, it does not take place without an intense struggle against concupiscence; those traveling along the way of peace must be weaned eventually from the sweetness of lesser, inferior pleasures as was John,[190] the beloved friend of Christ, the Bridegroom.[191]

---

[187] ". . . iste ascensus fit per vigorem et commotionem fortissimam Spiritus sancti; sicut dicitur de Elia: *Ecce, spiritus subvertens montes et conterens petras . . . .*" *Hex*, coll. 2, n. 33 (V, 342b).

[188] *Sabbato Santo*, 1 (IX, 269a).

[189] *Hex*, coll. 2, n. 5- 6 (V, 337a-b).

[190] *Comm Jn*, prooem, n. 3 (VI, 240a). In this text Bonaventure uses the word "ablactare" that is, "to wean," to describe the necessary movement away from the "milk" of terrestial consolation which opens the poor to the Holy Spirit and consequently to an understanding of spiritual realities. See also: *De donis*, coll. 8, n. 3 (V, 494b). Although the Johannine way of peace relies primarily on grace, it also demands human effort if the poor are to wean, or seperate, themselves from that which would impede union with God, see: *Hex*, coll. 2, n. 30 (V, 341a). See also: Longpré, "Bonaventure," 1826. Bonaventure speaks in a similar fashion of the ascent into God along the "via negationis" of negative theology. Just as the affections should be kept from finding final rest in anything less than God, on the theological level the contemplative is called to resist the attempt to posit the qualities of God in a final manner. The Dionysian way of ascent "per ablationem" is clearly superior to the Augustinian way "per affirmationem;" yet, both are dependent on each other; see: *Trip via,* c. 3, n. 13 (VIII, 17b). Concerning the methodology of the "via negationis" Bonaventure says: "Iste autem ascensus fit . . . per *ablationem*, ab infimo usque ad summum; et iste modus est conveniens magis, ut: non est hoc, non est illud; nec privo ego a Deo quod suum est, vel in ipso est, sed attribuo meliori modo et altiori, quam ego intelligo. - Ablationem sequitur amor semper. Unde Moyses primo a senioribus *sequestratur*, secundo *ascendit* in montem, tertio *intrat caliginem*. Aliud exemplum: qui sculpit figuram nihil ponit, immo removet et in ipso lapide relinquit formam nobilem et pulcram. Sic notitia Divinitatis per *ablationem* relinquit in nobis nobilissimam dispositionem." *Hex*, coll. 2, n. 33 (V, 342b). On the "viam negationis" in Bonaventure's teaching, see: Schlosser, "Lux Inaccessibilis. Zur negativen Theologie bei Bonaventura," 3-139, esp. 48-58. On "ablatio" and the ecstasy of nuptial theology, see: Balthasar, *Studies in Theological Styles: Clerical Styles,* 269-279.

[191] *De S. Ioanne Evan,* 2 (IX, 495b).

The element of struggle in Johannine contemplation is better appreciated in light of the Cross.[192] The anagogical effect brought about by spiritual desire inevitably draws the poor into the mystery of the Cross: ". . . the one who wishes to find the Lord finds him on the Cross . . . the one who burns with desire for the Cross and for the Lord finds him there . . . ."[193] The Cross of Christ connotes the bitter struggle of penance; yet, it is also the Tree of Life offering the promise of abundant grace, justice, and wisdom.[194] When viewed through the prism of the Cross, the penitential struggle against concupiscence becomes an expression of baptismal union with Christ[195] effected by the Holy Spirit. It is the Spirit who brings about this union of the soul with the Crucified by planting Christ within the soul and the soul into Christ.[196]

As Francis of Assisi's encounter with the Crucified on La Verna indicates, the willingness to carry the Cross and the corresponding desire to be conformed to the Crucified are related intrinsically to the ecstatic transformation of the soul by the Crucified.[197] Francis, who played out the

---

[192] On Bonventure's theology of the cross, see: Werner Hülbusch, *Elemente einer Kreuzestheologie in den Spätschriften Bonaventuras* (Düsseldorf: Patmos Verlag, 1968).

[193] ". . . qui vult invenire Dominum invenit eum in cruce . . . qui desiderio fervet ad crucem et ad Dominum invenit ibi eum . . . ." *De S. Andrea*, 1 (IX, 465b).

[194] *De S. Andrea*, 1 (IX, 464a-467a) and *De S. Andrea*, 1 (Collatio) (IX, 467a-470a). The Cross was the sign of penance for Francis of Assisi; see: *Leg maj*,. prol., n. 2 (VIII, 504b). Because of Francis' penitential lifestyle, God chose to seal his flesh with the sign of the Cross on Mount La Verna; see: *De S. P. Franc*, 4 (IX, 587a).

[195] *De S. Andrea*, 1 (IX, 464b-465a). Although baptism is not mentioned, Francis of Assisi's struggle against concupiscence is said to have flowed from his union with Christ; see: *Leg maj*, c. 5, n. 1 (VIII, 516a).

[196] *Plant par*, n. 8 (V, 577a).

[197] This point is developed by Balthasar in: *Studies in Theological Style: Clerical Styles,* 270-276 and 352-362.

drama of his life in the shadow of the Cross, looked upon the life of the Crucified as the model for his own life. Bonaventure writes in the *Major Life of St. Francis* that: "[Francis] wished in all respects to be in conformity to Christ Crucified, who poor, suffering, and naked, hung upon the cross."[198] Francis' wish to be like the Crucified was realized on Mount La Verna[199] where, while in the midst of solitary prayer, he saw a vision of a six-winged Seraph resembling the Crucified. Inflamed with divine love, Francis' flesh was sealed with the stigmata through the grace of the Holy Spirit.[200] In this mystical-eschatological event, the Poor Man of Assisi was transformed by the power of love[201]and the manifest sign of Christian wisdom,[202] which is the

---

[198] "Voluit certe per omnia Christo crucifixo esse conformis, qui pauper et dolens et nudus in cruce pependit." *Leg maj,* c. 14, n. 4 (VIII, 546b).

[199] *Leg maj,* c. 13, n. 3 (VIII, 542b-543a). For Bonaventure's interpetation of the stigmatization, see also: *De S. P. Franc,* 4 (IX, 585b-590b). It is appropriate that the Seraph appear in the context of this mystical encounter where the soul experiences the fullness of the gift of wisdom in union with God because the Seraph represents the plentitude of delight and knowledge; see: *II Sent,* d. 9, au., q. 4, concl. ad 6 (II, 249b). Thus, the Seraph can be considered as symbolic of Christ, who is the cause of delight; see: *Perf vitae,* c. 5, n. 5 (VIII, 119a) and source of all correct knowledge and wisdom; see: *Christus mag,* n. 1 (V, 567a). According to Bonaventure, the Seraph represents the union of the soul in the mystical ascent into God; see: *Hex,* coll. 22, n. 27 (V, 441b) as well as the integration of the triple way of peace because of its purgative, illuminative and unitive action; see: *Leg maj,* c. 13, n. 7 (VIII, 544a). It should also be pointed out that the six wings of the Seraph symbolize the six degrees of speculative prayer outlined in the *Itin;* see: *Itin,* c. 1, n. 5 (V, 297b). On the ascent to God and the Seraph as representative of Christ (with reference to the *Hex* and the *Itin),* see: Fischer, *De Deo trino et uno,* 48-57.

[200] ". . . verum etiam irrefragabili veritatis testificatione confirmat *signaculum similitudinis* Dei viventis, Christi videlicet crucifixi, quod in corpore ipsius fuit impressum non per naturae virtutem vel ingenium artis, sed potius per admirandam potentiam Spiritus Dei vivi." *Leg maj,* prol., n. 2 (VIII, 504b-505a) and *De S. P. Franc,* 4 (IX, 590a-b).

[201] On the tranforming power of love in Francis' life, see: *Leg maj,* c. 13, n. 3 (VIII, 542b); *De S. P. Franc,* 1 (IX, 574b) and *De S. P. Franc,* 2 (IX, 580a). On the transforming power of love in general, see: *I Sent,* d. 15, dub. 5 (I, 275b) and *Dom 14 post Pent,* 1 (IX, 408a). See also: Prentice, *The Psychology of Love according to St. Bonaventure,* 53-58.

[202] *Leg maj,* c. 13, n. 10 (VIII, 545b).

crucified image of his Beloved, appeared in his flesh.[203] Francis' unique encounter with the Crucified serves as a paradigm for all who desire to pass over with him into ecstatic peace.[204] To experience such ecstatic peace or wisdom is to know the fullness of mercy sought by the poor in prayer.

4. 4. Summary

This chapter began by equating the culmination of divine mercy sought in prayer with the ecstatic peace experienced in contemplation by Francis of Assisi on Mount LaVerna. In the *Commentary on Luke,* Bonaventure proposes to the poor a three-fold way to arrive at this ecstatic peace of contemplation: the way of James, the way of Peter, and the way of John. Those who follow the way of these disciples accompany Christ up Mount Tabor and arrive eventually at the summit of contemplation. Each one of these ways signifies a form of prayer since Bonaventure considers every contemplative act to be an expression of prayer. While these ways of prayer leading to the fullness of mercy are distinct, they are not mutually exclusive, as the poor are called to walk along all of them as they ascend with Christ.

The first way of peace, which was examined in this chapter, was that of James or Jacob. The name "Jacob" means "wrestler," thereby, indicating that Jacob's way of contemplation is marked by the struggle against sin. The

---

[203] *De S. P. Franc,* 2 (IX, 580a) and *Leg maj,* c. 13, n. 5 (VIII, 543b). According to Bonaventure, the stigmata is also a reflection of the friendship between Francis and Christ; see: *De trans S. Franc* (IX, 534a-535a). Like the Apostle John, Francis is a friend of the Bridegroom; see: *Leg maj,* prol., n. 1 (VIII, 504b).

[204] *Itin,* prol., n. 2-3 (V, 295a-296a) and c. 7, n. 3 (V, 312b). See also: *Hex,* coll. 22, n. 22-23 (V, 440b-441a). On the academic debate surrounding the mystical-eschatological interpretation of the stigmata with reference to this section of the *Hex,* see: David Burr, "Bonaventure, Olivi and Franciscan Eschatology," *CF* 53 (1983): 29-35.

struggle against sin in general, and concupiscence in particular, unfolds with the painful recognition of the poverty of sin and is accompanied by tears of sorrow. As such, it is reminiscent of the Eastern Christian way of compunction. The recognition of sin and tears of sorrow on the part of the poor is crucial in the contemplative ascent, for it is impossible for them to ascend into God unless they first descend into their own poverty by humbly acknowledging their sinfulness. While Christ himself was without sin, he cried for those immersed in the poverty of sin and interceded for them. His prayer for mercy, which he offers now as eternal high priest, is shared in by the Virgin Mary and all the blessed. Despite the fact that the struggle against sin dominates the way of Jacob, it does not overshadow the virtue of hope which empowers the poor to await the blessings God has promised them. By placing their hope in God, they are raised up in contemplation into God.

The second way of peace is that of Peter. Bonaventure, who interprets the name Peter to mean "one who knows," describes the way of Peter as that of intellectual speculation leading to an ever-deepening knowledge of God. This way of Peter is also spoken of as the "way of splendor," which Bonaventure says is taught by Augustine. It is typified as the ascent of the soul into God through the consideration of the trinitarian God as reflected first in the external, material world of nature and then in the internal, spiritual world of the soul. This prayerful ascent of the soul or intellect into God is the thematic of the *Journey of the Soul into God*. The Petrine manner of ascent is impossible without the assistance of the virtue of faith and the gift of understanding. Faith is the solid foundation of the ascent to God; it fosters a knowledge of God as Trinity by illuminating the intellect to vestiges of the Trinity present throughout Creation. For its part, the gift of understanding affords a deeper contemplative knowledge of the trinitarian God because it

235

enables the poor to perceive the reflection of the Trinity in the soul. They arrive at the heights of the Petrine way of splendor when they receive the contuition of God proper to the pure of heart and contemplate Christ, the eternal splendor of the Father.

The third way of peace is the way of John and is taught by Pseudo-Dionysius. According to Bonaventure, the name "John" signifies "the one in whom grace resides;" therefore, the way of John is said to be characterized by the action of divine grace evidenced in the virtue of charity. Such charity or love unites the poor to God and transforms them into a divine similitude. The process of union and transformation is grounded in the very dynamic of love since love by nature unites the lover with the beloved as well as transforms the lover into an image of the beloved. The process of union and transformation belonging to the Johannine ascent to God is accompanied by an intimate knowledge of God, whereby, the poor taste and delight in the goodness of God. This experiential knowledge of God is synonymous with the gift of wisdom or ecstatic peace experienced by Francis of Assisi on Mount LaVerna. Francis, who was filled with a burning desire for union with Christ, was transformed into the image of Christ and sealed with the sacred stigmata. These wounds of the Crucified, carved as they were by the grace of the Holy Spirit, testify to Francis' intimate knowledge of Christ, the wisdom of God.

Conclusion

Prayer is the object of continual theological reflection on the part of Saint Bonaventure. Throughout his works, he turns time and time again to examine the role of prayer in the spiritual life. The present dissertation has developed his teaching on prayer by giving special attention to his thought on petitionary prayer. This has been done by exploring the prayer of petition against the background of some of the major themes in Bonaventure's theology. In light of the research found in this dissertation, the following conclusions can be drawn as to Bonaventure's teaching on prayer:

1. Prayer does not stand out as an isolated phenomena in the spiritual life. Instead, it is a constant, all-embracing element of the spiritual journey. As the supplication of the poor for divine mercy, it is found at every stage of the pilgrimage back to God.

2. Prayer is born in the acknowledgment of ontological poverty as well as in the experience of moral poverty. Only those who are moved by grace to recognize their two-fold indigence as creatures will turn, as mendicants, to the Creator in prayer.

3. Prayer finds its historical point of convergence in the advent of Christ. In response to the prayer of those who long for salvation, Christ descended, as a gift from the Father, into the womb of the Virgin. This gift of the Son is the most wondrous alms that the poor could ever hope to receive from the Father.

4. Prayer is modeled on the example of Christ, who, himself, often

237

turned to the Father in prayer. All people, regardless of social class or occupation, are called to follow his example of prayer and to be conformed to him as a son or daughter of God. One way of approaching the Father in prayer is with the classical prayer Christ taught his disciples: the "Our Father." When they pray in this manner, the poor ask for everything that they need for their salvation.

5. Prayer seeks the outpouring of the Holy Spirit upon the poor. The advent of the Holy Spirit, which is, at times, identified with the reception of the seven gifts of the Holy Spirit, renders the poor rich in grace and conforms them to Christ. As a result, they are transformed into the sons and daughters of God. The "Our Father" is one privileged way to ask for the advent of the Holy Spirit.

6. Prayer can neither be reduced to any specific form or activity, nor can it be limited to any particular time or place. Instead, it is the richly-diverse, continuous cry of the poor, which embraces a multitude of expressions such as the recitation of the Liturgy of the Hours, the desire for good, and the effort to live justly. It also includes the battle against concupiscence, symbolized by Christ's struggle with the Devil in the desert.

7. Prayer is expressed both vocally and mentally. While vocal prayer is important in its own right, it takes on added significance in the spiritual life of the poor because it can foster an interior dialogue between the heart and God. Mental prayer is another name for this prayer of the heart.

8. Prayer culminates in the contemplative experience of God. The struggle against concupiscence, the intellectual consideration of divine truth, and the desire for God, are all unique paths of prayer along which the poor, like the apostles James, Peter, and John, ascend Mount Tabor with Christ. On the heights of the mountain, they experience in contemplation the fullness of

divine mercy. The stigmatization of Francis of Assisi on Mount LaVerna serves as a paradigm for those wishing to ascend by means of contemplation into God.

Selected List of Works Consulted

Primary Sources: The Works of Saint Bonaventure

Critical Editions

Doctoris Seraphici S. Bonaventurae Opera Omnia. Ed. PP. Collegii a S. Bonaventura. 10 vols. Quaracchi: Collegium S. Bonaventurae, 1882-1902.

Collationes in Hexaëmeron et Bonaventuriana quaedam selecta. Ed. Ferdinandus Delorme. Quaracchi: Collegium S. Bonaventurae, 1934.

Sancti Bonaventurae Sermones Dominicales. Ed. Jacques Guy Bougerol. Grottaferrata: Collegio S. Bonaventura, 1977.

Metodologia del sapere nel sermone di s. Bonaventura "Unus est magister vester Christus." Ed. Renato Russo. Grottaferrata: Editiones Collegii S. Bonaventurae, 1982.

Translations

Works of St. Bonaventure. Vol. I: *De reductione artium ad theologiam.* Intro., Trans., and Comm. Emma Thérèse Healy. Saint Bonaventure, N. Y.: The Franciscan Institute, 1955.

Works of St. Bonaventure. Vol. 2: *Itinerarium mentis in Deum.* Intro., Trans., and Comm. Philotheus Boehner. Saint Bonaventure, N. Y.:

The Franciscan Institute, 1956.

Works of St. Bonaventure. Vol. 3: *Disputed Questions on the Mystery of the Trinity.* Intro. and Trans. Zachary Hayes. Saint Bonaventure, N. Y.: The Franciscan Institute, 1979.

The Works of St. Bonaventure. 5 Vols. Trans. José de Vinck. Paterson, N. J.: St. Anthony Press, 1960-1970.

Obras de San Buenaventura. 6 Vols. Trans., Intro., and Notes. Leon Amorós, Bernardo Aperribay, Miguel Oromí and Ignacio Omaechevarría. Madrid: La Editorial Católica, 1945-1949.

Bonaventure. The Soul's Journey into God, The Tree of Life, The Life of St. Francis. Trans. and Intro. Ewert Cousins. Pref. Ignatius Brady. New York: Paulist Press, 1978.

Bonaventura. Itinerarium Mentis in Deum. De Reductione Artium ad Theologiam. Trans., Intro., and Comm. Julian Kaup. München: Kösel Verlag, 1961.

Bonaventura. Das Sechstagewerk. Trans. and Intro. Wilhelm Nyssen. München: Kösel Verlag, 1964.

Saint Bonaventure. Breviloquium. 8 Vols. Trans., Intro., and Notes Jacques Guy Bougerol and others. Paris: Éditions Franciscaines, 1966-1967.

Bonaventura. Itinerario dell'anima a Dio, Breviloquio, Riconduzione delle arti alla teologia. Trans, Intro., Pref., and Notes. Letterio Mauro. Milano: Rusconi, 1985.

San Bonaventura. La Sapienza Cristiana: Le Collationes in Hexaemeron. Trans., Intro., and Notes. Vincenzo Bigi. Milano: Jaca Book, 1985.

San Bonaventura. I sette doni dello Spirito Santo. Trans., Intro., and Comm. Eliodoro Mariani. Vicenza: L.I.E.F, 1985.

The Disciple and the Master. St. Bonaventure's Sermons on St. Francis of

Assisi. Trans., Ed., and Intro. Eric Doyle. Chicago: Franciscan Herald Press, 1983.

Bringing forth Christ, the Son of God. Five Feasts of the Child Jesus. St Bonaventure. Trans. and Intro. Eric Doyle. Oxford: SLG Press, 1984.

Other Primary Sources

Biblical: Translations of the Bible

Bibliorum sacrorum iuxta vulgatam Clementinam. Ed. Aloisius Gramatica. Cologne: Benziger, 1914.

New Catholic Edition of the Holy Bible. Translated from the Latin Vulgate. Ed. Catholic Scholars and others. New York: Catholic Book Publishing Company, 1949-1950.

Nova vulgata bibliorum sacrorum. Ed. Second Vatican Council. Roma: Liberia Editrice Vaticana, 1979.

The New Oxford Annotated Bible with the Apocrypha. Ed. Herbert May and Bruce Metzger. New York: Oxford University Press, 1977.

Patristic and Medieval

Anselm. *Cur deus homo.* Vol. 2 of *S. Anselmi Opera Omnia.* Ed. Franciscus Schmitt. Rome: 1940.

Apophthegmata Patrum. PG 65. 1864.

Augustine. *De diversis quaestionibus octoginta tribus. CChr* 44 A. Ed. Almut Mutzenbecher.

_____. *De natura et gratia. PL* 44. 1845.

_____. *In Iohannis Evangelium Tractatus 1244. CChr* 36. Ed. Radbodus Willems. 1954.

Bede. *In Lucae Evangelium Expositio. CChr* 120. Ed. D. Hurst. 1960.

Bernard. *Semones super Cantica Canticorum.* Vol. 1 and 2 of *Sancti Bernadi Opera.* Ed. Jean Leclercq, Henri Rochais, and Charles Talbot. Rome: Editiones Cistercienses, 1957-1958.

Boethius. *De arithmetica. PL* 63. 1847.

David of Augsburg. *De exterioris et interioris hominis compositione.* Ed. PP. Collegii S. Bonaventurae. Quaracchi: Collegium S. Bonaventurae, 1899.

De oratione. MS Codex Vatic. Palat. lat. 612. Rome: Vatican Library.

De oratione, satisfactionis parte. Printed in *Alexandri Alensis Universae Theologiae Summa in quattour partes ab ipsomet authore distributa.* Cologne: 1622.

Ekbert of Schönau. *De humanitate Christi.* Printed among the works of Anselm as Meditatio 9 in *Liber Meditationum et Orationum. PL* 158. 1853.

Francis of Assisi. *Die Opuscula des hl. Franziskus von Assisi. Neue textkritische Edition.* Ed. Kajetan Eßer. Grottaferrata: Collegium S. Bonaventurae, 1976.

Gennadius of Marseille. *De ecclesiasticis dogmatibus.* Printed among the works of Augustine. *PL* 42. 1845.

Gillebertus of Hoilandia. *Sermones in Cantica. PL* 184. 1854.

Glossa Ordinaria. PL 113-114. 1852.

Gregory the Great. *Homilia 36. PL* 76. 1849.

_____. *Moralia in Iob Libri XI-XXII. CChr* 143 A. Ed. Marc Adriaen. 1979.

_____. *Moralia in Iob Libri XXIII-XXXV. CChr* 143 B. Ed. Marc Adriaen. 1985.

Gunther of Paris. *De oratione, jejunio et eleemosyna. PL* 212. 1855.

Hugh of St. Victor. *De modo orandi. PL* 176. 1854.

_____. *De sacramentis christianae fidei. PL* 176. 1854.

_____. *De quinque septenis. PL* 175. 1854.

_____. *Eruditionis didascalicae. PL* 176. 1854.

Jerome. *Liber interpretationis hebraicorum nominum. CChr* 72. Ed. Paul de LaGarde. 1959.

_____. *Liber de nominibus hebraicis. PL* 23. 1845.

John of Damascus. *De fide orthodoxa. PG* 94. 1864.

Miscellanea. Printed among the works of Hugh of St. Victor. *PL* 177. 1854.

Origen. *De oratione. PG* 11. No date.

_____. *Selecta in primum librum Regnorum. PG* 12. 1862.

Pseudo-Dionysius. *De divinis nominibus. PG* 3. 1889.

_____. *De theologia mystica. PG* 3. 1899.

Richard of St. Victor. *De Trinitate. PL* 196. 1855.

_____. *De gratia contemplationis. PL* 196. 1855.

_____. *De quatuor gradibus violentae charitatis. PL* 196. 1855.

Thomas of Celano. *Vita secunda S. Francisci Assisiensis.* Vol. 10 of *Analecta Franciscana.* Ed. PP. Collegii S. Bonaventurae. Quaracchi: Collegium S. Bonaventurae, 1927.

William of Middleton. *Opusculum super Missam.* Ed. Willibrod Lampen. Quaracchi: Collegium S. Bonaventurae, 1931

Secondary Sources

Research Aids

A Latin Dictionary. Ed. Charlton T. Lewis and Charles Short. Oxford: The
Clarendon Press, 1879.

Lexicon latinitatis medii aevi. Ed. Albert Blaise. Turnholt: Brepols, 1975.

The New American Roget's College Thesaurus. New York: The New
American Library, Inc., 1958.

Webster's New Collegiate Dictionary. Springfield, Mass.: G & C Meriam
Co., 1973.

Books

Alszeghy, Zoltan. *Grundformen der Liebe. Die Theorie der Gottesliebe bei
dem hl. Bonaventura.* Roma: Typis Pontificae Universitatis
Gregorianae, 1946.

Armstrong, Regis J. *The Spiritual Theology of the "Legenda Major" of Saint
Bonaventure.* Fordham U. Ann Arbor: UMI, 1978.

Auer, Johann. *Die Entwicklung der Gnadenlehre in der Hochscholastik I.
Das Wesen der Gnade.* Freiburg: Herder, 1942.

_____. *Die Entwicklung der Gnadenlehre in der Hochscholastik II. Das
Wirken der Gnade.* Freiburg: Herder, 1951.

Balthasar, Hans Urs von. *Studies in Theological Styles: Clerical Styles.* Vol. 2
of *The Glory of the Lord. A Theological Aesthetics.* Trans. Andrew

Louth, Francis McDonagh, and Brian McNeil. Ed. John Riches. San Francisco: Ignatius Press, 1984.

Barth, Hans-Martin. *Wohin - woher mein Ruf. Zur Theologie des Bittgebets.* München: Chr. Kaiser Verlag, 1981.

Bissen, Jean-Marie, *L'exemplarisme divin selon saint Bonaventure.* Paris: J. Vrin, 1929.

Boeckl, Karl. *Die sieben Gaben des heiligen Geistes in ihrer Bedeutung für die Mystik nach der Theologie des 13. und 14. Jahrhunderts.* Freiburg: Herder, 1931.

Bonnefoy, Jean François. *Le Saint-Esprit et ses dons selon Saint Bonaventure.* Paris: J. Vrin, 1929.

____. *Une somme bonaventurienne de théologie mystique: Le 'De triplici via.'* Paris: Libraire Saint-François, 1934.

Bougerol, Jacques Guy. *Introduction to the Works of Bonaventure.* Trans. José de Vinck. Paterson, N.J.: St. Anthony Guild Press, 1964.

____. *La théologie de l'espérance aux XII et XIII siècles.* Vol. 1 of *Etudes.* Paris: Études Augustiniennes, 1985.

Boving, Remigius. *Bonaventura und die französische Hochgotik.* Werl/Westfalen: Franziskus - Druckerei, 1930.

Bradshaw, Paul F. *Daily Prayer in the Early Church.* New York: Oxford University Press, 1982.

Brümmer, Vincent. *What are we doing when we pray? A Philisophical Inquiry.* London: SCM Press, 1984.

Butler, Dom Cuthbert. *Western Mysticism.* Intro. David Knowles. London: Constable, 1967.

Caba, José. *La oración de petición. Estudio exegético sobre los evangelios sinópticos y los escritos joaneos.* Rome: Biblical Institute Press, 1974.

247

Chenu, M. D. *Nature, Man and Society in the Twelfth Century. Essays on New Theological Perspectives in the Latin West.* Trans. and Ed. Jerome Taylor and Lester K. Little. Pref. Etienne Gilson. Chicago: The University of Chicago Press, 1979.

Chiettini, Emanuele. *Mariologia S. Bonaventurae.* Romae: Officium Libri Catholici, 1941.

Chitty, Derwas J.. *The Desert a City. An Introduction to the Study of Egyptian and Palestinian Monasticism under the Christian Empire.* London: Mowbrays, 1977.

Cipriani, Nello. *La pedagogia della preghiera in s. Agostino.* Palermo: Edizioni Augustinus, 1984.

Clasen, Sophronius. *Der hl. Bonaventura und das Mendikantentum.* Werl/Westfalen: Franziskus Druckerei, 1940.

Corcoran, Gervase. *Prayer and St. Augustine.* Vol. 25 of the *Living Flame Series.* Ed. Thomas Curran. Dublin: Carmelite Centre of Spirituality, 1983.

Courth, Franz. *Trinität in der Scholastik.* Vol 2, Faszikel 1b of *HDG.*

Cousins, Ewert H. *Bonaventure and the Coincidence of Opposites.* Chicago: Franciscan Herald Press, 1978.

Curtius, Ernst Robert. *Europäische Literatur und lateinisches Mittelalter.* Bern: A Francke A. G. Verlag, 1948.

D'Avary, D. L. *The Preaching of the Friars,* Oxford: Clarendon Press, 1985.

De Champeaux, Gérard and Sébastien Sterckx. *I simboli del medioevo.* Trans. Monica Girardi. Milano: Jaca Book, 1981.

De Wachter, Maurits. *Le péché actuel selon saint Bonaventure.* Paris: Éditions Franciscaines, 1967.

Dhont, René Charles. *Le problème de la préparation à la grâce: débuts de l'école franciscaine.* Paris: Éditions Franciscaines, 1946.

Di Cristina, Salavtore. *Preghiera e devozione a Cristo nei Padri.* Milano: Edizioni O.R., 1987.

Distelbrink, Balduinus. *Bonaventurae scripta, authentica dubia vel spuria critice recensita.* Roma: Istituto Storico Cappuccini, 1975.

Dölger, Franz Joseph. *Sol Salutis. Gebet und Gesang im christlichen Altertum.* Münster: Verlag der Aschendorffschen Verlagsbuchhandlung, 1920.

Egenter, Richard. *Gottesfreundschaft. Die Lehre von der Gottesfreundschaft in der Scholastik und Mystik des 12. u. 13. Jahrhunderts.* Augsburg: Dr. Benno Filser Verlag, 1928.

Eilers, Erwin. *Gottes Wort. Eine Theologie der Predigt nach Bonaventura.* Freiburg: Heder, 1941.

Eßer, Kajetan. *Franziskus und die Seinen.* Werl/Westfalen: Dietrich Coelde Verlag, 1963.

Fischer, Konrad. *De Deo trino et uno. Das Verhältnis von productio und reductio in seiner Bedeutung für die Gotteslehre Bonaventuras.* Göttingen: Vandenhoeck & Ruprecht, 1978.

Forstner, Dorothea. *Die Welt der Symbole.* Innsbruck: Tyrolia Verlag, 1961.

Gerken, Alexander. *Theologie des Wortes. Das Verhältnis von Schöpfung und Inkarnation bei Bonaventura.* Düsseldorf: Patmos Verlag, 1963.

Gerster, Thomas Villanova a Zeil. *Das Gebet nach der Lehre des hl. Bonaventura.* Bolzano: 1931.

Gessel, Wilhelm. *Die Theologie des Gebetes nach <De Oratione>von Origenes.* München: Verlag Ferdinand Schöningh, 1975.

Gilson, Etienne. *The Philosophy of St. Bonaventure.* Trans. Dom Illtyd

Trethowan and Frank J. Sheed. Paterson, N.J.: St. Anthony Guild Press, 1965.

Gonzáles, Olegario. *Misterio Trinitario y existencia humana: estudio histórico teológico en torno a san Buenaventura.* Madrid: Rialp S. A., 1966.

Gössmann, Elisabeth. *Glaube und Gotteserkenntnis im Mittelalter.* Vol. 1, Faszikel 2b of *HDG.*

Grün, Anselm. *Gebet und Selbsterkenntnis.* Münsterschwarzach: Vier Türme Verlag, 1985.

Grünewald, Stanislaus. *Franziskanische Mystik: Versuch zu einer Darstellung mit besonderer Berücksichtigung des hl. Bonaventura.* München: Naturrechts - Verlag, 1932.

Guardini, Romano. *Die Lehre des hl. Bonaventura von der Erlösung.* Düsseldorf: L. Schwann, 1921.

____. *Systembildende Elemente in der Theologie Bonaventuras.* Ed. Werner Dettloff. Leiden: E. J. Brill, 1964.

Hamesse, Jacqueline. *Itinerarium mentis in Deum. De reductione artium ad theologiam.* Vol. 1 of *Thesaurus Bonaventurianus.* Louvain: CETEDOC, 1972.

Hartnett, Joanne. *Doctrina Sancti Bonaventurae de deiformitate.* Mundelein, Illinois: Seminarii Sanctae Mariae ad Lacum, 1936.

Hausherr, Irénée. *The Name of Jesus.* Trans. Charles Cummings. Kalamazoo, Michigan: Cistercian Publications, 1978.

____. *Penthos. The Doctrine of Compunction in the Christian East.* Trans. Anselm Hufstader. Kalamazoo, Michigan: Cistercian Publications, 1982.

Hayes, Zachary. *The Hidden Center. Spirituality and Speculative Christology in St. Bonaventure.* New York: Paulist Press, 1981.

Heiler, Friedrich. *Das Gebet.* München: Verlag von Ernst Reinhardt, 1923.

____. *Prayer.* Trans. Samuel McComb and J. Edgar Park. London: Oxford University Press, 1932.

Hellmann, J. A. Wayne. *Ordo. Untersuchung eines Grundgedankens in der Theologie Bonaventuras.* München: Verlag Ferdinand Schöningh, 1974.

Hülsbusch, Werner. *Elemente einer Kreuzestheologie in den Spätschriften Bonaventuras.* Düsseldorf: Patmos Verlag, 1968.

Imle, F. *Das geistliche Leben nach der Lehre des hl. Bonaventura.* Werl/Westfalen: Franziskus - Druckerei, 1939.

____. *Die Theologie des heiligen Bonaventura.* Werl/Westfalen: Franziskus - Druckerei, 1931.

Jeremias, Joachim. *The Prayers of Jesus.* Trans. John Bowden, Christoph Burchard and John Reumann. Norwich: SCM Press, 1967.

Jungmann, Josef Andreas. *Die Stellung Christi im liturgischen Gebet.* Münster: Verlag der Aschendorffschen Verlagsbuchhandlung, 1925.

____. *Christliches Beten in Wandel und Bestand.* München: Verlag Ars Sacra, 1969.

____. *Missarum Sollemnia.* Freiburg: Herder, 1958.

Kerkhoff, Radbert. *Das unablässige Gebet. Beiträge zur Lehre vom immerwährenden Beten im Neuen Testament.* München: Karl Zink Verlag, 1954.

Klawek, A. *Das Gebet zu Jesus. Seine Berechtigung und Übung nach den Schriften des neuen Testaments.* Münster: Verlag der Aschendorffschen Verlagsbuchhandlung, 1921.

Köpf, Ulrich. *Religiöse Erfahrung in der Theologie Bernhards von*

Clairvaux. Tübingen: J. C. B. Mohr, 1980.

Köster, Heinrich. *Urstand, Fall und Erbsünde in der Scholastik.* Vol. 2, Faszikel 3b of *HDG.*

Lapsanski, Duane. *Perfectio evangelica. Eine begriffsgeschichtliche Untersuchung im frühfranziskanischen Schrifttum.* München: Verlag Ferdinand Schöningh, 1974.

Lavatori, Renzo. *Lo Spirito santo dono del Padre e del Figlio.* Bologna: Edizioni Dehoniane, 1987.

Leclercq, Jean. *Études sur le vocabulaire monastique du moyen âge.* Romae: Pontificium Institutum S. Anselmi, 1961.

____. *The Love of Learning and the Desire for God. A Study of Monastic Culture.* Trans. Catharine Marsh. London: SPCK, 1978.

____. and François Vandenbroucke and Louis Bouyer. *The Spirituality of the Middle Ages.* Vol 2 of *A History of Christian Spirituality.* Trans. Benedictines of Holme Eden Abbey, Carlisle. New York: The Seabury Press, 1968.

LeFevre, Perry. *Understandings of Prayer.* Philadelphia: The Westminister Press, 1981.

Lehmann, Leonard. *Tiefe und Weite. Der universale Grundzug in den Gebeten des Franziskus von Assisi.* Werl/Westfalen: Dietrich Coelde Verlag, 1984.

Leinsle, Ulrich Gottfried. *Res et Signum. Das Verständnis zeichenhafter Wirklichkeit in der Theologie Bonaventuras.* München: Verlag Ferdinand Schöningh, 1976.

Longpré, Ephrem. *La théologie mystique de saint Bonaventure.* Quaracchi: Collegium S. Bonaventurae, 1921.

Louth, Andrew. *The Origins of the Christian Mystical Tradition. From Plato to Denys.* Oxford: Clarendon Press, 1972.

Marchel, W. *Abba, Père! La prière du Christ et des chrétiens.* Rome: Biblical Institute, 1971.

McGinn, Bernard. *The Golden Chain. A Study in the Theological Anthropology of Isaac of Stella.* Washington, D.C.: Cistercian Publications, 1972.

Mirabent, Antonio Briva. *La Gloria y su relación con la Gracia según las Obras de San Buenaventura.* Barcelona: Editorial Casulleras, 1957.

Monti, Dominic. *Bonaventure's Interpretation of Scripture in his Exegetical Works.* Diss. The University of Chicago, 1979.

Müller, Gerhard Ludwig. *Gemeinschaft und Verehrung der Heiligen. Geschichtlich-systematische Grundlegung der Hagiologie.* Freiburg: Herder, 1986.

Nédoncelle, Maurice. *The Nature and Use of Prayer.* Trans. A. Mason. London: Burns & Oates, 1964.

O'Connell, Patrick Francis. *The "Lignum Vitae" of Saint Bonaventure and the Medieval Devotional Tradition.* Diss. Fordham U. Ann Arbor: UMI, 1985.

Pelikan, Jaroslav. *The Growth of Medieval Theology (600-1300).* Vol. 3 of *The Christian Tradition. A History of the Development of Doctrine.* Chicago: The University of Chicago: 1978.

Pesch, Otto Hermann. *Das Gebet.* Augsburg: Verlag Winfried Werk, 1972.

Peter, Karl. *Die Lehre von der Schönheit nach Bonaventura.* Werl/Westfalen: Dietrich Coelde Verlag, 1964.

Prentice, Robert. *The Psychology of Love according to St. Bonaventure.* St. Bonaventure, N.Y.: The Franciscan Institute, 1951.

Ratzinger, Joseph. *The Theology of History in St. Bonaventure.* Trans.

Zachary Hayes. Chicago: Franciscan Herald Press, 1971.

Rauch, Winthir. *Das Buch Gottes. Eine systematische Untersuchung des Buchbegriffes bei Bonaventura.* München: Max Hueber Verlag, 1961.

Reist, Thomas. *Saint Bonaventure as Biblical Commentator.* Lanham, Md.: University Press of America, 1985.

Rorem, Paul. *Biblical and Liturgical Symbols within the Pseudo-Dionysian Synthesis.* Toronto: Pontifical Institute of Medieaval Studies, 1984.

Rotzetter, Anton. *Selbstverwirklichung des Christen.* Zürich: Benziger, 1983.

Ruppert, Lothar. *Das Buch Genesis. Geistliche Schriftlesung.* Vol. 6/2 of *Erläuterungen zum Alten Testament für die geistliche Lesung.* Ed. Hermann Eising and Hans Lubsczyk. Düsseldorf: Patmos Verlag, 1984.

Sabugal, Santos. *Abba' . . . La oración del Señor.* Madrid: La Editorial Católica, 1985.

Sakaguchi, Fumi. *Der Begriff der Weisheit in den Hauptwerken Bonaventuras.* München: Verlag Anton Pustet, 1968.

Sauer, Edgar. *Die religiöse Wertung der Welt in Bonaventuras Itinerarium Mentis in Deum.* Werl/Westfalen: Franziskus - Druckerei, 1937.

Schachten, Winfried. *Intellectus Verbi. Die Erkenntnis im Mitvollzug des Wortes nach Bonaventura.* Freiburg: Verlag Karl Alber, 1973.

Schalück, Hermann F. *Armut und Heil. Eine Untersuchung über den Armutsgedanken in der Theologie Bonaventuras.* München: Verlag Ferdinand Schöningh, 1971.

Schmucki, Oktavian. *Gotteslob und Meditation nach Beispiel und Anweisung des hl. Franziskus von Assisi.* Luzern: St. Fidelis - Druckerei, 1980.

Schnurr, Klaus Bernhard. *Hören und handeln. Lateinische Auslegungen des*

Vaterunsers in der Alten Kirche bis zum 5. Jahrhundert. Freiburg: Herder, 1985.

Spargo, Emma Jane Marie. *The Category of the Aesthetic in the Philosophy of Saint Bonaventure.* St. Bonaventure, N. Y.: The Franciscan Institute, 1953.

Stanley, David. *Boasting in the Lord. The Phenomenon of Prayer in Saint Paul.* New York: Paulist Press, 1973.

_____. *Jesus in Gethsemane. The Early Church Reflects on the Suffering of Jesus.* New York: Paulist Press, 1980.

Stoevesandt, Hinrich. *Die letzen Dinge in der Theologie Bonaventuras.* Zürich: EVZ Verlag, 1969.

Stohr, Albert. *Die Trinitätslehre des heiligen Bonaventura. I. Die wissenschaftliche Trinitätslehre.* Münster: Verlag der Aschendorffschen Verlagsbuchhandlung, 1923.

Strack, Bonifatius. *Christusleid im Christenleben.* Werl/Westfalen: Dietrich Coelde Verlag, 1960.

Taft, Robert. *The Liturgy of the Hours in East and West. The Origins of the Divine Office and Its Meaning for Today.* Collegeville, Min.: The Liturgical Press, 1986.

Tavard, George H. *Transiency and Permanence. The Nature of Theology According to St. Bonaventure.* Louvain: The Franciscan Institute, 1954.

Trexler, Richard. *The Christian at Prayer. An Illustrated Prayer Manual Attributed to Peter the Chanter (d.1197).* Binghamton, New York: Center for Medieval and Early Renaissance Studies, 1987.

Ulanov, Ann and Barry. *Primary Speech. A Psychology of Prayer.* Atlanta: John Knox Press, 1982.

Vagaggini, Cipriano, Penco, Gregorio and others. *La preghiera nella bibbia e nella tradizione patristica e monastica.* Roma: Edizioni Paoline, 1964.

Wilmart, André. *Auteurs spirituels et textes dévots du moyen âge latin.* Paris: Études Augustiniennes, 1971.

Wright, John. *A Theology of Christian Prayer.* New York: Pueblo Publishing Company, 1979.

Articles

Adnès, Pierre. "Garde du cœur." Vol. 6 of *DS*, 110-117.

____. "Garde des sens." Vol. 6 of *DS*, 117-122.

Alszeghy, Zoltan. "Die Theologie des Wortes Gottes bei den mittelalterlichen Theologen." *GR* 39 (1958): 685-705.

Andres, Friedrich. "Die Stufen der Contemplatio in Bonaventuras Itinerarium mentis in Deum und im Benjamin maior des Richard von St. Viktor." *FS* 8 (1921): 189-200.

Aperribay, Bernardo. "La vida activa y la vida contemplativa según San Buenaventura." *VV* 2 (1944): 655-689.

____. "Prioridad entre la vida activa y la vida contemplativa según San Buenaventura." *VV* 5 (1947): 65-97.

Bardy, Gustave. "Dons du Saint-Esprit I. Chez le Pères." Vol. 3 of *DS*, 1579-1587.

Beirnaert, Louis. "Le symbolisme ascensionnel dans la liturgie et la mystique chrétiennes." *EJ* 19 (1950): 41-63.

Bernard, Charles André. "La doctrine mystique de Denys L'Aréopagite." *Greg* 68 (1987): 523-566.

Bissen, Jean-Marie. "La contemplation selon saint Bonaventure." *FF* 14 (1931): 175-192.

____. "Les degrés de la contemplation selon saint Bonaventure." *FF* 15 (1932): 87-105.

____. "L'importance de la contemplation selon saint Bonaventure." *FF* 15 (1932): 437-454.

____. "Les conditions de la contemplation selon saint Bonaventure." *FF* 17 (1934): 387-404.

____. "Des effets de la contemplation selon saint Bonaventure." *FF* 19 (1936): 20-29.

Bougerol, Jacques Guy. "Amor." *LSB*, 16-18.

____. "Ascensus." *LSB*, 21.

____. "Contemplatio." *LSB*, 40-41.

____. "Descensus." *LSB*, 52.

____. "Frui." *LSB*, 73.

____. "Habitus." *LSB*, 79-80.

____. "Imago." *LSB*, 84-86.

____. "Synderesis." *LSB*, 125.

____. "Saint Bonaventure et Guillaume de Saint-Thierry." *Ant* 46 (1971): 298-321.

____. "Le rôle de l'*influentia* dans la théologie de la grâce chez Bonaventure." *RTL* 5 (1974): 274-300.

____. "L'aspect original de l'Itinerarium mentis in Deum et son influence sur la spiritualité de son temps." *Ant* 52 (1977): 309-325.

____. "Saint Bonaventure et le Pseudo-Denys l'Aréopagite." *EF* 18 (Supplément annuel 1968): 33-123.

Brady, Ignatius. "The Edition of the <<Opera Omnia>> 1882-1902 of Saint

Bonaventure." *AFH* 70 (1977): 352-376.

_____. "The Writings of Saint Bonaventure regarding the Franciscan Order." *SBM*, 89-112.

_____. "The Opera Omnia of St. Bonaventure revisited." *Proceedings of the Seventh Centenary Celebration of the Death of Saint Bonaventure.* Ed. Pascal F. Foley. St. Bonaventure, N.Y.: The Franciscan Institute, 1975, 47-59.

_____. "St. Bonaventure's Theology of the Imitation of Christ." *Proceedings*, 61-72.

Burns, J. Patout. "Grace: The Augustinian Foundation." Vol. 16 of *WS*, 331-349.

Burr, David. "Bonaventure, Olivi and Franciscan Eschatology." *CF* 53 (1983): 23-40.

Buscaroli, Silvano. "La povertà francescana secondo S. Bonaventura." *MF* 78 (1978): 357-412.

Cacciari, Antonio. Introduction. *S. Agostino d'Ippona La Preghiera*. Intro., Trans., and Notes by Antonio Cacciari. Roma: Edizioni Paoline, 1981.

Campenhausen, Hans Freiherr von. "Gebetserhörung in den überlieferten Jesusworten und in der Reflexion des Johannes." *KD* 23 (1977): 157-171.

Carr, Aidan. "Poverty in perfection according to Saint Bonaventure." *FSt* 7 (1947): 313-323; 415-425.

Châtillon, Jean. "Prière III. Dans la tradition chrétienne C. Prière au moyen âge." Vol. 12 of *DS*, 2271-2288.

_____. "Devotio." Vol. 3 of *DS*, 702-716.

_____. "Cor et cordis affectus 3. Cordis affectus au moyen âge." Vol. 2 of *DS*, 2288-2300.

_____. "Richard de Saint Victor." Vol. 13 of *DS*, 593-654.

Clasen, Sophronius. "Der hl. Bonaventura als Prediger." *WW* 24 (1961): 85-113.

Cousins, Ewert. "Francis of Assisi: Christian Mysticism at the Crossroads." *Mysticism and Religious Traditions*. Ed. Steven T. Katz. New York: Oxford University Press, 1983. 163-190.

Da Gama Caeiro, Francisco José. "L'interprétation du texte bonaventurien 'Sermo de S. Antonio.' Le problème historique et doctrinal." *EF* 18 (Supplément annuel 1968): 149-159.

Daniel, E. Randolph. "The Desire for Martyrdom: A Leitmotiv of St. Bonaventure." *FSt* 32 (1972): 74-87.

Delhaye, Philippe. "Peccatum originale." *LSB*, 106-107.

Del Zotto, Cornelio. "Gesù Cristo senso e speranza della storia in san Bonaventura." Vol. 2 of *La speranza. Atti del Congresso promosso dal Pontificio Ateneo "Antonianum" 30 maggio-2 giugno 1982*. Ed. Bruno Giordani. Roma: Ed. Antonianum, 1984. 483-547.

Dettloff, Werner. "Incipit speculatio pauperis in deserto." *FS* 66 (1984): 57-67.

_____. "Das officium praelationis." *Ius Sacrum. Klaus Mörsdorf zum 60. Geburtstag*. Ed. Audomar Scheuermann and Georg May. München: Verlag Ferdinand Schöningh, 1969. 207-229.

_____. "Die Geistigkeit des hl. Franziskus in der Theologie der Franziskaner." *WW* 19 (1956): 197-211.

_____. "'Christus tenens medium in omnibus.' Sinn und Funktion der Theologie bei Bonaventura." *WW* 20 (1957): 28-42; 120-140.

De Villalmonte, Alejandro. "El Padre Plenitud fontal de la Deidad." *SB*, Vol. 4, 221-242.

Doucet, Victorinus. "De quaestionibus S. Bonaventurae adscriptis in Cod. Vaticano Palatino lat. 612." *AFH* 26 (1933): 487-496.

____. "The History of the Problem of the Authenticity of the Summa." *FSt* 7 (1947): 26-41; 274-312.

Dufeil, Michel. "La prière implicite dans les textes universitaires." *La prière au moyen âge*. Aix-en-Provence, 1981.

Dupuy, Michael. "Oraison." Vol. 11 of *DS*, 831-846.

Dürig, Walter. "Die Deutung der Brotbitte des Vaterunsers bei den lateinisches Vätern bis Hieronymus." *LitJ* 18 (1968): 72-86.

Epping, Adelhard. "Zur Bonaventuras Schrift De reductione artium ad theologiam." *WW* 27 (1964): 100-116.

Eßer, Kajetan. "Mysterium paupertatis. Die Armutsauffassung des hl. Franziskus von Assisi." *WW* 14 (1951): 177-189.

Frank, Isnard W. "Gebet VI. Mittelalter." Vol. 12 of *TRE*, 65-71.

Gardeil, A. "Dons du Saint-Esprit." Vol. 4/2 of *DThC*, 1728-1781.

Grelot, Pierre. "Prière II. La prière dans la Bible." Vol. 12 of *DS*, 2217-2247.

Greshake, Gisbert. "Theologische Grundlagen des Bittgebets." *ThQ* 157 (1977): 27-40.

Guillaume, Paul-Marie. "Jacob." Vol. 8 of *DS*, 1-19.

Guillaumont, Antoine. "Le problème de la prière continuelle dans le monachisme ancien." *L'experience de la prière dans les grandes religions*. Ed. Henri Limet and Julien Ries. Louvain-la-Neuve: Centre d'Histoire des Religions, 1980. 285-294.

Hanes, Keith. "The Death of St. Francis of Assisi." *FS* 58 (1976): 27-46.

Hauschild, Wolf Dieter. "Gnade IV. Dogmengeschichtlich." Vol. 13 of *TRE*, 476-495.

Hellmann, Wayne. "Poverty: the Franciscan way to God." *TD* 22 (1974): 339-345.

Hülsbusch, Werner. "Die Theologie des Transitus bei Bonaventura." Vol. 4 of *SB*, 533-565.

Iammarrone, Giovanni. "La 'Sequela di Cristo' nelle Fonti Francescane." *MF* 82 (1982): 417-461.

Jean de Dieu. "Contemplation et contemplation acquise d'après S. Bonaventure." *EF* 43 (1931): 401-429.

Johnson, Timothy J. "Contemplative Prayer and the Constitutions of the Order of Friars Minor Conventual." *MF* 87 (1987): 96-113.

Johnston, Raymond. "Une question d'équilibre: le rôle du désir dans la pensée primitive de saint Bonaventure." *EF* 21 (Supplément annuel 1971): 75-86.

Köpf, Ulrich. "Hoheliedauslegung als Quelle einer Theologie der Mystik." *Grundfragen christlicher Mystik.* Ed. Margot Schmidt and Dieter R. Bauer. Stuttgart-Bad Cannstatt: Friedrich Frommann Verlag, 1987. 50-72.

Leclercq, Jean. "Ways of Prayer and Contemplation II. Western." Trans. Dennis Tamburello. *Christian Spirituality 1.* Vol. 16 of *WS*, 415-426.

Longpré, Ephrem. "Bonaventure." Vol. 1 of *DS*, 1768-1843.

Marcucci, Bruno. "La virtù dell'obbedienza nella perfezione secondo la dottrina di S. Bonaventura." *StFr* 50 (1953): 3-30.

Marthaler, Berard. "Original Justice according to St. Bonaventure." *Franciscan Approach to Education.* Ed. Sebastian Miklas. Washington, D.C.: The Franciscan Education Conference,1958. 166-175.

Matanic, Atanasio. "'Beatitudo est in unione.' La felicità dell'uomo alla luce del magistero bonaventuriano." Supplement II of *SBM*, 269-280.

McEvoy, James. "Microcosm and Macrocosm in the Writings of St. Bonaventure." Vol. 2 of *SB*, 309-343.

McGinn, Bernard. "The Human Person as Image of God II. Western Christianity." Vol. 16 of *WS*, 312-330.

____. "Ascension and Introversion in the Itinerarium mentis in Deum." Vol. 3 of *SB*, 535-552.

Meier, Ludger. "Zwei Grundbegriffe augustinischer Theologie in der mittelalterlichen Franziskanerschule." *Fünfte Lektorenkonferenz der deutschen Franziskaner für Philosphie und Theologie.* Werl/Westfalen: Franziskus - Druckerei, 1930. 53-74.

____. "Evangelische Lebensform und mündliches Beten." *FS* 32 (1950): 261-271.

Ménard, André. "Spiritualité du Transitus." Vol. 4 of *SB*, 607-635.

Mitzka, Franz. "Die Lehre des hl. Bonaventura von der Vorbereitung auf die heiligmachende Gnade." *ZKT* 50 (1926): 27-72; 220-252.

Monti, Dominic. "A Reconsideration of the Authorship of the Commentary of the Book of Wisdom attributed to St. Bonaventure." *AFH* 79 (1986): 359-391.

Pompei, Alfonso. "Amore ed esperienza di Dio nella mistica bonaventuriana." *DtS* 33 (1986): 5-27.

Prunières, Louis. "Contuitio." *LSB*, 41-46.

Pyfferoen, Hilaire. "L'abnégation-renoncement dans la spiritualité bonaventurienne." *LR* 15 (1974): 97-153.

Rahner, Karl. "Zum theologischen Begriff der Konkupiszenz." Vol. 1 of *Schriften zur Theologie*. Einsiedeln: Benziger Verlag, 1954. 377-414.

Rézette, Jean Pierre. "Caritas." *LSB*, 29-32.

____. "Gratia." *LSB*, 74-77.

_____. "Grâce et similitude de Dieu chez saint Bonaventure." *ETL* 32 (1956): 46-64.

_____. "L'espérance, vertu du pauvre, selon S. Bonaventure." Vol. 2 of *La speranza. Atti del Congresso promosso dal Pontificio Ateneo "Antonianum" 30 maggio-2 giugno 1982*. Ed. Bruno Giordani. Roma: Ed. Antonianum, 1984. 357-380.

Riedlinger, Helmut. "Zur buchstäblichen und mystischen Schriftauslegung Bonaventuras." *Grundfragen christlicher Mystik*. Margot Schmidt and Dieter R. Bauer. Stuttgart-Bad Cannstatt: Friedrich Frommannn Verlag, 1987. 139-156.

Rivera de Ventosa, Enrique. "Amour personnel et impersonnel chez saint Bonaventure." *EF* 18 (Supplément annuel 1968): 191-203.

Rordorf, W. "Le 'pain quotidien' (Mt 6, 11) dans l'exégèse de Grégoire de Nysse." *Aug* 17 (1977): 193-197.

Sagne, Jean-Claude. "Du besoin à la demande, ou la conversion du désir dans la prière." *MD* 109 (1972): 87-97.

Schalück, Hermann. "Armut und Heil. Die theologischen Implikationen des Armutsgedankens bei Bonaventura." *SB*. Vol. 4, 673-683.

Scheffczyk, Leo. "Brautsymbolik." Vol. 2 of *LM*, 589-591.

Schlachmuylders, Berthold. "Concupiscentia." *LSB*, 37-38.

Schlosser, Marianne. "Lux Inaccessibilis. Zur negativen Theologie bei Bonaventura." *FS* 68 (1986): 3-140.

Schmaus, Michael. "Die Trinitätskonzeption in Bonaventuras Itinerarium Mentis in Deum." *WissWb* 15 (1962): 229-237.

Schmucki, Oktavian. "Die Stellung Christi im Beten des hl. Franziskus." *WW* 25 (1962): 128-145; 188-212.

Solignac, Aimé. "Piété II. Moyen âge." Vol. 12 of *DS*, 1714-1725.

Splett, Jörg. "Der Geist der Gaben." *WW* 45 (1982): 72-79.

Szabó, Titus. "Extase IV. Chez les theologiens du 13e siècle." Vol. 4 of *DS*, 2120-2131.

Tavard, George. "La structure de l'expérience fruitive." *EF* 34 (1952): 205-211.

Vandenbroucke, François. "Dons du Saint-Esprit IV. Le moyen âge." Vol. 3 of *DS*, 1587-1603.

von Severus, Emmanuel. "Gebet I." Vol. 8 of *RAC*, 1134-1258.

Ward, Benedicta. Intro. *The Prayers and Meditations of Saint Anselm with the Proslogion*. Trans. and Intro. Benedicta Ward. Forw. R. W. Southern. Bungay, Suffolk: The Chaucer Press, 1984.

Wulf, Friedrich. "Das innere Gebet (oratio mentalis) und die Betrachtung (meditatio)." *GL* 25 (1952): 382-390.

Zafarana, Zelina. "Pietà e devozione in san Bonaventura." *Da Gregorio VII a Bernardino da Siena: saggi di storia medievale*. Ed. O. Capitani, C. Leonardi, E. Menestò, and R. Rusconi. Firenze; "La Nouva Italia" Editrice, 1987, 111-157.

Zinn Jr., Grover A. "Book and Word. The Victorine Background of Bonaventure's Use of Symbols." Vol. 2 of *SB*, 143-169.

Index of Proper Names

266

Gillebertus of Hoilandia, 229, 244
Gilson, E., 44, 116, 181, 198, 204, 206, 213, 248, 249
Giordani, B., 189, 259, 263
Girardi, M., 112, 248
Gonzales, O., 250
Gössmann, E., 201, 250
Gramatica, A., 59, 243
Gregory the Great, 125, 145, 147, 148, 149, 152, 153, 168, 244
Grelot, P., 21, 260
Greshake, G., 44, 260
Grün, A., 185, 250
Grünewald, S., 24, 144, 209, 250
Guardini, R., 20, 106, 107, 108, 250
Guillaume, P., 183, 260
Guillaumont, A., 136, 260
Gunther of Paris, 135, 141, 245

Hamesse, J., 199, 250
Hanes, K., 186, 260
Hartnett, J., 34, 250
Hauschild, W., 45, 260
Hausherr, I., 114, 136, 157, 182, 186, 250
Hayes, Z., 21, 30, 36, 38, 61, 66, 67, 68, 69, 78, 80, 82, 84, 91, 93, 94, 103, 105, 108, 113, 213, 242, 250, 254
Healy, E., 116, 241
Heiler, F., 22, 23, 152, 251
Hellmann, W., 27, 29, 36, 251, 261
Hufstader, A., 182, 250
Hugh of St. Cher, 115

Hugh of St. Victor, 30, 40, 120, 140, 193, 210, 245
Hülsbusch, W., 216, 232, 251, 261
Hurst, D., 244

Iammarrone, G., 81, 261
Imle, F., 22, 24, 105, 108, 251
Isaac, 173
Isaiah, the Prophet, 120
Israel, 185, 186, 197

Jacob, 182, 183, 184, 185, 186, 187, 188, 189, 191, 196, 197, 205, 228, 234, 235
James, the Apostle, 172, 182, 183, 234
Jeremias, J., 77, 78, 251
Jean de Dieu, 183, 184, 199, 261
Jerome, 100, 198, 218, 245
John Chrysostom, 111
John of Damascus, 139, 172, 191, 192, 205, 245
John of La Rochelle, 20, 146
John, the Apostle, 109, 172, 182, 183, 218, 219, 220, 228, 234, 236, 238
John the Baptist, 41
Johnson, T., 88, 261
Johnston, R., 148, 149, 181, 261
Jungmann, J., 114, 115, 139, 251

Katz, S., 72, 259
Kaup, J., 242
Kerkhoff, R., 136, 251
King David, 124, 207

Claudia Rüegg

David von Augsburg
Historische, theologische und philosophische
Schwierigkeiten zu Beginn des Franziskanerordens in
Deutschland

Bern, Frankfurt/M., New York, Paris, 1989
Deutsche Literatur von den Anfängen bis 1700. Bd. 4
ISBN 3-261-03939-6 br. DM 49.--/sFr. 42.30

Deutschlands 13. Jahrhundert ist durch Umbrüche in verschiedensten
Gebieten gekennzeichnet: politische und soziale Verlagerungen
schwächen einerseits das herkömmliche klerikale System, schaffen
aber gerade auch dadurch ein Vakuum, welches durch neue Institu-
tionen und Gesetzgebungen gefüllt werden muß; auch auf geistig- reli-
giösem Gebiet ist nach dem Bekanntwerden der Aristoteles-Texte eine
Neuorientierung unumgänglich. Die Arbeit versucht, diese Spannun-
gen anhand einer bedeutenden Pesönlichkeit konkret darzulegen.

Aus dem Inhalt: Geschichtliche Daten und Fakten aus dem Raume
Augsburg im 13. Jahrhundert - Soziale Zuordnung David von Augs-
burgs anhand linguistischer Untersuchungen - Davids franziskanische
Ideen - Sein philosophischer Hintergrund und dessen individuelle
Deutung.

Verlag Peter Lang Frankfurt a.M. · Bern · New York · Paris
Auslieferung: Verlag Peter Lang AG, Jupiterstr. 15, CH-3000 Bern 15
Telefon (004131) 321122, Telex pela ch 912 651, Telefax (004131) 321131
– Preisänderungen vorbehalten –

Joseph Overath

Kirchengeschichte
Orientierungshilfen, Standpunkte, Impulse für heute

Frankfurt/M., Bern, New York, 1987. 234 S.
Europäische Hochschulschriften. Reihe 23, Theologie. Bd. 294
ISBN 3-8204-9697-1   br./lam. DM 60.--/sFr. 50.--

Die elf Beiträge verstehen sich als Orientierungshilfen und Impulse für heute. Sie versuchen die Gegenwart der Kirche im Lichte der Vergangenheit zu deuten, fordern auch zu einer Stellungnahme heraus. Kirchengeschichte als theologische Disziplin leistet damit einen Beitrag zur Klärung des Verhältnisses von Tradition und Fortschritt in der Kirche.

Aus dem Inhalt: Sentire ecclesiam - Weichenstellungen im 19. Jahrhundert - Gegenwart aus der Kirchengeschichte verstehen.

Verlag Peter Lang Frankfurt a.M. · Bern · New York · Paris
Auslieferung: Verlag Peter Lang AG, Jupiterstr. 15, CH-3000 Bern 15
Telefon (004131) 321122, Telex pela ch 912 651, Telefax (004131) 321131
- Preisänderungen vorbehalten -